Diesel Aerosols and Gases in Underground Mines: Guide to Exposure Assessment and Control

Department of Health and Human Services: Centers for Disease Control and Prevention, Anonymous

RI 9687

REPORT OF INVESTIGATIONS/2011

Diesel Aerosols and Gases in Underground Mines:
Guide to Exposure Assessment and Control

Department of Health and Human Services
Centers for Disease Control and Prevention
National Institute for Occupational Safety and Health

Report of Investigations 9687

Diesel Aerosols and Gases in Underground Mines: Guide to Exposure Assessment and Control

By Aleksandar D. Bugarski, Samuel J. Janisko, Emanuele G. Cauda, James D. Noll, and Steven E. Mischler

DEPARTMENT OF HEALTH AND HUMAN SERVICES
Centers for Disease Control and Prevention
National Institute for Occupational Safety and Health
Office of Mine Safety and Health Research
Pittsburgh, PA • Spokane, WA

October 2011

Disclaimer

Mention of any company or product does not constitute endorsement by the National Institute for Occupational Safety and Health (NIOSH). In addition, citations to Web sites external to NIOSH do not constitute NIOSH endorsement of the sponsoring organizations or their programs or products. Furthermore, NIOSH is not responsible for the content of these Web sites.

The findings and conclusions in this report are those of the authors and do not necessarily represent the views of the National Institute for Occupational Safety and Health.

Ordering Information

To receive documents or other information about occupational safety and health topics, contact NIOSH at

> Telephone: **1–800–CDC–INFO** (1–800–232–4636)
> TTY: 1–888–232–6348
> e-mail: cdcinfo@cdc.gov

> or visit the NIOSH Web site at **www.cdc.gov/niosh**.

For a monthly update on news at NIOSH, subscribe to NIOSH *eNews* by visiting **www.cdc.gov/niosh/eNews**.

DHHS (NIOSH) Publication No. 2012–101

October 2011

SAFER • HEALTHIER • PEOPLE™

Contents

Figures

Tables

Acronyms and Abbreviations Used in This Guide

ACGIH	American Conference of Governmental Industrial Hygienists
Al	aluminum
Al_2TiO_5	aluminum titanate
ANSI	American National Standards Institute
APF	assigned protection factor
API	American Petroleum Institute
APR	air-purifying respirator
AQE	Air Quality Estimator
ASC	ammonia slip catalyst
ASR	air-supplying respirator
ASTM	ASTM International, originally known as American Society for Testing and Materials
B5	biodiesel blend containing 5% biodiesel and 95% petroleum diesel
B20	biodiesel blend containing 20% biodiesel and 80% petroleum diesel
B99	biodiesel blend containing 99% biodiesel and 1% petroleum diesel
B100	neat biodiesel
BPT	balance point temperature
BQ9000	National Biodiesel Accreditation Program standards
BSFC	brake-specific fuel consumption
BTH	2,6-di-t-butyl-p-cresol
C	carbon
CARB	California Air Resources Board
Ce	cerium
CCRT™	catalyzed continuously regenerating trap (registered trademark of Johnson Matthey PLC)
CCV	closed crankcase ventilation
CDPF	catalyzed diesel particulate filter systems
CFR	Code of Federal Regulations
CH_4	methane
CJ4	API grade for low-ash lubricating oil
CO	carbon monoxide
CO_2	carbon dioxide
Cr	chromium
CRT™	continuously regenerating trap (registered trademark of Johnson Matthey PLC)
DEEP	Diesel Emissions Evaluation Program
DEF	diesel exhaust fluid
DFE	disposable filter element
DHHS	U.S.Department of Health and Human Services
DOC	diesel oxidation catalyst
DOE	U.S. Department of Energy

DPF	diesel particulate filter
DPM	diesel particulate matter
EC	elemental carbon
ECM	engine control module
ECU	electronic control unit
EGR	exhaust gas recirculation
EGS	electrochemical gas sensor
EPA	U.S. Environmental Protection Agency
FAME	fatty acid methyl ester
FBC	fuel-borne catalyst
Fe	iron
Fed.Reg.	Federal Register
FID	flame ionization detector
FOEN	Swiss Federal Office of the Environment
FTIR	Fourier transform infrared (spectrometer)
H_2	hydrogen
H_2O	water
H_2S	hydrogen sulfide
HC	hydrocarbon
H_XC_Y	generic hydrocarbon compound
HC-SCR	hydrocarbon selective catalyst reduction
HD	heavy-duty
He	helium
HEI	Health Effects Institute
HEPA	high-efficiency particulate air
HPCR	high-pressure common rail
HR	hazard ratio
HTDFE	high-temperature disposable filter elements
ID	identification (number)
IR	infrared
ISO	International Standards Organization
LD	light-duty
LHD	load-haul-dump (vehicle)
LLSP	laser light scattering photometry
LNC	lean NO_X catalyst
LSD	low-sulfur diesel
LTDFE	low-temperature disposable filter elements
MERV	Minimum Efficiency Reporting Value
Mg	magnesium
$Mg_2Al_4Si_5O_{18}$	cordierite
M/NM	metal and nonmetal (mines)
Mo	molybdenum
MSDS	material safety and data sheet
MSHA	U.S. Mine Safety and Health Administration
Mtb	mycobacterium tuberculosis

N_2	nitrogen
N_2O	nitrous oxide
NBAC	National Biodiesel Accreditation Commission
NBB	National Biodiesel Board
NDIR	nondispersive infrared
NH_3	ammonia
$(NH_2)_2CO$	urea
NIOSH	National Institute for Occupational Safety and Health
No. 1-D	light middle grade of diesel fuel in the U.S.
No. 2-D	middle grade of diesel fuel in the U.S.
No. 4-D	heavy middle grade of diesel fuel in the U.S.
NO	nitric oxide
NO_2	nitrogen dioxide
NO_X	nitric oxides
NPPTL	National Personal Protective Technology Laboratory
NREL	National Renewable Energy Laboratory
O_2	chemical formula for oxygen
OC	organic carbon
OEM	original equipment manufacturer
OSHA	U.S. Occupational Safety and Health Administration
PADEP	Pennsylvania Department of Environmental Protection
PAH	polycyclic aromatic hydrocarbon
PAPR	powered air-purifying respirator
Pd	palladium
PDM	personal dust monitor
PEL	Personal Exposure Limit (OSHA)
PF	partial filter
PI	particulate index
PM	particulate matter
PPE	personal protective equipment
ppm	parts per million
Pt	platinum
REL	Recommended Exposure Limit (NIOSH)
Rh	rhodium
RME	rapeseed methyl ester
RTD	resistance temperature detector
S	sulfur
SAE	Society of Automotive Engineers
SCR	selective catalytic reduction
SCRT™	catalyzed continuously regenerating trap with selective catalyst reduction (registered trademark of Johnson Matthey PLC)
Si	silicon
SiC	silicon carbide
SM	sintered metal
SME	soy methyl ester (biodiesel)

SMF	sintered metal filter
SO_2	sulfur dioxide
SOF	soluble organic fraction (of DPM)
Sr	strontium
SUVA	Swiss National Accident Insurance Organization
SVOC	semivolatile organic compounds
T_{30}	temperature that exhaust gas exceed for 30% of operating time
TB	tuberculosis
TC	total carbon
TLV	ACGIH Threshold Limit Value
TPM	total particulate matter
TWA	time-weighted average
ULSDF	ultralow sulfur diesel fuel
U.S.	United States (of America)
V	vanadium
V_2O_5/TiO_2	vanadium oxide/titanium oxide wash-coat catalyst in SCR systems
VERT	Verminderung der Emissionen von Real-Dieselmotoren im Tunnelbau (Curtailing Emissions from Diesel Engines in Tunnel Construction)
VGT	variable geometry turbocharger
VOC	volatile organic compound
VOF	volatile organic fraction (of DPM)
WRAP	Western Regional Air Partnership
WVDEC	West Virginia Diesel Equipment Commission

Unit of Measure Abbreviations Used in this Guide

cfm	cubic feet per minute
g	gram
in^2	square inch
lpm	liter per minute
kPa	kilopascal
mbar	millibar
mg	milligram
mg/m^3	milligram per cubic meter
psig	pound-force per square inch gauge
r^2	coefficient of determination
$\mu g/cm^2$	microgram per square centimeter
$\mu g/m^3$	microgram per cubic meter

Diesel Aerosols and Gases in Underground Mines: Guide to Exposure Assessment and Control

Aleksandar D. Bugarski, Samuel J. Janisko, Emanuele G. Cauda,
James D. Noll, and Steven E. Mischler

Office of Mine Safety and Health Research
National Institute for Occupational Safety and Health

1 Introduction

Diesel engines are a major contributor to concentrations of submicron aerosols, CO, CO_2, NO_X, SO_2 and hydrocarbons (HC) in underground coal and metal/nonmetal mines. The extensive use of diesel-powered equipment in underground mines makes it challenging to control workers' exposure to submicron aerosols and noxious gases emitted by those engines. In order to protect workers, mines need to establish a comprehensive program based on a multifaceted and integrated approach. This program should include a concerted effort to:

- Curtail emissions of the diesel particulate matter (DPM) and toxic gases at the source;
- Control pollutants after they are released in the underground mine environment; and
- Use administrative controls to reduce exposures of underground miners to pollutants.

Many of the technologies and strategies available to the coal and metal/nonmetal underground mining industries to control exposures of underground miners to diesel pollutants are similar. However, the differences in the U.S. regulations limiting DPM exposures of miners in underground coal mines [66 Fed. Reg. 27864 (2001)[1]] and metal/nonmetal mines [71 Fed. Reg. 28924 (2006)] have a major bearing on how those technologies and strategies are implemented. In underground coal mines, achieving compliance is based on implementing technologies developed to control DPM and gaseous emissions directly at their source and providing sufficient quantities of fresh air to dilute criteria gases emitted by diesel engines [61 Fed. Reg. 55411 (1996)]. In contrast, the metal/nonmetal performance-based regulations enforce personal exposure limits (PEL) and provide much more latitude in the selection of technologies and strategies to control miners' exposures to DPM and gases [MSHA 2008].

The effort to reduce the exposure of underground miners to diesel pollutants requires the involvement of several key departments of mining companies, including those responsible for health and safety, engine/vehicle/exhaust aftertreatment maintenance, mine ventilation, and production, as well as the departments responsible for acquiring vehicles, engines, exhaust aftertreatment systems, fuel, and lubricating oil. Due to the complexity of this problem and the involvement of personnel from various departments in an underground mine, a program coordinator is crucial to the success of diesel control programs [McGinn et al. 2004; Conard et al. 2006; Schnakenberg 2006; Mischler and Colinet 2009]. The program coordinator must have adequate knowledge of issues related to exposure to diesel aerosols and gases, as well as the authority to coordinate all the efforts throughout various mine departments. The program

---

[1] *Federal Register.* See Fed. Reg. in references

coordinator must build a team of qualified personnel and solicit genuine support from workers as well as from corporate and mine management.

The diesel pollutants control program plan and execution of this plan should be dynamic and based on information gathered through surveillance efforts. This surveillance should include gathering information on parameters pertinent to planning, execution, and coordination of the program (e.g., size of the diesel-powered fleet, role of diesel-powered equipment in the mining process, type of engine emissions, contribution of diesel-powered equipment to exposure of underground miners to DPM and criteria gases, quality of diesel fuel and lubricating oil, and ventilation supply and demand). Surveillance efforts should also help to identify and quantify the extent of the problem, identify and evaluate potential solutions, and identify and establish a hierarchy of potential solutions. The adopted solutions should be instituted and implemented in a manner that takes the costs and benefits into consideration. The surveillance efforts should be continued throughout the implementation phase of the program, and the results should be used to constantly re-evaluate the effectiveness of the program and adjust actions accordingly.

Establishing a hierarchy of solutions is critical to the success of a multifaceted diesel pollutants control program. Certain technologies and strategies have a greater chance of success if their implementation is preceded by implementation of the prerequisite solutions. For example, the first step in retrofitting exhaust aftertreatment control systems to existing vehicles or equipment is to implement an effective maintenance and fuel/lubricating-oil supply program. This will provide sufficient information on engine emissions, quality of fuel and lubricating-oil, and lubricating oil consumption to allow for adequate design and performance monitoring while avoiding damage to the aftertreatment device(s) due to sulfate or ash formation.

A relatively wide variety of technologies and methodologies is available to the underground mining industry to reduce exposures to DPM and toxic gases. Those that are effective in curtailing DPM and toxic gaseous emissions at their source are discussed in detail in Section 2 of this handbook. Correspondingly, a detailed description of effective technologies and strategies for controlling pollutants after they are released in the underground mine environment is provided in Section 3. The methods and tools for monitoring ambient concentrations and personal exposures of underground miners to diesel particulate matter and toxic gases are described in Section 4. Various administrative controls and practices available to the mining industry to reduce emissions and exposures to DPM and toxic gases are discussed in Section 5.

2 Source Control of Diesel Particulate Matter (DPM) and Gases

2.1 Formation and Composition of Harmful Diesel Engines Emissions

2.1.1 Diesel Particulate Matter (DPM)

Introduction

The U.S. Environmental Protection Agency (U.S. EPA) defines diesel particulate matter (DPM) as any material being emitted from a diesel engine that can be collected on a filter through cooled and diluted exhaust (with the filter temperature held below 52°C, 126°F) [EPA 2002a]. This definition generally corresponds with any solid matter emitted or any liquid matter which is emitted or adsorbed onto the surface of these solid particles. This largely includes four byproducts of diesel combustion: elemental carbon (EC), organic carbon (OC), ash, and sulfuric compounds. These substances will quickly combine to form DPM aerosols (see Figure 1).

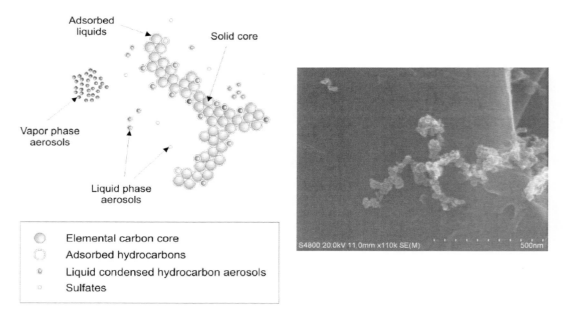

Adsorbed liquids
Solid core
Vapor phase aerosols
Liquid phase aerosols

◯	Elemental carbon core
◌	Adsorbed hydrocarbons
⊚	Liquid condensed hydrocarbon aerosols
○	Sulfates

S4800 20.0kV 11.0mm x110k SE(M)   500nm

Figure 1. (left) A graphical depiction of the composition of diesel particulate matter and (right) a microscopic image of a typical diesel particle agglomerate.

Diesel particles are, in general, one order of magnitude smaller than other respirable dust aerosols in underground mines (typically less than one micron in size) [Kittelson 1998; Cantrell and Volkwein 2001]. Due to their small size, DPM aerosols behave similarly to the surrounding gases. They have much longer residence times in a mine atmosphere than larger mechanically generated particles, which are removed from the atmosphere quite quickly by gravitational settling. In addition, a large portion of diesel particles is deposited in the human respiratory tract in comparison to larger aerosols. These small diesel aerosols will

3

penetrate deeply into regions of the human lung where gas exchange occurs [Pietikäinen et al. 2009; Morawska et al. 2005], potentially increasing the health risks associated with long-term exposure to diesel aerosols. For these reasons, control of exposure to DPM particles is both an important and challenging task. The following section outlines the composition and formation of diesel particulate matter.

Elemental Carbon (EC)

Diesel engines function by allowing a mixture of fuel (a hydrocarbon, C_XH_Y) and intake air, which includes oxygen (O_2), nitrogen (N_2), and carbon dioxide (CO_2), to ignite under high temperatures and pressures formed by compression [Diesel 1895]. This form of combustion allows overall cylinder conditions to be "lean"(fuel poor or oxygen rich), which promotes good efficiency and, as a result, a high conversion of fuel (C_XH_Y) into carbon dioxide (CO_2) and water vapor (H_2O) [Heywood 1988c]. However, fuel injection (typically used in diesel engines) also creates "rich" regions, or localized areas within the fuel injection plume that lack the amount of oxygen necessary for proper combustion of fuel. If temperatures are hot enough, fuel will burn without the presence of oxygen within these regions, creating charred remains, or solid carbon soot [EPA 2001a].

Another term for this soot is elemental carbon (EC). Once the EC is formed, most of it will combine with oxygen and burn during later stages of the combustion process [Kittelson et al. 1986; EPA 2001a; Kittelson 1998]. However, the remainder will be emitted from the engine exhaust as solid particulate matter, forming the core of a typical diesel-particle agglomerate. The formation of EC during combustion and expulsion is therefore driven by three primary factors: temperature, residence time, and availability of oxidants [EPA 2001a].

EC formation is reduced at the source by increasing the surface area contact of fuel and air during combustion so that the conversion rate of fuel into carbon dioxide and water vapor is high. This includes promoting lower local fuel/air ratios in contemporary engines through a number of in-cylinder controls (see Section 2.2.1) and using biodiesel fuels (see Section 2.3.1). Secondary reduction strategies for EC emissions involve capturing these particles within the exhaust system using diesel particulate filters (DPFs) (see Section 2.2.2.2).

Organic Carbon (OC)

On a mass basis, EC is the largest contributor to particulate matter (PM) emissions produced by a diesel engine [Noll et al. 2007]. Another large contributor is organic carbon (OC), or compounds that form when hydrocarbons (in fuel and lubricating oil) are consumed but not fully oxidized during the combustion process [Heywood 1988c]. Sources of OC emissions include fuel that is present in overly lean regions (where the ratio of fuel to air is too low to support efficient combustion), fuel that is post-injected ("leaked") into the chamber too late during the combustion process, or lubrication oil that is scraped from cylinder walls or introduced into the combustion chamber from other sources. In these instances, temperatures may be high enough to vaporize the hydrocarbons, but not high enough to convert them into carbon dioxide and water vapor.

OC compounds are partially composed of volatile material rather than nonreactive elemental carbon, and will react and change in both composition and phase during emission. If these

4

compounds are not in the gas phase, they are considered a component of DPM. Typically, this scenario occurs when organic compounds condense and adsorb onto the surface of larger EC particles, but they can also condense and form smaller nanoparticulates without the presence of EC [Kittelson 1998; Plumley 2005]. If OC remains in the gas phase, it is often referred to as an "HC" or "vapor-phase OC" emission, which is a pollutant that is regulated by the U.S. EPA. OC in the nongas phase is often referred to, by engine manufacturers, as the volatile organic fraction (VOF) or soluble organic fraction (SOF), depending on the measurement process used [Majewski and Khair 2006a]. It is important to note that, in the mining industry, the terms "organic carbon" or "OC" almost always refer to nongas-phase organics or to those substances that have mass and, therefore, contribute to total DPM mass.

Control of OC emissions at the source is accomplished by reducing oil consumption, improving fuel and oil formulations, and improving fuel injection design and timing (see Section 2.2.1). Diesel oxidation catalysts (DOCs) are often used within the exhaust system as a secondary control of OC emissions (see Section 2.2.2.1) [EPA 2007a; EPA 2004; Miller et al. 1997]. DPFs can also play a role in reducing OC emissions by capturing entire DPM particles, which may include adsorbed particle-bound OC (see section 2.2.2.2).

Ash

Fuel and lubricating oil often contain a number of additives (detergents, dispersants, etc.), which are composed of metallic elements. When these fluids are consumed during combustion, these metallic elements can form inorganic solids known as ash [Whitacre et al. 2010; Jung et al. 2003; Aravelli and Heibel 2007]. Normal wear of metallic engine components are another, though less substantial, source of ash generation. Although its contribution to DPM mass is often lower in comparison with other forms of particulate matter emissions [Kittelson 1998], ash cannot oxidize in secondary reactions with aftertreatment devices and may accumulate within the exhaust system and cause maintenance issues over time [Miller et al. 2007a; Vouitsis et al. 2007]. Reduction of ash formation can be accomplished by reducing the metallic fraction of the fuel and lube oil formulations, and by lowering the amount of oil consumed during the combustion process (see Section 2.3).

Sulfuric Compounds

Sulfur containing compounds is another contributor to DPM emissions. Sulfur dioxide, which forms when sulfur in the fuel and lubrication oil oxidizes during the combustion process [Kittelson et al. 2008; Whitacre et al. 2010; EPA 2004; Kittelson 1998], is a gaseous emission that can damage or deactivate expensive exhaust catalysts in contemporary diesel engines. During the emissions process, sulfur dioxide can react with other compounds in the exhaust and form solid sulfates, which contribute to overall DPM emissions. The transition toward ultralow sulfur diesel fuels (ULSDF) and low-sulfur content lubricants (e.g., CJ-4 oil, the newest API class) has promoted control over these emissions (see Section 2.3).

5

Total Carbon and EC:TC Ratio

Total carbon (TC) is a term used to describe the sum of the EC and OC fractions of DPM (TC = EC + OC). Likewise, the EC:TC ratio defines the fraction of EC in TC.

This relationship between EC and OC fractions depends on engine operating conditions, engine type, fuel type, and a number of other parameters. Because EC and OC make up over 80% of total DPM mass [Pierson and Brachaczek 1983; Kittelson 1998], the EC:TC ratio helps to quickly describe the general composition of DPM as well as the condition under which it was formed. For instance, if the EC:TC ratio is low, the aerosol contains more organic carbon and, if the source was a heavy-duty diesel engine fueled with a petroleum diesel fuel, it is likely that the DPM was formed under lower-load, lower-speed conditions, which is a typical operating mode approximation that corresponds with high OC formation.

2.1.2 Gases

Nitrogen Oxides (NO and NO_2)

At high temperatures, molecular nitrogen (N_2) from the intake air will react with oxygen (O_2) and hydrocarbons (HC) to form gaseous NO_X emissions, or oxides of nitrogen (NO and NO_2). During combustion, NO_X is formed in an area outside the fuel-rich region of the fuel plume where the proportion of fuel to air is optimal for efficient, high-temperature combustion [Dickey et al. 1998]. The rate of formation of NO_X is exponentially related to the temperature of combustion [Heywood 1988c]. Therefore, in-cylinder controls aimed at decreasing NO_X formation are almost always intended to lower the peak temperatures during the combustion process. In contemporary diesels, this is largely accomplished through exhaust gas recirculation (see Section 2.2.1) [Dickey et al. 1998]. Secondary control through various aftertreatment technologies, such as lean NO_X catalysts (LNCs) and selective catalyst reduction (SCR), may also be employed to further reduce NO_X emissions to acceptable levels (see Section 2.2.2.5 and Section 2.2.2.6).

NO_X/DPM Tradeoff

In conventional diesel combustion, almost any attempt to lower NO_X emissions through in-cylinder techniques results in an increase in DPM, and the converse is true as well. Referred to as the "NO_x/DPM" or "NO_X/PM" tradeoff, this correlation is controlled by the fact that NO_X formation increases at higher combustion temperatures and lean conditions, while DPM mass formation (driven by increased EC formation), will increase at lower combustion temperatures and rich conditions [Horibe and Ishiyama 2009; Heywood 1988c; Majewski and Khair 2006b; EPA 2001a; Helmantel and Golovitchev 2009; Kook et al. 2005]. Because of this correlation, it is very difficult to simultaneously reduce NO_X and DPM without combining various in-cylinder and aftertreatment technologies. For this reason, contemporary diesel-engine designs aimed at meeting U.S. EPA emissions regulations (which stipulate simultaneous reductions in NO_X and DPM emissions) have become particularly complex.

Carbon Monoxide

Carbon monoxide (CO) results from a non-ideal combustion. Its production is correlated to an incomplete oxidation of carbon in the fuel to carbon dioxide, most often from a lack of available oxygen or low gas temperatures. Therefore, under conditions which might produce locally fuel-rich mixtures, such as overloading and overfueling, diesel engines may produce higher concentrations of CO.

Compared to the CO emissions of a gasoline engine, the CO concentration in diesel exhaust is minimal due to the fact that diesel engines have a higher amount of available oxygen, or overall lean mixtures. Nevertheless, the extremely high toxicity related to human exposure to CO has prompted several regulatory agencies to limit the emission of CO from diesel engines [ACGIH 1991].

In diesel engines, reduction of CO emissions is achieved by improving the overall combustion efficiency by limiting any fuel-rich conditions within the cylinder (see Section 2.2.1) and using diesel oxidation catalysts (DOCs) within the exhaust system to convert CO to CO_2 in secondary reactions (see Section 2.2.2).

Gas-Phase Hydrocarbons (HC)

As a general guideline, hydrocarbons in the gas phase are typically referred to as volatile (VOC) and semivolatile organic compounds (SVOC). These are a complex mixture of many chemical species. Among them are polycyclic aromatic hydrocarbons (PAHs), which are widely investigated due to their toxicity. The formation of gas-phase hydrocarbons is outlined in Section 2.1.1. Likewise, control of gas-phase OC emissions at the source is accomplished in the same manner as nongaseous OC control—by reducing oil consumption, improving fuel and oil formulations, and improving fuel-injection design and timing (see Section 2.2.1). In addition, DOCs within the exhaust system are often used as a secondary control (see Section 2.2.2.1) [EPA 2007a; EPA 2004; Miller et al. 1997].

Sulfur Dioxide (SO_2)

As mentioned previously, sulfur dioxide forms when sulfur in the fuel and lubrication oil oxidizes during the combustion process [Kittelson et al. 2008; Whitacre et al. 2010; EPA 2004; Kittelson 1998]. This gaseous emission can damage or deactivate expensive exhaust catalysts in contemporary diesel engines. The transition toward ultralow sulfur diesel fuels (ULSDF) and low-sulfur content lubricants (CJ-4 oil) has promoted control over these emissions (see Section 2.3).

2.2 Engine Control Technologies

2.2.1 In-Cylinder Control Technologies

Introduction

In an effort to meet increasingly stringent worldwide emissions regulations, engine manufacturers have integrated a number of control technologies into new engine designs. Generally, these techniques are split into two categories: in-cylinder controls and aftertreatment. For the purposes of this manual, aftertreatment is defined as any technology that is incorporated into the exhaust system to physically or chemically alter or trap particulate and gaseous emissions (see Section 2.2.2). In-cylinder control technologies are designs or processes that are incorporated into the engine and its subsystems in an effort to prevent or manipulate the formation of unwanted emissions.

Mine operators have limited say in selecting in-cylinder controls because these technologies are usually incorporated during the design stage by the original equipment manufacturer (OEM). This is increasingly common in contemporary diesel engines intended to meet EPA nonroad emissions regulations [40 CFR 89[*]]. For this reason, the discussion on how in-cylinder control technologies can reduce mineworker exposure to diesel pollutants focuses on maintaining these technologies to the original OEM specifications and monitoring their performance rather than retrofitting or altering them. This is best accomplished through a stringent preventative maintenance program. This section provides an overview of the role in-cylinder controls play in emissions formation as well as suggested practices for maintaining the proper function of these technologies.

Technologies

Charge-Air Compression

Charge-air compressors (e.g., turbochargers and superchargers) allow more air to be introduced into the chamber before combustion, thus increasing the amount of fuel that can be injected and burned and, subsequently, enhancing the power output of the engine [Heywood 1988a; Majewski and Khair 2006c]. From an emissions perspective, the compression of charge air leads to leaner conditions within the cylinder during combustion (or situations where the fuel to air ratio is low), which promotes efficient, higher temperature oxidation of the fuel. Under these conditions, DPM formation is limited at the expense of increased NO_X gas emissions [Helmantel and Golovitchev 2009]. In addition, the compression of charge air may increase turbulence within the cylinder during induction, enhancing the mixing between fuel and air [Majewski and Khair 2006c] and further reducing DPM formation.

Charge-Air Cooling

The role of the intercooler is to combat the heating effects that charge compression systems have on intake air. Intercoolers decrease charge air temperature with minimal pressure loss.

---

[*] *Code of Federal Regulations.* See CFR in references.

This acts to decrease peak flame temperatures during combustion, assisting in the reduction of NO_X formation [EPA 2001a; Heywood 1988c].

Exhaust Gas Recirculation (EGR)

EGR is the most effective in-cylinder technology for reducing the formation of NO_X and is implemented on nearly all modern, electronically-controlled diesel engines. EGR involves routing a portion of the exhaust stream into the combustion chamber before ignition. Replacing charge air with exhaust gases increases the specific heat capacity of the mixture and reduces the amount of oxygen available to the fuel. This acts to lower peak in-cylinder temperatures during combustion and reduce NO_X formation at a rate that is proportional to the amount of EGR flow [Majewski and Khair 2006b; Ladommatos et al. 1996a,b; Ladommatos et al. 1997a,b]. Studies have shown that increasing the rate of EGR may result in possible increases in HC, CO, and DPM formation as well as thermal efficiency losses due to increased pumping work [Jacobs et al. 2003; Horibe and Ishiyama 2009; Heywood 1988c; Kook et al. 2005; Majewski and Khair 2006b].

There are a variety of EGR configurations, but two basic setups exist—internal EGR and external EGR. Internal EGR uses extended or extra exhaust valve lifts during the intake stroke to pull exhaust gases back into the chamber before compression. External EGR systems use plumbing to route exhaust gases to a position in the intake system, often downstream of the compressor, to avoid long-term fouling of intake components. In external EGR systems, an advanced turbocharger design, such as a variable geometry turbocharger (VGT), may be implemented to help maintain a positive-pressure differential across the exhaust and intake manifolds while a computer-controlled EGR valve may be used to regulate the amount of EGR flow in response to engine-loading conditions [Majewski and Khair 2006c; Arnold et al. 2001; Filipi et al. 2001]. Some engines may incorporate both internal and external EGR simultaneously. Additionally, external EGR systems may also include a dedicated EGR cooler to reduce the temperature of the recirculation gases. This cooling provides additional NO_X reduction capability at the expense of added complexity to the engine system, increased maintenance demand, and potential reductions in the time-response of EGR flow.

Fuel Delivery and Injection

Contemporary diesels use increasingly higher fuel-injection pressures. These high-pressure fuel delivery systems, such as high-pressure common rail (HPCR), allow a finer mist of fuel to be injected into the chamber, which increases the overall surface area contact between fuel and air during combustion. Additionally, high-pressure fuel injection allows the fuel spray to penetrate further into the chamber, enabling a greater dispersion of the fuel spray. These combined benefits increase the amount of oxygen available to the fuel during combustion and, therefore, help to reduce the formation of DPM [Roels et al. 2009; Busch et al. 2007; DEEP 1999; Majewski and Jääskeläinen 2010].

Fuel injectors themselves are designed with spray angles and timing events that coordinate with the position of the piston bowl within the chamber (so as to prevent fuel impingement on the cooler metal surfaces within the chamber) [Roels et al. 2009; Heywood 1988b; Vanegas et al. 2009; Horibe et al. 2007;

9

Majewski and Jääskeläinen 2010; Helmantel and Golovitchev 2009; Horibe and Ishiyama 2009; Han et al. 1996; EPA 2001a]. Any disruption to this calibration (typically caused by coking or by fouling of injector nozzles) can result in increased OC or vapor-phase HC emissions (see Section 2.1). Additionally, needle valve bounce or injector-fuel leakage might also contribute to increased OC or vapor phase HC emissions. Likely sources of failure in this area are the contamination of fuel from dirt, debris, water, and certain additives, and the overheating of injector tips [BHB Billiton 2005; Argueyrolles et al. 2007; Leedham et al. 2004]. Preventative maintenance of fueling systems for emissions reduction is, therefore, focused largely on ensuring the integrity of filters and fuel delivery components, and maintaining reasonable fuel temperatures.

Crankcase Filtration

Important and often overlooked sources of diesel emissions are crankcase ventilation systems, or breather systems. During combustion, high-pressure byproducts (CO, CO_2, NO_X, O_2, H_2O, HC, and DPM) can leak through the seal of the piston rings or through passages in the lubrication system and into the crankcase [Froelund and Yilmaz 2004, 2003]. These byproducts, combined with the mechanical shearing of lubrication oil in the crankshaft and the boiling of lube on piston and cylinder surfaces, form an aerosol mixture of gas, liquid, and particulate matter within the crankcase known as "blowby" [Jaroszczyk et al. 2006]. Over time, blowby pressure builds up within the crankcase and has to be vented. Because tailpipe DPM emissions from modern diesel engines are now at extremely low levels, the fraction of crankcase emissions to total DPM output can be significant in contemporary diesels. Consequently, for tier 4 regulations, the EPA began regulating crankcase ventilation emissions as a part of the total engine PM emissions [69 Fed. Reg. 38957-39006 (2004)]. As a result, improved crankcase filtration methods, utilizing coalescing filters, were developed [Nelson 2009]. Solid particulates that are not drained from coalescing filters can build up over long periods. This accumulation can cause pressure drops across the filter and an increase beyond the saturation pressure. This leads to excessive backpressures within the crankcase, which can cause damage to seals and gaskets in the engine. Therefore, it is important to follow the manufacturer's recommended maintenance schedule when employing crankcase filtration systems.

2.2.2 Exhaust Aftertreatment Controls

2.2.2.1 *Diesel Oxidation Catalysts (DOC)*

Introduction

Diesel oxidation catalyst (DOC) technology is extensively used to control CO and HC emissions from diesel engines. DOCs use a catalyst to support reactions where CO and hydrocarbons are converted into water vapor and CO_2 (see Figure 2). In addition, DOCs are also sometimes used by advanced aftertreatment technologies in modern diesels to support diesel particulate filter (DPF) regeneration strategies. Another favorable byproduct of a DOC installation is the reduction of offensive odors typically associated with diesel emissions.

DOC Technology

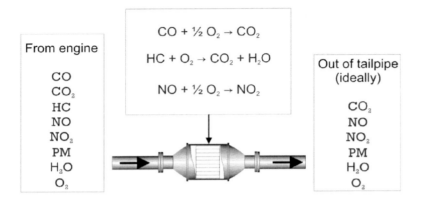

From engine

CO
CO_2
HC
NO
NO_2
PM
H_2O
O_2

$$CO + \tfrac{1}{2} O_2 \rightarrow CO_2$$

$$HC + O_2 \rightarrow CO_2 + H_2O$$

$$NO + \tfrac{1}{2} O_2 \rightarrow NO_2$$

Out of tailpipe
(ideally)

CO_2
NO
NO_2
PM
H_2O
O_2

Figure 2. The fundamental chemical reactions within a DOC.

The core of a DOC is an open-channel ceramic monolith or metallic honeycomb substrate that provides support to the catalyst. Cordierite ($2MgO\text{-}2Al_2O_3\text{-}5SiO_2$) is the most popular ceramic material used for DOC substrates [DieselNet 1997]. The cordierite monolith honeycomb substrates are characterized by a high geometric surface area, large open frontal area, low thermal mass and heat capacity, high temperature durability, low coefficient of thermal expansion, good coatability, washcoat compatibility, strength, and oxidation resistance.

Metallic substrates are an alternative to ceramic cordierite substrates and are made of thin metal foils that are flat or corrugated and formed into a honeycomb structure [DieselNet 2003]. Iron (Fe), chromium (Cr), and aluminum (Al) alloys are commonly used to make these substrates. They have higher cost than ceramic substrates and are characterized by their high geometric surface area and low pressure drop. Metallic substrates also have a lower heat capacity, which results in a reduced "light-off" temperature (the temperature at which the conversion begins to take place). Additionally, metallic substrates cause turbulent flow within these DOCs, resulting in homogeneous reacting conditions and, consequently, a better mass transfer coefficient. New designs, such as a permeable cross-corrugated structure, allow for a more compact DOC substrate and improved performance [Mucha et al. 2008].

The other important component of a DOC is the catalyst. By definition, a catalyst is a substance that increases the rate of a reaction without being consumed in the process. The most common catalysts used in DOCs are those formulated with noble metals such as platinum (Pt), palladium (Pd), and rhodium (Rh). During the manufacturing of a DOC, catalysts are applied to the substrate using a two-step washcoating and impregnation procedure [DieselNet 2005a]. In the first step, a washcoat (usually Al_2O_3, SiO_2, CeO_2, TiO2, ZrO_2, V_2O_5, La_2O_3 or zeolites) is applied to the substrate from a water-based slurry to form a porous, high surface area layer on the substrate. The washcoat helps to hold the catalyst to the substrate and increase reaction efficiency by maximizing the amount of active catalyst that can be accepted during the impregnation phase of the process [Görsmann 2008]. Impregnation then involves applying the catalyst to the washcoat. Catalyst formulations are typically specific to the particular product and are often proprietary.

The volume of a DOC is typically close to that of the engine displacement [Khair and McKinnon 1999]. Because the performance of a DOC is strongly dependent on exhaust temperatures, DOCs are typically installed as close to the exhaust manifold as possible. In some space-saving designs, the DOC is integrated with a muffler into a single device that provides reductions in both emissions and sound.

More recently, the development of advanced integrated exhaust emission control systems such as continuously regenerating trap (CRT™) systems [Walker et al. 2002; Kittelson et al. 2006; Biswas et al. 2008], continuously regenerating trap systems with a catalyzed DPF (CCRT™), selective catalyst reduction (SCR) systems [Katare et al. 2007; Biswas et al. 2008], and partial filter (PF) systems [Mayer et al. 2009; Yoon et al. 2009] has spawned alternative formulations for these applications. The catalysts used in CRT, CCRT, SCR, and PF systems are primarily formulated to promote oxidation of NO to NO_2 (the third reaction shown in Figure 2) [Allansson et al. 2002; Görsmann 2008]. Generated NO_2 is used to help oxidize DPM that is accumulated in DPFs and, therefore, supports the regeneration of DPF systems. In SCR systems, DOCs are also used to help improve low-temperature performance of the system.

To avoid potential deactivation of the catalyst, the use of ultra-low sulfer diesel fuel (ULSDF) is recommended and frequently required for the majority of engines equipped with DOCs and for other catalyzed exhaust aftertreatment systems. The oxidation performance of catalysts has been shown to severely degrade with excessive DPM accumulation in the DOC because the DPM acts as a barrier between the catalytic surface and gases [Eaton et al. 2009].

Effects of a DOC on Emissions

The United States Environmental Protection Agency (U.S. EPA) [EPA 2010] and the California Air Resources Board (CARB) [CARB 2010] have evaluated several types of DOCs for retrofit applications. The EPA verified several DOC products as 40% efficient at removing CO and 50% efficient at removing HC. Depending on design and catalyst formulation, DOCs were verified to reduce total DPM emissions by 20% to 35% [EPA 2010]. CARB listed several DOC-type products as Level 1 DPM control technologies with a DPM reduction of 25% [CARB 2010]. The EPA and CARB both require that DOCs should not increase on-average NO_2 emissions by more than 20% from the baseline [EPA 2007b; CARB 2009a,b].

The performance of a DOC varies widely based on catalyst formulation and effective surface area. In addition, because chemical reactions in a DOC depend on exhaust temperatures, the performance of a DOC is critically dependent upon the engine design and duty cycle. Due to these dependencies, the actual effects of a DOC on the emissions may vary with application. Still, most catalysts should be effective in reducing CO and

HC at temperatures exceeding 250°C (482°F), which are typical for engines operating in underground mines at medium- and heavy-duty conditions [McClure et al. 1988; Katare et al. 2007]. One study showed that CO and total hydrocarbons can be reduced by low-activity catalysts by 13%–40% and 55%, medium-activity catalysts by 57%–70% and 55%, and high-activity catalysts by 77%–80% and 97%, respectively [Khair and McKinnon 1999]. Additionally, the low-temperature performance of a DOC can also be enhanced by oversizing the DOC for the application [McClure 1992].

DOCs have also been found to be effective in reducing the soluble organic fraction (SOF) / organic carbon (OC) fractions of DPM as well as vapor-phase organics / gas-phase hydrocarbons emitted by heavy-duty diesel engines [Bagley and Gratz 1998; Bagley et al. 1998; Vaaraslahti et al. 2006; Shah et al. 2007; Bugarski et al. 2009] and light-duty diesel engines [Klein et al. 1998; Ålander et al. 2004]. Additionally, the effects of DOCs on the concentrations of EC have been found to be a function of engine operating conditions and fuel type [Bugarski et al. 2010]. In general, the overall effectiveness of a DOC as a DPM control is primarily dependent on the fraction of OC present in the engine exhaust (i.e., the total DPM reduction efficiency increases with increased OC content [Shah et al. 2007]). Considering this factor, DOCs may be particularly effective in reducing DPM emissions from engines operated on fatty acid methyl ester (FAME) biodiesel fuels (see Section 2.3.1).

When fuels with a relatively high sulfur content (> 500 ppm) are used, an increase in sulfate emissions has been shown to offset the advantages of Pt-catalyzed DOCs [McClure et al. 1988; McClure 1992; Majewski et al. 1995; Majewski 2009a]. Sulfates, as well as other gaseous and solid DPM components can be trapped within the washcoat and be released during high-load operating conditions (a process known as the "storage and release" phenomenon [Kittelson et al. 2006; Kawano et al. 2007; Majewski 2009a]). This complicates the measurement of DOC efficiency. Additionally, sulfur in the fuel can lead to sulfate formation, which can poison the catalyst and adversely affect the longevity of a DOC. The use of ULSD fuels and/or modern catalyst formulations designed to suppress sulfate formation (base-metal oxides and Pd) can help to minimize these issues [Majewski 2009a].

One potential adverse effect of using certain types of DOCs is an increase in secondary NO_2 emissions [Watts et al. 1998; NIOSH 2006a,b], which might result from enhanced oxidation of NO to NO_2 in the presence of Pt-based catalyst formulations. This phenomenon is temperature- and catalyst-formulation dependent [McClure et al. 1988; Ambs and McClure 1993; Mayer et al. 2003; Katare et al. 2007; Czerwinski et al. 2007; Lorentzou et al. 2008; Johansen et al. 2007; Khair et al. 2008]. In underground mining applications, the catalyst formulations that should be selected are those that minimize secondary NO_2 emissions while preserving an acceptable conversion efficiency for CO and HC over an anticipated duty cycle.

In the case of a typical Pt-based catalyst, the oxidation of NO to NO_2 reaches the highest rate between 300°C (572°F) and 450°C (842°F). At temperatures higher than approximately 500°C (932°F), the process is reversed by thermal dissociation of NO_2. Because a typical catalyst is relatively inefficient at temperatures below 250°C (482°F), the secondary NO_2 emissions are relatively low for DOC-equipped engines operated at light load conditions. Due to the presence of other constituents in diesel exhaust, the NO_X reactions in a DOC are more complicated than a simple conversion of NO to NO_2 [Ambs and McClure 1993; Majewski et al. 1995]. Because DOCs have been shown to not produce NO_2 until most of the CO and hydrocarbons have been consumed [Katare et al. 2007], the issue of secondary NO_2 emissions should theoretically be more pronounced for lower emitting engines. However, DOCs that are used to control CO and HC emissions, from modern, low-emitting engines are designed with relatively low Pt-content formulations (< 0.4 g/liter) and, consequently, the rate of NO to NO_2 oxidation is substantially lower [Ambs and McClure 1993]. An aged, low-activity DOC has even shown to be a net consumer of NO_2 over a wide range of temperatures and space velocities [Katare et al. 2007]. DOCs with Pd [Majewski et al. 1995] and base-metal-Pd catalysts [Johansen et al. 2007] have been found to not produce secondary NO_2 emissions within typical exhaust temperature ranges. However, similar catalysts have shown to have significantly higher light-off temperatures for CO and HC than Pt catalysts [Majewski et al. 1995].

Regulations

DOCs are used in underground coal and metal/nonmetal mining applications as stand-alone devices and as an integral part of various exhaust aftertreatment systems [Watts et al. 1998; Khalek et al. 2003; MSHA 2009f]. In Pennsylvania and West Virginia regulations require the use of DOCs on underground diesel-powered coal-mining vehicles [PADEP 2009; WVDEC 2004].

2.2.2.2 Diesel Particulate Filters (DPF)

Introduction

Diesel particulate filter (DPF) technology was introduced in the late 1970s as a method for controlling particulate matter emissions from diesel engines [Howitt and Montierth 1984; Mathur et al. 2008]. Because of their ability to significantly reduce DPM mass emissions, these systems play an increasingly important role in meeting current emissions standards for heavy-duty (HD) onroad and nonroad diesel-powered vehicles [66 Fed. Reg. 5001 (2001); 69 Fed. Reg. 38957 (2004); EC 1999/96/EC (2000); EC 595/2009 (2009)]. DPFs are commercially available in both retrofit and original equipment manufacturer (OEM) applications for both onroad and nonroad engines [Mayer et al. 2000; Allansson et al. 2002; Eberwein 2008; Mayer 1998; Mayer et al. 1999; Hug 2008; Shah et al. 2006]. Additionally, manufacturers are implementing them into the majority of new HD highway truck engines in the U.S. [Johnson 2009; Liu et al. 2009b; Khalek et al. 2009].

DPF Technology

DPM Filtration

The heart of a DPF system is the filtration media, which captures DPM within its fine porous microstructure, preventing expulsion into the environment. The actual filtration

14

process depends on filter media and DPM loading. Eventually, these trapped particles will be burned off of the DPF in a secondary oxidation process known as "regeneration."

Several types of filtration media are currently being used or researched: extruded ceramics, sintered metal, and metal foams are the most common. Extruded ceramic monoliths are made of ceramic oxides such as cordierite ($Mg_2Al_4Si_5O_{18}$, used in both heavy-duty (HD) and light-duty (LD) applications) and aluminum titanate (Al_2TiO_5, used in LD applications), as well as silicon carbide (SiC) (used in HD and LD applications) [Konstandopoulos and Papaionnou 2008; Boger et al. 2008a; Johnson 2009]. Extruded ceramic monoliths have a "wall-flow" filtration design, or a design that is composed of a large number of small channels (resembling that of catalytic converter monoliths) whose alternating ends are plugged to force exhaust flow through the wall of the monolith (see Figure 3). In general, these ceramic monolith substrates are characterized with high geometric surface area, large open frontal area, low thermal mass and heat capacity, high-temperature durability, low coefficient of thermal expansion, good coatability, washcoat compatibility, strength, and oxidation resistance.

However, the two classes of ceramic materials (ceramic oxides and SiC) differ in several critical physical properties. Due to higher porosity, the SiC monoliths typically generate less backpressure than monoliths made of ceramic oxides [Lorentzou et al. 2008]. Also, SiC monoliths can withstand higher thermal stresses than ceramic-oxide materials. This advantage makes SiC monoliths the preferred choice for applications requiring short-term and high-peak temperature regeneration, whereas DPFs made with ceramic-oxide materials are almost exclusively used in systems designed for thermally moderate regeneration processes. SiC also has a higher melting temperature, which makes it more durable than ceramic-oxide materials in the event of uncontrolled regeneration [Weltens and Vogel 2008]. Ceramic oxides have lower thermal conductivity than SiC, which allows these monoliths to regenerate more efficiently at any given temperature than SiC monoliths [Boger et al. 2008a].

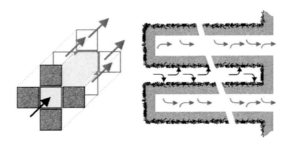

Figure 3. Extruded ceramic wall-flow monolith used in DPF systems.

Monoliths with a higher cell density, or number of channels per cross-sectional area, generally have a higher filter surface area and, therefore, generate less flow restriction. However, these are much more prone to clogging due to ash accumulation. Wall-flow monoliths with 100 cells/in² are typically used (as retrofits) on older, higher emitting engines [Weltens and Vogel 2008]. Wall-flow monoliths with 200 cells/in² are often used in contemporary diesel engines that are fueled and lubricated with low-ash-forming fluids (ULSDF and CJ-4 oils).

The DPM cake that builds in the channels and on the surface of wall flow monolith filters plays an important role in the filtration process [Schmidt et al. 2007; Konstandopoulos and Papaionnou 2008]. As DPM accumulates within the filter, it becomes the governing filtration medium and can improve the overall filtration efficiency of the DPF by two to three orders of magnitude [Gieshaskiel et al. 2007; Schmidt et al. 2007; Lorentzou et al. 2008; Yang et al. 2009].

The alternative to DPFs made with ceramic monoliths are wall-flow filters made of sintered metal media [Zelenka et al. 1998; Konstandopoulos et al. 2005; Schrewe et al. 2008]. The core of a sintered metal filter (SMF) is composed of a number of sintered metal plates, or pockets, welded together to form a filter unit. The plates are made of a formed and expanded stainless steel substrate coated with sintered metal powder [Schrewe et al. 2008]. Flow is typically channeled from the outside to the inside of the plates. The system is designed to allow for easy access to the element for ash cleaning [Steigert 2008]. The prominent characteristics of SMF systems are flexibility in forming/shaping, relatively low pressure drop, relatively high ash-holding capacity, and relatively simple DPM and ash cleaning.

Safety, Reliability, and Durability of DPF Systems

It has been demonstrated that DPF systems have a useful life of several thousand hours [McGinn et al. 2004; WRAP 2005; Conard et al 2006; D'Urbano and Mayer 2007; Mayer et al. 2008]. Typical causes of useful-life failures of DPF elements include stresses induced by mechanical vibrations, stresses from high exhaust temperatures generated during normal operation as well as uncontrolled regenerations, and catalyst degradation from thermal stress or chemical poisoning [Stroia et al. 2008; Kim et al. 2008; Dabhoiwala et al. 2009]. In the case of uncontrolled regeneration, the exhaust temperatures can reach in excess of 925°C (1,697°F) [Watts et al. 1995; DieselNet 2005b]. The potential for uncontrolled regeneration of a DPF system can be minimized by ensuring operation of the system within design parameters. The risk of uncontrolled regeneration is typically minor if the DPM mass accumulation within the filter does not exceed 5 g (grams) of DPM per liter of the element volume [Mayer 2008b; Mathur et al. 2008].

To avoid potential problems with engine and filtration media, all DPF systems should be equipped with a visible engine backpressure sensor, monitor, and data-logging system. These systems are primarily used to monitor the regeneration process and the accumulation of ash in the DPF. The exhaust backpressure monitor can also be used to identify instances of unusually low pressure drop across the DPF system, which may indicate potential failures [DieselNet 2005b; Dabhoiwala et al. 2009].

Other potential safety issues related to the use of DPF systems are related to hot surfaces, additional noise, and reduced visibility. The temperatures of the DPF system components during the regeneration process can reach 800°C (1,472°F) [Mathur et al. 2008; Boger et al. 2008b], substantially exceeding normal exhaust temperatures. In order to minimize potential safety issues, all hot surfaces of the components of DPF systems should be guarded or insulated.

Verification of DPF Systems

DPF systems are verified by a number of government bodies in the United States [CARB 2009a,b; EPA 2009; MSHA 2009b] and worldwide [D'Urbano and Mayer 2007]. The approved DPM removal efficiencies of various models of noncatalyzed and catalyzed DPFs for controlling DPM emissions from underground mining equipment are available from the Mine Safety and Health Administration (MSHA) [MSHA 2009b]. However, the MSHA list of DPFs is not all inclusive and only contains products submitted for consideration by the manufacturers. According to the list, DPF systems with ceramic oxide and SiC wall flow monoliths are generally considered to be either 85% or 87% efficient in removing total DPM mass, depending on the product. Similarly, sintered metal DPFs are considered to be either 81% or 99% efficient in removing total DPM mass. The MSHA list primarily includes noncatalyzed DPFs regenerated using electrical energy as well as passively regenerated DPF systems. The majority of the DPF efficiencies were established using low-sulfur diesel (LSD) fuel. Additional information on the efficiency of verified diesel emissions control strategies for on-road and off-road applications is also available from CARB [CARB 2009a,b] and the U.S. EPA [EPA 2009]. Also, the Swiss Federal Office of the Environment (FOEN) and Swiss National Accidents Insurance Organization (SUVA) have a list of retrofit filters that were thoroughly tested in occupational applications, including retrofit mining and tunneling [D'Urbano and Mayer 2007].

Effects of DPF Systems on Emissions

Effects on DPM Emissions

The following list highlights key findings from research performed to validate the efficiency of various DPF systems. In general, a number of independent tests have found that DPF systems are highly efficient at removing DPM on a mass basis.

- Clean, noncatalyzed ceramic oxides and SiC monolith DPFs are reported to be, on average, approximately 75% efficient in filtering the mass of diesel aerosols of all sizes [Lorentzou et al. 2008; Dabhoiwala et al. 2009]. However, DPM-loaded ceramic monoliths DPF systems, as well as DPM-loaded sintered metal DPF systems, have been shown in a number of studies to be ten times more effective at removing DPM when compared to clean DPFs [Warner et al. 2003; Liu et al. 2008; Biswas et al. 2008].

- Warner et. al [2003] found that Pt-washcoated/impregnated catalyzed DPF (CDPF) systems remove 93.8% to 96.7% of the TC, 94.7% to 99.5% of the EC, and 84.8% to 97.8% of the OC, depending on engine operating conditions.

- A CRT system was shown to reduce total DPM mass and number of solid diesel aerosol particle emissions by 90% [Mayer et al. 2000; Zarling et al. 2005; Shah et al. 2007] and 99%, respectively [Mayer et al. 2000]. Similarly, Zarling and coauthors [2005] showed a CRT system was capable of reducing EC emissions, on average, by 95%. Shah and coauthors [2007] observed 89.7% and 93.6% reductions in EC and OC for a CRT system.

- A study conducted by Liu and coauthors [2009b] showed that CCRT systems reduced the EC emissions by 99.7% and OC emissions by 99.4%.

- Several studies [Warner et al. 2003; Khalek et al. 2009] showed that DPF systems reduce emissions of metals (primarily originating from lubricating oil) by more than 85%. Richards [Richards et al. 2006] showed that a base-metal-catalyzed SiC wall-flow monolith is effective in removing metals from the exhaust of an engine fueled with ULSD that is treated with an Fe/Sr-based fuel-borne catalyst (FBC).

- CCRT systems were found to reduce high molecular weight compounds derived from incomplete combustion of lubricating oil by more than 95% [Liu et al. 2008; Liu et al. 2009b]. CCRT systems were also found to reduce a selection of particularly hazardous organic compounds (polycyclic aromatic hydrocarbons, aldehydes, formaldehydes, acetaldehydes, flouranthene and its derivatives) by more than 90% [Khalek et al. 2009].

- The release of sulfates was found to impact the effectiveness of aged DPF systems [Mayer et al. 2003; Mayer et al. 2008]. Sulfate formation can be minimized using fuels and lubricating oil with low-sulfur content and catalysts formulated with less Pt and more Pd, Rh, and base metals [Johansen et al. 2007; Czerwinski et al. 2007; Lorentzou et al. 2008; Khair et al. 2008; Morgensen et al. 2009].

However, DPF systems appear to be much more effective in controlling the DPM mass concentration than the total number concentration emissions of diesel aerosol particles [Biswas et al. 2008; Bugarski et al. 2009; De Filippo and Maricq 2008]. Several studies have shown that DPF systems can potentially increase the number of particles emitted from the engine (these particles are often very small and, therefore, are not a major contributor in mass-based efficiency measurements). This is an area of concern and currently a topic of ongoing research [Warner et al. 2003; Vaaraslahti et al. 2004; Grose et al. 2006; Kittelson et al. 2006; Biswas et al. 2008; Bugarski et al. 2009].

Effects on Gas Emissions

Typically, noncatalyzed DPF systems have minor effects on CO, HC, NO, NO_2, and SO_2 emissions [Herner et al. 2009]. At DPF temperatures over 250°C (482°F), however, a fraction of NO_2 might get consumed in a chemical reaction with DPM accumulated in the DPF [Richards et al. 2006].

The effects of catalyzed DPF systems on CO, HC, NO, NO_2, and SO_2 emissions are primarily a function of catalyst formulation, catalyst load, and operating temperature [Warner et al. 2003; Richards et al. 2006; Herner et al. 2009]. Noble- and base-metal-catalyzed DPF systems are efficient in lowering CO and HC emissions by oxidizing them to CO_2. In Pt-group-catalyst formulations, the highest reductions in CO, HC, SO_2, and the highest NO_2 / NO_X ratio emissions can be expected at high catalyst loadings and high exhaust temperatures.

Some catalysts in catalyzed DPF systems may oxidize NO to NO_2. This is desirable because NO_2 assists in the process of removing DPM from the filter. However, under certain conditions the catalyst may oxidize more NO to NO_2 than can be consumed by DPM. Under these circumstances, NO_2 slip, or the unwanted emission of NO_2, occurs. These secondary emissions of NO_2 are a major issue related to DPF/DOC systems using Pt-based catalysts [MSHA 2002; Mayer et al. 2003; Conard et al. 2005; Bugarski et al. 2006; Czerwinski et al. 2007; Johansen et al. 2007]. Noble- and base-metal-catalyst formulations in DPF systems typically have minor effects on total NO_X emissions [Mayer et al. 2003; Warner et al. 2003; Herner et al. 2009; Richards and Chadderton 2003; Richards et al. 2006], but may have a major impact on the split between NO and NO_2 fractions in total NO_X [Czerwinski et al. 2007; Johansen et al. 2007; Khalek et al. 2009; Richards and Chadderton 2003; Richards et al. 2006].

Effects of Failed DPF Systems on Emissions

The cracks that develop in the DPF media due to excessive mechanical and thermal stresses can diminish the efficiency of DPF systems [Seiler et al. 2008; Dabhoiwala et al. 2008]. However, the extent of efficiency depletion depends on the level of damage. In some cases, minor damage was found to have only a minor influence on the effectiveness of the DPF, especially in a loaded state [Seiler et al. 2008]. At least one study investigated cracks in the DPF element of CDPF and CCRT systems and concluded that these failures had minor effects on gaseous emissions [Dabhoiwala et al. 2008]. However, it is important to state that more significant damage would likely have a substantial effect on the performance of these systems. Because it is extremely difficult to gauge the level and impact of a DPF failure, mine's should have any damaged DPFs replaced immediately, regardless of the extent of the damage.

DPF Regeneration

The engine backpressure generated by DPF systems is, in general, substantially higher than the typical pressure drop across exhaust piping, bands, mufflers, and DOCs. The maximum allowable exhaust backpressure is determined for each engine by the engine manufacturer. The maximum allowable exhaust backpressures for MSHA-approved engines that are not equipped with DPF systems range from 4.7 kPa (47 mbar, 19 in H_2O) to 15 kPa (150 mbar, 60 in H_2O) [MSHA 2009a]. The issue of increased engine backpressure should be discussed with both the engine and DPF suppliers to avoid potential issues with engine warranties during retrofit applications.

Removing DPM captured in the DPF element on a continuous or periodic basis is critical to sustaining engine backpressures at reasonable levels. The carbonaceous fraction of DPM trapped in the DPF element (EC and OC) is effectively removed by an oxidation process called DPF regeneration. The metallic ash fraction of DPM, however, cannot be oxidized. Therefore, DPF systems still need periodic servicing to remove ash buildup.

DPF regeneration is based on the oxidation of DPM in the presence of heat. The DPM is ignited by raising the exhaust temperature, which subsequently oxidizes it to CO and CO_2. The main parameters governing the regeneration process in DPF systems are exhaust or media temperature, the availability of oxidants, DPM load and morphology, and the thermal properties of filter material [Setten van et al. 2001; Boger et al. 2008a; Schrewe et al. 2008]. The temperature at which the rate of DPM accumulation in the DPF is equal to the rate of DPM oxidation is known as balance point temperature (BPT). The BPT is usually slightly higher than the light-off temperature, which is the temperature at which the conversion of DPM begins.

The two oxidizers typically available in diesel exhaust are oxygen (O_2) and nitrogen dioxide (NO_2). Because diesel combustion is inherently lean, O_2 is abundant in the exhaust under most engine operating conditions (as high as 10% or 100,000 ppm). In contrast, the concentration of NO_2 in the exhaust of a typical diesel engine is usually below 100 ppm. NO_2, however, is a much stronger oxidizer than O_2. In the presence of sufficient NO_2, the DPM is oxidized at exhaust temperatures as low as 200°C (392°F) [Görsmann 2008]. In contrast, DPM oxidization by O_2 takes place at exhaust temperatures that often exceed 550–600°C (1,022-1,112°F) [Jelles et al. 1999; Görsmann 2008; Chilumukuru et al. 2009]. For this reason, noble-metal catalysts are often used to substantially increase the fraction of NO_2 in NO_X [McClure et al. 1988; Ambs and McClure 1993; Mayer et al. 2003; Katare et al. 2007; Czerwinski et al. 2007; Johansen et al. 2007; Lorentzou et al. 2008; Khair et al. 2008].

The excessive accumulation of DPM in the DPF element (e.g., during prolonged periods of operation at light engine loads, such as idle), followed by the initiation of regeneration, can result in spikes of extremely high temperatures—a condition known as uncontrolled regeneration. Under these circumstances, DPM burns too quickly, and the exhaust flow rate is not sufficient to dissipate the heat. Uncontrolled regeneration may cause catastrophic failure of the DPF element and pose significant safety risks. For this reason, periods of excessive idling as well as buildup of excessive DPM mass within the DPF must be prevented. Implementation of administrative measures and close monitoring of engine backpressure can help prevent these dangerous scenarios. The risk of uncontrolled regeneration is typically minor if the DPM burden does not exceed 5 g (grams) of DPM per liter of the element volume [Mayer 2008b; Mathur et al. 2008].

In terms of regeneration processes, DPF systems are often divided into two groups: passive systems and active systems. In passive systems, the regeneration occurs during the normal operation of the vehicle. The process does not require any external assistance and depends solely on the energy and temperatures available in the exhaust gases. Passive systems are typically used for DPFs deployed over HD cycles. On the other hand, active systems are needed when the application requires an external source of energy to reach exhaust temperatures high enough to support the regeneration. Active systems are generally used in LD applications and are more complex as well as more expensive than passive systems.

Passive Regeneration Systems

Passive regeneration is typically achieved with the help of a catalyst. The catalyst is either a compound deposited in the DPF (catalyzed DPF or CDPF) or an additive present in the diesel fuel (fuel-borne catalyst, FBC) and is used to lower the onset temperature of the regeneration process.

The majority of compounds used in CDPF systems exhibit activity at temperatures below 200°C (392°F) [Allansson et al. 2002]. The most common catalyst formulations are based on platinum group metals (Pt, Pd) and base metals (V, Fe, Sr, Mg, Mo, Cr) [Johansen et al. 2007; Czerwinski et al. 2007; Lorentzou et al. 2008; Khair et al. 2008; Morgensen et al. 2009; Richards et al. 2006]. Pt-based catalysts induce regeneration at onset temperatures as low as 280°C (536°F) [Allansson et al. 2002], although base-metal catalysts initiate regeneration at 350–400°C (662-752°F) [Johansen et al. 2007; Steigert 2008; Görsmann 2008].

A fuel-borne catalyst (FBC) that is used as an additive in the diesel fuel improves the direct contact between the catalyst and the DPM [Jelles et al. 1999]. During combustion, the FBC forms very small particles that mix directly with or deposit onto the DPM, which is later beneficial during DPF regeneration. The most widely used FBCs have Pt, Ce, Fe, and Sr for an active component [Bach et al 1998; Seguelong and Quigley 2002; Richards et al. 2006; D'Urbano and Mayer 2007; Naschke et al. 2008]. The concentrations of metals in FBC additives are relatively low, between a few ppm and a few tenths of a ppm. FBCs can initiate passive regeneration of a DPF at onset temperatures between 330°C (626°F) and 430°C (806°F), even in the case where temperatures are in this range for only short time periods [Bach et al. 1998; Jelles et al. 1999; Schrewe et al. 2008]. This relatively low onset temperature, combined with the absence of NO_2-slip-related issues, are the major reasons for the popularity of FBC/DPF systems in U.S. underground mines [Richards et al. 2006; Czerwinski et al. 2007; MSHA 2009c; Noll and Patts 2009].

The FBC is generally added to the fuel via onboard dosing systems [Seguelong and Quigley 2002; Naschke at al. 2008]. These systems are equipped with closed-loop safety systems that prevent dosing of the FBC if a DPF failure is detected. Alternatively, the FBC can be added directly to the fuel supply [McGinn et al. 2004]. When this approach is used, strict administrative controls must be implemented in order to prevent dispensing fuel treated with FBC to vehicles that are not designated to receive this fuel. The use of FBC-doped fuel in a vehicle without a DPF could potentially generate harmful metal-oxide particle emissions.

Some potential drawbacks of using FBCs include: (1) long-term effects of increased ash accumulation due to the FBC, (2) potential metal-oxide particle emissions in the event of system malfunction or tampering, and (3) the added complexity of a reliable onboard computer-controlled dosing system.

An alternative approach to these passive regeneration strategies is a continuously regenerating trap (CRT). This system is composed of a precatalyst followed by a noncatalyzed DPF [Allansson et al. 2002; Görsmann 2008]. The catalyst formulation in

21

the precatalyst (a DOC) is designed to promote the oxidation of NO to NO_2 and supply the DPF with enough NO_2 needed for the regeneration of DPM. These systems can support continuous regeneration at exhaust temperatures between 250°C (482°F) and 500°C (932°F) [Görsmann 2008].

Due to the presence of a DOC, the CRT requires more space than a simple CDPF. The performance of a CRT system also depends on the abundance of engine-out NO_2 emissions (NO_X/DPM ratio for sustainable regeneration should be over 50) [Jaussi 2008]. Additionally, the use of a catalyst within the DPF to support regeneration in such a system is also available (CCRT) [Allansson et al. 2002; Görsmann 2008]. This method can be used for applications where exhaust temperatures frequently exceed 200°C–250°C (392°F- 482°F) [Görsmann 2008]. However, NO_2 slip (as high as 500 ppm) [Mayer et al. 2003] has prevented the use of these systems in occupational environments where there is concern about high exposure to NO_2.

Two approaches are currently being deployed to minimize NO_2 slip from CRT and CCRT systems [O'Sullivan et al. 2004; Görsmann 2008]: (1) NO_2 reduction using hydrocarbon injection and an NO_2 decomposition catalyst, and (2) NO_2 and NO reduction using urea injection and selective catalyst reduction (SCR) (see Section 2.2.2.5). A CRT system equipped with an SCR (SCRT™ system, Johnson Matthey PLC) is being evaluated in an underground salt mine in Germany [Saelhoff 2010].

Active Regeneration Systems

Although advancements in catalyst formulations and design of passive DPF systems have significantly reduced onset regeneration temperatures in passive systems, there are still a large number of applications where vehicles are operated over LD cycles with exhaust temperatures that remain below DPM light-off temperatures the majority of the time. Such applications require the use of active DPF systems. In these systems, regeneration is achieved by temporarily raising exhaust temperatures above 600°C (1,112°F) through the use of an external energy source. The most common sources of external energy are: (1) electrical heaters, (2) diesel fuel burners, and (3) catalytic burners. The major advantage of these systems is that the regeneration does not depend on vehicle duty cycle.

Offboard Active Regeneration

Active systems use heater sources, which can either be located offboard or onboard of the vehicle. When offboard, the DPF is temporarily removed from the vehicle and taken to a regeneration station or kiln either when the engine backpressure reaches a predetermined limit or at scheduled time intervals. This regeneration station needs to be installed in a safe, well-ventilated area to prevent exposure of workers to pollutants emitted during the regeneration process. The electrical power requirement for such stations is typically between 3.5 and 10 kW [Schrewe 2008].

During the process of offboard DPF regeneration, an electrical element is used to heat a stream of compressed air, which is then forced through the DPF to initiate oxidation of the DPM. The air temperature is controlled to ensure that the regeneration is initiated and supported safely, without causing excessive stress to the DPF elements, which are often exposed to temperatures above 1,000°C (1,832°F) [Steigert 2008]. Typically, SiC monolith DPFs, which can withstand high thermal stresses, can be regenerated in approximately two hours. Ceramic-oxide monoliths can require up to eight hours. After the DPF is thermally regenerated and cooled, compressed air is used to clean ash from the DPF element. In order to minimize worker exposure, a vacuum system is normally used to collect the ash during this process.

The major disadvantages of offboard regeneration systems are: (1) the requirement for downtime and labor needed for disassembling and reassembling the system, (2) the requirement for a regeneration system infrastructure (including the potential added expense of additional DPFs), and (3) the need for strong discipline in performing regeneration procedures in a timely manner. Also, in order to minimize the effect that this process has on productivity, regeneration procedures must be optimized to coordinate with production cycles. Therefore, an offboard electric regeneration strategy is often most suitable for light-duty, nonproduction applications [Conard et al. 2006]. Handling issues related to the weight and size of the DPF units may also limit the applicability of these systems to engines with an output of approximately 150 hp or less [Schnakenberg and Bugarski 2002].

<u>Onboard active regeneration</u>

Onboard active regeneration strategies are desirable because there is no downtime or added labor associated with the removal of DPFs from the system. There are a number of embodiments of onboard active DPF regeneration systems, the most common of which are:

- **Electrical heaters onboard of the vehicle with electrical energy and compressed air supplied from a source offboard of the vehicle.** In this system, SiC monoliths are used to allow for the shortest possible regeneration time. In order to execute the regeneration, the vehicle must be parked in a designated area with its engine turned off. A stream of compressed air (supplied from offboard of the vehicle) is heated to 600°C (1,112°F) by the electrical coils mounted in the inlet section of the DPF. The major disadvantages of such onboard regenerated systems are: (1) requirement for vehicle downtime and labor required for bringing the vehicle to and from the regeneration station, (2) requirement for regeneration system infrastructure, and (3) potential reliability and durability issues with the system components, primarily electrical heaters.

- **Electrical heaters onboard of the vehicle with electrical energy and compressed air supplied by the vehicle power system.** The primary challenge in designing this system is the availability of electrical energy onboard of the vehicle. Approximately 55 kW of energy is needed to regenerate a typical DPF installed on a 6.6 liter nonroad engine under all engine operating conditions [Schrewe 2008]. If an FBC is added to the fuel, the regeneration of the same DPF system requires approximately 25 kW of electrical energy. This is still a sizeable amount of energy and is typically greater than what is available onboard most vehicles. To overcome this challenge, large DPFs are usually replaced with multiple smaller units mounted in parallel, which can then be regenerated one at a time. In such a system, a valve is used to divert the exhaust flow between DPF units. One of the units is isolated from the rest of the exhaust flow and regenerated using an onboard heater and electrical energy available on the vehicle. The heater is used to increase the temperature of the bypass air and support O_2 regeneration. Although regeneration is occurring in this unit, the others continue to filter the exhaust [Shah et al. 2007].The remaining units are then regenerated sequentially. Systems of this type are both complex and expensive. Additionally, systems regenerated using electrical energy supplied from the vehicle power system typically increase fuel consumption [Rembor 2007].

- **Direct ignition of the DPM layer via radiation heat produced by an electrical heater and power supplied by the vehicle systems.** This approach is based on direct ignition of the soot layer via radiation heat to activate regeneration in sintered metal DPF systems [Schewe et al. 2008]. Ignition is achieved with the help of an electrical heater placed in the raw gas side near the sintered metal (SM) filter outlet. A short-term increase in exhaust temperature is used to initiate O_2-supported regeneration. A base metal FBC is used to lower the light-off temperature and energy requirements [Schewe et al. 2008] Additionally, systems regenerated using electrical energy supplied from the vehicle power system typically increase fuel consumption [Rembor 2007].

- **Direct heating of the filter material using the vehicle power system.** DPF systems made with conductive sintered metal elements can also be regenerated by direct heating of the filter material [DePetrillo et al. 2007; Schrewe 2008] using power available onboard of the vehicle. However, because the power requirement for heating an entire filter is rather high, even at low exhaust flow rates, multiple filter units with sequential regeneration (as mentioned above) are also utilized in these systems. This design requires a rather elaborate system. In such systems, a temporary increase in secondary emissions of CO and HC during the regeneration is typically controlled by a DOC. Additionally, systems regenerated using electrical energy supplied by the vehicle power system typically increase fuel consumption [Rembor 2007].

- **In-line full-flow diesel fuel burner systems**. In-line full flow diesel fuel burner systems are a potential solution for applications that require unrestricted operation over the entire duty cycle [Houben et al. 1994; Zelenka et al. 2002]. In these systems, a diesel fuel burner is periodically used to provide the heat needed to increase the temperature of the entire exhaust and to support regeneration. Ideally, these systems regenerate independently of the vehicle duty cycle and irrespective of engine exhaust temperatures. The regeneration takes approximately five minutes and occurs every eight hours [Zelenka et al. 2002; Conard et al. 2006]. More details on the design and operation of in-line full-flow diesel fuel burner DPF systems are available elsewhere [Houben et al. 1994; Zelenka et al. 2002; Paterson et al. 2007; Majewski 2009b].

These systems are quite complex and expensive. Additionally, the energy demand for a full flow diesel burner during the regeneration process is approximately 20% to 50% of the entire engine power [Rembor 2008]. There is also up to a 2% fuel penalty associated with using this type of system.

DPF systems with inline full-flow diesel fuel burners are available in commercial HD applications [Majewski 2009b; Rembor 2007]. Prototypes of similar systems were extensively evaluated in underground metal mines [NIOSH 2006b, Conard et al. 2006]. However, these systems are not currently offered in the U.S. for retrofit applications.

- **Standstill full-flow diesel fuel burner systems.** Standstill full-flow diesel fuel burner systems are similar to in-line systems, but they are designed to regenerate (using heat from a diesel fuel burner) while the engine is turned off. This type of system is suitable for applications that have sufficient downtime to allow for regeneration. The exhaust flow rate through such a system is much lower, as are the energy use and corresponding fuel consumption, which amounts to an increase of less than 1% [Rembor 2008].

- **Catalytic burner regenerated DPF systems.** An alternative to diesel fuel burners are catalytic burners. Catalytic burner technology is used by the majority of LD and HD engine builders to establish regeneration over a wide range of transient operating conditions [Majewski 2003; Suresh et al. 2008; Khalek et al 2009]. In these systems, raw diesel fuel is post-injected into the exhaust system (either with an additional injector located downstream of the exhaust manifold or using late-stage injection within the cylinder). A specially designed DOC is then used to oxidize the fuel and generate heat. This heat increases the exhaust temperature upstream of the DPF system, which promotes regeneration within the DPF [Bouchez and Dementhon 2000; Rembor 2008; Suresh et al. 2008; Chilumukuru et al. 2009; Schaefer et al. 2009; Seguelong and Quigley 2002; Majewski 2003; Schrewe et al. 2008].

Implementation

Currently DPF systems are used by a number of underground mines in the U.S. [MSHA 2009c; Noll and Patts 2009] to attain emissions standards for nonpermissible[2] diesel-powered equipment in underground coal mines [66 Fed. Reg. 27864 (2001)] and to comply with DPM exposure standards in underground metal/nonmetal mines [71 Fed. Reg. 28924 (2006)]. The majority of the systems used in underground coal mines are either active offboard systems regenerated using electrical heaters or lightly catalyzed DPFs regenerated with the help of an FBC [MSHA 2009c]. The potential for increase in NO_2 emissions prevents wider implementation of catalyzed DPF systems in underground mines [MSHA 2002; Cauda et al. 2010].

Prerequisites for implementation of DPF systems

The effects of a selected DPF system on concentrations of criteria gases in the mine should be the first consideration when implementing such a system. The potential need to supply additional quantities of fresh ventilation air above the quantities currently

---

[2] Throughout this document, "permissible" and "nonpermissible" are descriptions used to classify diesel engines. The term permissible describes an engine that is certified by MSHA for use in all areas of a mine that have been deemed gaseous or potentially gaseous by MSHA. The term nonpermissible refers to those engines which are not certified for use in all areas.

provided should also be examined. This issue is particularly important if there is the potential for an increase in the fraction of NO_2 in total NO_X emissions [MSHA 2002]. For this reason, using DPF systems washcoated by catalyst formulations with high Pt content is not currently recommended for use in underground coal mines [MSHA 2002]. In general, these systems should be installed only on vehicles operated in the areas of an underground mine where sufficient quantities of fresh air are supplied for diluting NO_2 concentrations to or below the action or ceiling limits for NO_2 [30 CFR 70.1900; 30 CFR 57.5001].

The installation of DPF systems has a higher chance of success if the system is installed on a relatively new and well-maintained engine with low lubricating oil consumption. Repowering some vehicles should be considered when DPM emissions from the targeted vehicle are substantially higher than certification emissions and/or too high to ensure the reliable operation of the DPF system over the normal duty cycle. Good maintenance practices, and perhaps the measurement of engine emissions (see Section 2.4), should be used to verify that engine-out emissions remain at or below the requirements established by the DPF supplier throughout the engine's life.

Finally, a mine should establish good quality control over the supply and distribution of diesel fuels and lubricants. Engines equipped with DPFs should be fueled only with diesel fuels having low-sulfur content and lubricated using only low-ash-content oils.

Selecting Applications for DPF Installation

DPF installation should be evaluated on a case-by-case basis in terms of cost/benefits and level of effectiveness as compared with other available controls discussed in this document. Some important factors to consider include:

- Operators of HD production diesel-powered vehicles, such as shield haulers, load-haul-dump (LHD) vehicles, and haulage trucks, are the underground mine workers who typically encounter the highest personal exposures to DPM concentration. This is due to the types of engines used (high-output emitters), duty cycles, and the low supply of fresh air in the operation area. [Cantrell et al. 1991; Haney et al. 1997; 71 Fed. Reg. 28924 (2006)]. For this reason, HD diesel-powered vehicles with a high utilization factor appear to be the prime candidates for DPF installations.

- The majority of HD vehicles are operated over duty cycles that frequently produce exhaust temperatures high enough to support passive regeneration of certain types of DPF systems [Watts et al. 1995; McGinn et al. 2004; Conard et al. 2006].

- The HD vehicles in underground mines are typically operated continuously and are not considered suitable for DPF systems that require downtime for active DPF regeneration [McGinn et al. 2004].

- DPF systems are currently retrofitted to a number of HD nonpermissible underground coal applications [MSHA 2009c] and HD applications in metal and nonmetal mines. Due to engineering challenges related to meeting stringent surface and exhaust gas temperature requirements [26 Fed. Reg. 645 (1961); 61 Fed. Reg.

26

55412 (1996)], DPF systems are currently not available for HD underground coal permissible vehicles.

- LD vehicles have been found to be responsible for 47% of the underground DPM burden in metal mines [Rubeli et al. 2004]. One of the reasons for such a significant contribution is the fact that the LD vehicles are typically powered by relatively small engines with relatively high power-specific emissions [MSHA 2009a]. The duty cycle of LD vehicles typically does not generate exhaust temperatures high enough to support passive regeneration of the majority of DPF systems [Conard et al. 2006]. However, these vehicles are operated infrequently, and active DPF systems, regenerated during the vehicle downtime, are found to be suitable for these types of applications [Conard et al. 2006; MSHA 2009c].

- The actual contribution of a targeted vehicle to overall DPM concentrations (as well as personal exposures) can be established by conducting ambient and personal exposure monitoring for different production scenarios or for simulated isolated-zone scenarios [McGinn et al. 2004; NIOSH 2006a,b].

Design, Selection, Optimization, and Installation of DPF Systems

DPF systems are currently available to underground mining industries almost exclusively as aftermarket retrofits for existing and new diesel-powered vehicles and equipment. Because DPF systems are expected to play a major role in advanced exhaust aftertreatment systems in the foreseeable future, the mining industry will soon have the option of using OEM-supplied engines equipped with DPF systems. However, for underground coal mines, these Tier 4 engines will first need to be certified by MSHA before being introduced into the mine [61 Fed Reg. 55412 (1996)]. At the time this document was compiled, only one engine equipped with an OEM DPF system had been certified by MSHA [2009a].

Exhaust Temperature Distribution

The duty cycle of the engine has a major impact on the temperatures in the exhaust system. This temperature distribution is critical information that the DPF supplier needs when selecting an adequate DPF size, catalyst strategy, and regeneration concept. This information can be obtained relatively easily by outfitting the targeted vehicle with exhaust temperature sensors and an onboard data logging system [Schnakenberg 2003; McGinn et al. 2004; Conard et al. 2006]. The temperature sensor, typically a thermocouple [Schnakenberg 2003] or resistance temperature detector (RTD) [McGinn et al. 2004; Conard et al. 2006], should be installed in the exhaust system as close as possible to the location of the future DPF installation. The exhaust temperature profile should be obtained for the targeted vehicle over several days of operation, making sure that the recorded duty cycle(s) are well represented [Conard et al. 2006]. In addition, this information can be used to assess the availability of time periods when the vehicle is shut down allowing active regeneration of a DPF system to occur (see Figure 4).

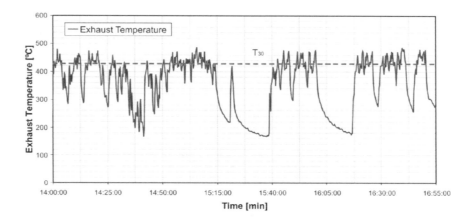

Figure 4. An exhaust temperature profile example.

The exhaust temperature data should be analyzed statistically to obtain the basic exhaust temperature distribution information needed for the DPF selection process. Some useful analyses are histograms, cumulative frequency, moving averages [Schnakenberg 2003], and the duration of high-temperature events (see Figure 5) [Conard et al. 2006]. The cumulative temperature distribution curve is used to estimate T_{30}, the temperature at which exhaust gases exceed the filter regeneration temperature for 30% of the operating time. The T_{30} value is typically used to assess the potential for passive regeneration of a DPF system.

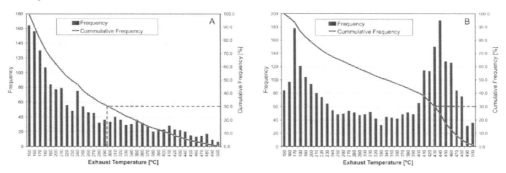

Figure 5. Exhaust temperature histograms typical for: (A) an LD application, and (B) an HD application.

Engine Backpressure

Engine backpressure information is also crucial in the DPF design process. It helps to determine the size and regeneration strategy for the system. In general, the short-term average pressure drop across the DPF, when loaded with DPM and ash (determined for

28

worst-case operating conditions), should not exceed the maximum engine backpressure allowed by the manufacturer for that particular engine.

The maximum allowable backpressure for all MSHA-approved engines is available from MSHA [MSHA 2009a]. The engine backpressure limits determined by the manufacturers of DPF systems, however, are not necessarily identical to those specified by engine manufacturers [D'Urbano and Mayer 2007]. Engine backpressure limits currently range between 4.7 kPa (47 mbar, 19 in H_2O) and 15 kPa (150 mbar, 60 in H_2O) for MSHA-approved engines [MSHA 2009a]. Relatively large DPF units are needed to keep engine backpressures below those limits. DPF manufacturers typically favor higher engine backpressure limits, because this allows for the use of smaller, less expensive units and also helps to maintain the higher exhaust temperatures needed for the regeneration process. Operators should discuss the topic of engine backpressure with both the engine supplier and the DPF supplier before installation to avoid potential engine warranty issues.

Once installed, an engine backpressure monitoring system is an essential component of the DPF system. The information on exhaust backpressure should be displayed in a prominent, highly visible place for the operator during normal equipment operation. Warning signals related to the level of backpressure should be incorporated into the system to allow for adequate action by the operator.

<u>Engine-Out DPM and Gaseous Emissions</u>

Engine-out DPM and gaseous emissions are design parameters that influence the size of the DPF element. DPM mass emissions, potentially available from various engine certification processes or engine manufacturers, should be used to determine the needed storage capacity of the DPF element. However, these values are established during certification testing procedures and duty cycles [DieselNet 2009], which may not be representative of the prevailing duty cycle for the targeted vehicle. Therefore, although this may be the most practical information available to guide mines in DPF sizing, it should be considered a best available estimate and not necessarily an exact representation of in-use emissions.

In addition, the effects of engine age, inadequate maintenance, and altitude [Rubeli et al. 2007] on DPM and gaseous emissions should also be taken into consideration in the DPF sizing process. The DPM mass emissions for engines certified by MSHA under Part 7 are available at MSHA [2009a]. These emissions are established as a weighted average for eight modes of the ISO 8178-C1 steady-state test following the procedure outlined in §7.88 of 61 FR 55412 [1996].

For catalyzed DPF systems requiring NO_2 for passive regeneration, a NO_X / DPM ratio of 50 is desired for sustainable regeneration [Jaussi 2008].

<u>Physical and Dimensional Considerations</u>

For active, offboard regeneration systems, the DPF should be designed to a size that allows for accumulation of DPM over a whole shift without imposing excessive exhaust backpressure. This allows regeneration to be performed between shifts, which can eliminate vehicle downtown. Similarly, onboard active DPF systems should have elements large enough to accommodate DPM collected between regeneration events without imposing excessive exhaust backpressures.

Passive DPF systems, in which regeneration performance depends on exhaust temperature, should be installed as close to the exhaust manifold as possible to minimize the loss of exhaust temperature and heat. Thermal insulation of exhaust pipes between the exhaust manifold and DPF can also be used to minimize exhaust cooling.

The DPF system and other exhaust components should be mounted high on the vehicle to prevent mud and water from entering the system, and they should be installed away from fire-suppression actuators [Conard et al. 2006]. Stresses on the components of the exhaust aftertreatment system that are related to engine and vehicle vibrations should be minimized through some form of dampening. Finally, the DPF installation should allow for easy access to engine systems as well as assembly and disassembly of the DPF system components for inspection and cleaning [McGinn et al. 2004; Conard et al. 2006].

The availability of space for the installation of exhaust aftertreatment and cooling systems is one of the major challenges in designing future underground mining vehicles [Saelhoff 2010]. Mechanics should identify what options are available (considering all of the previous design requirements) and coordinate with vehicle operators to ensure that vision is not obstructed and that the selected location does not put the DPF at risk for physical damage during operation. One thing to remember is that DPF systems can also provide noise reduction—which may potentially eliminate the need for a muffler in some installations. However, no scientific information was found in the literature on the effectiveness of noise reduction in DPF/Muffler systems.

<u>Fuel and Lubricating Oil Properties and Quality</u>

The performance of contemporary diesel engines and advanced exhaust aftertreatment systems is highly sensitive to the properties and quality of fuel and lubricants. Issues with fuel properties have been identified as a potential source of DPF failures [WRAP 2005; Mayer 2008b]. Fortunately, recent EPA regulations have forced improvements in the quality of diesel fuels and lubricants [66 Fed. Reg. 5001 (2001); 69 Fed. Reg. 38957 (2004)]. In particular, a reduction in the sulfur content of fuel to less than 15 ppm and the introduction of low-ash lubricating oils (i.e., API-grade CJ4 from the American Petroleum Institute, API) have enabled the implementation of catalyzed DPF technology.

The compatibility of advanced engines and exhaust aftertreatment systems with biodiesel fuels is another issue. At this time, there is limited information about operating contemporary diesel engines equipped with exhaust aftertreatment systems on high biodiesel blends (B20–B99), which are frequently used in underground metal and nonmetal mines in the U.S.

Some researchers have shown positive effects of biodiesel use. In particular, studies have indicated that soy methyl ester (SME) biodiesel lowers the light-off temperature of passively regenerated CDPF systems [Boehman et al. 2005; Williams et al. 2006a,b; Sappok and Wong 2008; Fukuda et al. 2008]. On the other hand, studies have also found that fuels with a high content of biodiesel can hinder regeneration in systems that use after- and post-injection of fuel [Fukuda et al. 2008]. Additionally, some research has shown that there is the potential for increased ash emissions with certain types of biodiesel [Sappok and Wong 2008]. Therefore, the use of biodiesel with advanced exhaust aftertreatment technologies remains a topic of ongoing research and an area of concern.

DPF System Operation and Maintenance

After the DPF system is installed, vehicle operators, mechanics, and other involved parties should receive training on performing all of the necessary tasks related to operating and maintaining DPF systems. A detailed understanding of the critical design and operating parameters, as well as the potential modes of failure, is crucial to the success of the DPF system installation. Detailed plans of preventive actions should also be established. It is particularly important for vehicle operators to be able to recognize and respond to high engine-backpressure warnings.

DPF maintenance should be performed in accordance with the recommendations from the manufacturer. Engines in underground mining vehicles are typically maintained in prescribed federal [61 Fed Reg. 55412 (1996)] and state requirements as well as self-imposed intervals. The routine assessment and preventive maintenance of an installed DPF system should be integrated with regular engine and vehicle preventive maintenance efforts.

Cost of DPF Systems

The total cost of a retrofit DPF system installation is equal to the sum of the initial investment and the operating cost. The initial costs are primarily associated with acquiring and installing the DPF system and the related infrastructure. In general, active systems are more expensive to acquire and operate than passive systems.

Retrofitting aftermarket DPF systems on a wide range of underground mining vehicles requires a relatively large level of customization and optimization for individual applications, which usually leads to a substantial increase in the installation cost [Mayer 2008a]. The initial cost of a retrofit DPF system depends on the engine-rated power, the vehicle category, and the duty cycle. In the case of OEM applications, DPFs and other advanced exhaust aftertreatment components integrated into some Tier 4 engines are expected to significantly increase the total cost of the off-road HD engine package [Stirling 2010].

The operating costs associated with DPF systems are primarily associated with the potential fuel penalty as well as the cost of additional engine and DPF maintenance. Fuel penalties associated with retrofit DPF systems are very difficult to quantify, but typically amount to a few percentage points or less [WRAP 2005].

2.2.2.3 Disposable Filter Elements (DFEs)

Introduction

DFE filtration systems are widely used by the underground coal mining industry for curtailing DPM emissions from HD diesel-powered permissible and nonpermissible equipment [66 Fed. Reg. 27864 (2001); MSHA 2009c; Ambs and Hillman 1992; Ambs et al. 1994]. These types of filtration systems have filter elements that cannot be regenerated, but must be removed and replaced (or, in certain cases, laundered to extend the usable life of the filter) once the element reaches a certain level of DPM loading.

By design, DFE systems incorporate other complex technologies which lead to high initial and operational costs. However, they have proven to be a viable technology for curtailing DPM emissions from permissible vehicles and from HD nonpermissible vehicles. This is in part, because DFEs are capable of removing a large fraction of the total DPM mass emissions without adversely affecting gaseous emissions. Due to potential fire hazards associated with using DFEs, it is imperative that the filter systems be properly engineered, approved by MSHA, and maintained in approved conditions.

Exhaust Conditioners

DFE filtration systems were originally developed to control DPM emissions from diesel-powered, permissible coal-mining equipment that already had exhaust cooling and surface temperature controls in place [26 Fed. Reg. 645 (1961); 61 Fed. Reg. 55412 (1996)]. Currently, the filtration systems available for permissible power packages [MSHA 2009d] condition the exhaust using: (1) water-bath exhaust conditioner systems (see Figure 6), and (2) dry exhaust conditioner systems (see Figure 7). Simplified versions of these systems have recently been developed for HD nonpermissible applications using paper and synthetic low-temperature disposable filter elements (LTDFEs) as the filtration medium. Synthetic high-temperature disposable filter elements (HTDFEs) were primarily developed for use in HD nonpermissible applications, but are currently also used in permissible applications.

Water-Bath Exhaust Conditioners

A water-bath exhaust conditioner system with DFE is shown in Figure 6. The water-bath exhaust conditioner, also known as a scrubber, has the dual purpose of cooling the exhaust below 77°C (171°F) and quenching flames and sparks while simultaneously maintaining an acceptable engine backpressure [61 Fed. Reg. 55412 (1996)]. A water trap, which is installed downstream of the water bath, allows for the condensation, capture, and return of the water evaporated by exhaust gases back to the water bath. This prevents condensation of water in the DFE.

32

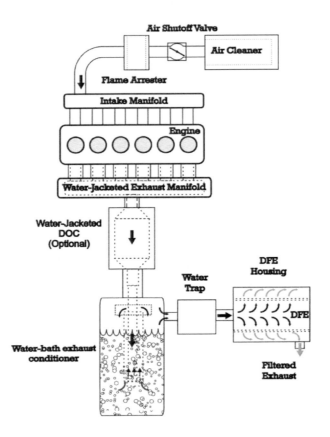

Figure 6. A simplified schematic of a permissible filtration system with water-bath exhaust conditioner.

Maintaining adequate water levels in the water-bath is critical to the performance of the system because loss of water can result in increased exhaust temperature. Water lost from the water-bath exhaust conditioner due to evaporation is replenished automatically using water from a makeup tank. An emergency shutdown system is incorporated to prevent engine operation should a failure cause the exhaust temperature at the exit of the water-bath scrubber to exceed 85°C (185°F) [Ambs et al. 1994].

Dry Exhaust Conditioners

A filtration system with a dry exhaust conditioner is shown in Figure 7. These systems use an air-to-liquid heat exchanger to cool the exhaust [26 Fed. Reg. 645 (1961); 61 Fed. Reg. 55412 (1996)]. A flame arrester downstream of the heat exchanger prevents the propagation of a flame or discharge of heated particles out of the exhaust system. An exhaust temperature sensor and an engine shutdown system are designed to shut off the fuel supply to the engine if the temperature of the exhaust at the exit of the dry exhaust conditioner exceeds 150°C (302°F). Additionally, a DOC is typically incorporated upstream of this type of system to control CO and HC emissions [Khalek et al. 2003].

33

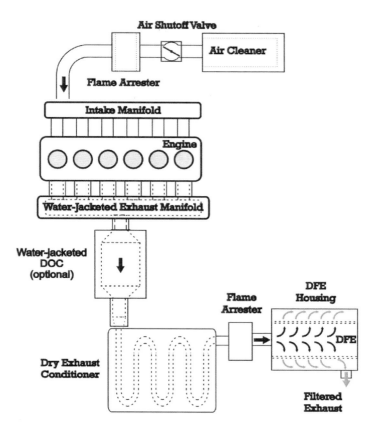

Figure 7. A simplified schematic of a permissible filtration system with a dry exhaust conditioner.

Temperature Considerations

The majority of exhaust system components of a permissible diesel engine and diesel power package are often water-jacketed to maintain the temperature of all surfaces below certain values specified in regulations [26 Fed. Reg. 645 (1961); 61 Fed. Reg. 55412 (1996)]. The coolant used in these systems is cooled using the engine cooling system and sometimes augmented by a larger radiator or fan to handle any additional heat load, especially in the case of dry exhaust conditioners.

In the case of certain HD nonpermissible underground coal applications, vehicles are not required to meet exhaust and surface temperature requirements and, therefore, exhaust conditioning systems are not typically installed on these engines. These vehicles should be retrofitted with a heat exchanger capable of cooling exhaust temperatures below that which is recommended by the HTDFE supplier. Because the heat rejection requirements are substantially lower than those for permissible systems, less elaborate and less expensive systems can be deployed.

Implementation

The major drawbacks of permissible filtration systems with DFEs are the high initial cost of the system, a high operational cost, and the large dimensions of the system. The operational costs are associated with the downtime and labor needed for the exchange of DFEs, the cost of new filter elements, and the relatively complex maintenance requirements. The requirements for maintaining a water-bath exhaust conditioning system are related to high water consumption, complex safety controls, sludge buildup, and damage caused by converting the SO_2 in the water box to corrosive sulfuric acid. Dry exhaust conditioning systems require the periodic cleaning of the heat exchanger components.

The major DPM trapping component of these filtration systems is the DFE. This filter medium is highly porous and creates relatively low exhaust backpressure when new. As filter loading increases, DFEs become more efficient as the pathways through the filter become smaller and more restrictive. However, the efficiency of these systems can be significantly affected by leaks. DFEs are designed to fit tightly in the housing so that all exhaust gases are forced through the filtration media. For this reason, it is critical that both mating surfaces of the DFE are properly sealed during installation of the DFE within the housing. The surfaces near seals should be periodically examined for signs of potential exhaust leaks. Potential flaws in the original permissible system design (such as the existence of an unfiltered water-bath scrubber overflow hole) in some systems should be corrected by the manufacturer or end user during installation [Schnakenberg and Bugarski 2002; MSHA 2009e].

DFEs used on permissible and nonpermissible diesel machines must be approved by MSHA for the specific application. MSHA [2009b] evaluated several types of paper/synthetic DFEs and deemed them to be compliant with current regulations which limit emissions from diesel-powered equipment used in underground coal mines [66 Fed. Reg. 27864 (2001)]. The majority of approved DFEs are suitable for use in water-bath scrubber-based systems with exhaust temperatures below 85°C (185°F). Several of the approved DFEs are suitable for use on dry heat-exchanger-type exhaust cooling systems with exhaust temperatures up to 150°C (302°F). In many instances, the user needs to contact the DFE supplier for information pertaining to the appropriate temperature limit. Typical backpressure requirements are below 150 mbar (60 in H_2O); however, the usable life of the DFE is actually determined by the maximum engine backpressure allowed by the engine manufacturer [MSHA 2009a].

In addition, a few suppliers offer fiberglass-type HTDFEs for nonpermissible applications [Mathur and Chavan 2008; MSHA 2009b]. These HTDFEs can be used in exhaust systems that never exceed 343°C (649°F) [MSHA 2009b]. It is important to note that, although the regular and HTDFEs used in DPM filtration applications resemble the intake air filters used on heavy-duty, on-highway vehicles, the filtration media is substantially different between these two types of elements. Therefore, it is important to acquire the models approved by MSHA for DPM emissions control [MSHA 2009b].

Another area of concern is the disposal of used DFEs. It is recommended that mines contact local waste management authorities to ensure proper disposal of these materials.

Effects of DFEs on emissions

MSHA reports that paper and synthetic LTDFEs provide reductions in total DPM mass similar to those provided by a "golden" standard paper DFE (~95%). However, the actual filtration efficiencies of these LTDFEs are not posted [MSHA 2009b]. Additionally, two types of HTDFEs evaluated by MSHA have been reported to provide 83% and 80% removal of total DPM mass if used at exhaust temperatures below 343°C (649°F) [MSHA 2009b]. The filtration efficiency of these HTDFEs is substantially higher at exhaust temperatures below 77°C (171°F), making them equivalent to other LTDFEs at these conditions.

Various studies have shown that DFE filtration efficiencies are quite high and that they correspond with system setup, mass accumulation within the filter element and engine-loading conditions. Studies have also shown that secondary emissions from DFEs are an area of concern. A summary of additional independent studies is given below.

- A field evaluation of a water-bath exhaust conditioner and paper LTDFEs (conducted in underground coal mines) showed that the installation of these systems may allow ambient mass concentrations of DPM to be reduced between 70% and 95% [Ambs and Hillman 1992; Ambs et al. 1994]. The usable DFE life during these evaluations ranged from 10 to 32 hours. In another study, a laboratory evaluation of just a water-bath exhaust conditioner showed that this system, by itself, reduces DPM mass emissions by up to 35% for certain particle sizes without affecting concentrations of the majority of regulated exhaust gases (the only exception being a slight decrease in NO_X emissions) [Cantrell and Rubow 1992].

- LTDFEs used with dry exhaust conditioning systems and a DOC were shown to remove 90% to 93% of DPM mass in at least one study [Khalek et al. 2003]

- LTDFE systems incorporating a dry heat exchanger and cellulose-based filtration (developed for city bus applications) were tested and shown to reduce total DPM mass between 81% for new and 91% for DPM-loaded conditions [D'Urbano and Mayer 2007; Colamussi 2008].

- An HTDFE from Donaldson Company, Inc. and a prototype DFE from Filter Services, Inc. were evaluated in an isolated zone of an underground metal mine [NIOSH 2006b]. The results showed that Donaldson DFE reduced concentrations of total particulate matter (TPM) mass and EC mass, on average, by 85% and 92%, respectively. The prototype HTDFE from Filter Service reduced concentrations of TPM mass and EC mass on average by 70% and 62%, respectively.

- Three types of HTDFEs were evaluated during a study conducted in an experimental mine [Bugarski et al. 2009]. Results showed that the efficiency of DFEs in filtering DPM mass increased substantially as particulate mass accumulated on the filter during several hours of de-greening. The same study investigated the effect that the laundering process has on DFE efficiency and found that a single laundering process did not substantially affect DFE performance.

- Both LTDFE and HTDFEs have been shown to, on their own, have minor effects on CO, CO_2, NO, and NO_2 emissions [Colamussi 2008; Bugarski et al. 2007].

- Studies have shown a substantial increase in the number of particles emitted during initial operation with a new DFE [Ambs and Setren 1995; Bugarski et al. 2009]. This process (known as "off-gassing") is due to the release of secondary emissions of various compounds and aerosols from the breakdown of the paper, synthetic filter material, and/or organic material binders. Some examples of secondary emissions include increased CO, HC, and formaldehyde. It is believed that the intensity and duration of the off-gassing process depends on a number of factors including exhaust temperatures and exhaust flow rate. A NIOSH study observed the release of presumed secondary emissions into the 18th hour of engine operation [Bugarski et al. 2009].

Safety Concerns

It is important to note that filtration systems with DFEs are approved by MSHA for use in permissible and nonpermissible applications under very specific operating constraints. Proper maintenance of water-bath and dry-exhaust conditioning systems and their associated safety systems is critical to maintaining exhaust temperatures at recommended levels and, therefore, the safe operation of DFEs. The paper and synthetic filter media in LTDFEs and trapped DPM can spontaneously combust if the exhaust temperatures exceed maximum allowable temperatures recommended by the manufacturers [MSHA 2009b]. For the same reasons, HTDFEs should never be exposed to exhaust gas temperatures above 343°C (649°F) [MSHA 2005; MSHA 2009b]. Although the filter media in HTDFEs by itself can sustain exhaust gas temperatures as high as 760°C (1,400°F), the DPM material trapped in the HTDFEs have the potential to spontaneously combust at exhaust gas temperatures above 343°C (649°F).

Because the rate of DFE loading depends on the engine DPM emissions, the operators have a strong incentive to improve engine maintenance and reduce emissions from engines retrofitted with these filtration systems. It is particularly important to minimize emissions of semivolatile and low-volatile hydrocarbons. These compounds, typically formed by the incomplete combustion of fuel and lubricating oil, contribute to the combustibility of the DPM trapped in the DFEs and increase the risk associated with spontaneous combustion of the DFE, particularly in high-temperature applications.

Regulations

LTDFEs and HTDFEs are approved by MSHA following Part 7 testing procedures [61 Fed. Reg. 55412 (1996)]. The installation of filtration systems on permissible and nonpermissible vehicles requires that either the machine manufacturer obtain MSHA approval for the system or that the mine operator obtain MSHA approval for a field modification [61 Fed. Reg. 55412 (1996)].

2.2.2.4 Partial Filter Systems (PF)

Introduction

Partial filter (PF) systems, also known as particulate oxidation catalysts, particulate reduction systems, or flow-through and open filters, are designed as a compromise between the filtration efficiency of DPFs and the operability of DOCs. Unlike DPF systems, where all of the exhaust is forced through a filtration media, PF systems allow some flow to escape unfiltered. Because this open structure allows PF systems to operate with less backpressure increase on the engine, PF systems do not use regeneration as a means to prevent plugging. Instead, regeneration is used to prevent a loss in the filtration efficiency due to the eventual release of accumulated DPM from the filtration media. Additionally, the open structure in PFs removes the need for ash cleaning.

Implementation

Several different designs of PFs are available on the market. The most popular designs consist of foil structures with indentations, openings, and metal fiber fleece [Yao et al. 2008; Babu et al. 2008; Mayer et al. 2009; Weltens and Vogel 2008]. In these PFs, the metal foil substrate is designed so that the exhaust gas flow is diverted through the fleece into adjacent channels, and the particles are temporarily retained in the fleece. Alternative designs are based on a pleated sintered metal DPF (that is perforated at the downstream side to provide relief for unfiltered exhaust) [Mayer et al 2009; Weltens and Vogel 2008], ceramic and metallic open-pore foams [Mayer et al 2009], and knitted wire mesh [CARB 2009a,b]. The sintered metal PF plates are similar in design to sintered metal DPF plates. The major difference is a protrusion that is introduced in the PF plates to allow a fraction of the flow to be redirected and bypass the filtration media [Weltens and Vogel 2008].

Because PF regeneration depends on the oxidation of DPM by NO_2, PFs are typically installed downstream of an existing or newly introduced DOC [Mayer et al. 2009; Yoon et al. 2009]. In the presence of the catalyst, NO from exhaust is converted to NO_2 and consequently used to oxidize DPM from the filter. These systems are designed to maintain turbulent flow and, therefore, intensify the conversion processes. Similar to those in other contemporary catalyzed aftertreatment devices, the catalyst in PFs requires the use of ULSD fuel to avoid potential poisoning and diminished performance [Johnson 2009].

PFs are deployed on a variety of utility vehicles, both as retrofits and as OEM (original equipment manufacturer) solutions [Weltens and Vogel 2008]. The California Air Resources Board (CARB) verified several PF systems as Level 2 devices (50% filtration efficiency) [CARB 2009a,b]. However, PFs are not verified or approved by MSHA [2009b] and FOEN/SUVA [D'Urbano and Mayer 2007].

Effects of PFs on Emissions

Several studies have shown that, at higher engine loads, PFs exhibit filtration efficiencies as high as 70% [Mayer et al. 2009; Yoon et al. 2009]. However, the same evaluations have also shown that the efficiency of PFs is substantially lower in the case of engines operated over light load cycles, dynamic cycles, and high space velocity (a ratio used to gauge exhaust flow rate versus catalyst area). The filtration efficiency of PFs was found to be strongly affected not only by engine operating conditions but also by prior history of DPM accumulation and regeneration [Mayer et al. 2009]. Therefore, due to the dynamics of the filtration, regeneration, and blowoff, it is very difficult to reproduce data and establish actual values.

Balancing the production and consumption of NO_2 in PFs over an actual duty cycle is a major challenge. NO_2 slip (or the unwanted release of NO_2 emissions) is, therefore, an area of concern for PF systems [Mayer et al. 2009]. Because conversion of NO to NO_2 is temperature dependent [McClure et al. 1988; Ambs and McClure 1993; Katare et al. 2007; Mayer et al. 2003; Czerwinski et al. 2007; Lozentzou et al. 2008, Johansen et al. 2007, Khair et al. 2008], the effect of PFs on NO_2 is relatively difficult to quantify. At least one study found NO_2 slip to be a problem for certain PF systems, particularly when engines are operated at high loads [Mayer et al. 2009].

Particle-size-distribution measurements have shown that PFs decrease DPM number concentrations across the entire particle size range [Mayer et al. 2009]. However, PF systems were found to remove some, but not all, of the metallic aerosols originating from the use of fuel-borne catalysts (FBCs) [Mayer et al. 2009]. Therefore, FBCs should not be used in engines equipped with PF systems.

Summary

Although PFs cannot provide filtration efficiencies comparable to those of DPFs, they can potentially be used to reduce DPM emissions from engines that are not suitable for DPF installation. PFs have an appeal because they are simpler, lighter, smaller, and less expensive than comparable DPFs. The specifics of the application and how those factors will correlate with the properties of a given PF all need to be carefully considered during the selection process. A loss of efficiency with accumulation of DPM, the potential for release of accumulated DPM from the filtration media at high space velocity conditions [Johnson 2009, Mayer et al. 2009], and the potential for NO_2 slip [Mayer et al. 2009] should all be taken into account when PFs are considered for an underground mining application.

2.2.2.5 Selective Catalytic Reduction (SCR) Technology

Introduction

Selective catalytic reduction (SCR) is an exhaust aftertreatment technology that is used to control NO_X emissions from stationary and mobile diesel-powered engine applications. The main goal of this technology is to convert nitric oxide (NO) and nitrogen dioxide (NO_2), present in the engine exhaust, to inert molecular nitrogen (N_2) and water. This conversion can be accomplished via a complex series of chemical reactions [Bosch and Janssen 1988; Cho 1994].

SCR Technology

In an SCR system, the reduction of NO_X compounds to N_2 and water is possible via a reaction with a specific reducing compound over a catalyst in the presence of oxygen. The reducing compound is generally injected as a liquid into the exhaust ahead of the aftertreatment SCR system. Historically, the common reducer used in SCR applications is ammonia (NH_3). Since 1990, urea, $(NH_2)_2CO$ has increasingly been used to replace ammonia as the reducing compound for reasons of safety in handling and storage for mobile applications [Gabrielsson 2004; Sullivan and Doherty 2005; Park et al. 2006]. An aqueous solution of urea (10% in volume) is currently the reducer of choice for mobile SCR systems, with the urea being converted to ammonia in the first part of the SCR system. Sometimes, in industrial applications, the reducer is called diesel exhaust fluid (DEF).

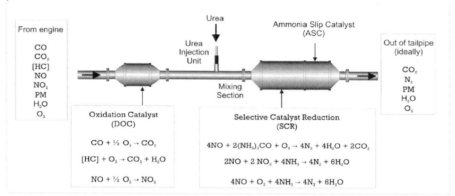

**Figure 8. The fundamental chemical reactions within a generic
SCR system for mobile sources.**

A generic SCR system for mobile source applications usually includes an auxiliary oxidation catalyst (DOC), a main SCR catalyst, and a secondary oxidation catalyst at the exit of the system (see Figure 8). The two oxidation catalysts have features and characteristics similar to a generic DOC (see section 2.2.2.1). The auxiliary oxidation catalyst in this system is used to increase the NO_2 concentration in the exhaust gases. Laboratory studies [Chandler et al. 2000; Gieshoff 2001] have confirmed that the efficiency in NO_X abatement increases with an elevated NO_2 concentration at the inlet of the main SCR catalyst. The optimum NO_2/NO ratio was reported to be near 1:1 [Gieshoff 2000; Koebel et al. 2002; Goo et al. 2007].

In a standard SCR system, the reducing compound is introduced after the auxiliary oxidation catalyst. The reducer is injected as a spray from a high-pressure nozzle system. The vaporization of the urea and proper distribution across the tailpipe diameter are crucial aspects of this phase. The urea is then hydrolyzed to ammonia at the entrance of the main SCR catalyst.

The main SCR catalyst is typically comprised of an extruded ceramic honeycomb monolith with a mixture of a carrier (titanium oxide) and an active catalyst. The catalyst mixture is either incorporated throughout the structure or coated on the substrate. Reduction of NO_X over the main SCR catalyst is dependent upon many factors, including catalyst formulation, temperature range, and the NO_2/NO_X ratio. The most efficient catalyst formulation for SCR systems to be used in mobile applications appears to be catalysts based on vanadium [Koebel et al. 2001; Madia et al. 2002] and zeolite [Gieshoff 2001].

40

The emission, or slip, of ammonia is a concern associated with the use urea injection in an SCR system. Ammonia that is not consumed in the main SCR catalyst (either due to imperfect tuning of the system or an overdosage of urea) can potentially be emitted into the atmosphere. To address this issue, an additional oxidation catalyst, known as an ammonia slip catalyst (ASC), is usually integrated at the outlet of the SCR system.

Studies have reported that the majority of the slipped ammonia (NH_3) undergoes complete oxidation to NO and NO_2 over the ASC [Havenith and Verbeek 1997]. NH_3 concentrations at the tailpipe, resulting from NH_3 slip [Chandler et al. 2000], have been found to be below 25 parts per million, the ambient ammonia ACGIH TWA/TLV (American Conference of Governmental Industrial Hygienists, time-weighted average / threshold limit value). Therefore, a possible NH_3 slip from an SCR system should not pose a problem and would not require additional ventilation air in underground work areas. However, urea dosing levels need to be optimized and subsequently monitored to achieve high NO_X reduction while minimizing NH_3 slip [Miller et al. 2000].

Implementation

SCR is a complex technology, and its implementation in underground mining requires preliminary investigation in several areas. The storage and handling of the reducing compound is one of the main areas of concern because a dedicated tank, a dosing system, and a nozzle vaporizer system (for the injection of the reducer) must be installed on each vehicle. Additionally, an underground or outside area for the storage and distribution of urea that accommodates urea's freezing temperature of $-11°C$ (12.2°F) must also be considered. Another area of concern is the deactivation of the catalyst in SCR systems. This deactivation, which is connected with the sulfur content of the fuel, has been observed in SCR systems using zeolite in the main catalyst [Cavataio et al. 2008]. Therefore, in situations where there is a risk for higher sulfuric emissions, vanadium SCRs may be a better option. However, it is important to mention that SCR systems should only be implemented on vehicles fueled with ultra-low sulfur diesel fuel and lubricated with low-sulfur content oils (see sections 2.3.1 and 2.3.2).

SCR systems are available as an original equipment manufacturer (OEM) product or as a retrofit package. In the case of an OEM product, the engine electronic control unit (ECU) manages the SCR system operations and optimizes its performance. For this reason, only electronically controlled diesel engines with an installed ECU or an electronic control module (ECM) will be equipped with an OEM SCR system.

SCR retrofit systems can be set up for two types of control: sensor feedback and map based. A sensor-feedback system measures exhaust NO_X directly using a zirconia sensor mounted at the engine exhaust outlet. The real-time NO_X concentration is then recorded by a stand-alone control unit which operates a urea injection pump to dose sufficient reducer into the exhaust stream. The urea injection rate is determined by a number of parameters (catalyst volume, NO_X emission, exhaust temperature, etc). Alternatively, map-based SCR retrofit systems are controlled by a stand-alone unit that contains controlling information that is based on a contour plot (3D map) of the engine NO_X emissions versus engine speed and operating load. The unit receives this real-time engine loading data and determines the expected NO_X emission rate from the calibration map. A predetermined amount of reducer (that corresponds with the required emission reductions at that condition) is then delivered. Additionally, predictive control techniques may be used to facilitate quicker response times for increased NO_X reduction.

Some disadvantages of map-based systems are that a NO_X map may be difficult to obtain and that the accuracy of these systems is highly dependent upon the quality of this engine mapping procedure. Additionally, the SCR controller must receive engine-loading data from the engine computer, which adds a slight complexity to these systems.

Effects of an SCR on Emissions

The performance of an SCR system is a function of many factors (temperature profile, type of catalyst used, NO_2/NO_X ratio, etc.). Typically, expected reductions in NO_X emissions from heavy-duty engines equipped with SCR systems ranges from 55% to 90%, depending on the application and test method used [Havenith and Verbeek 1997; Fritz et al. 1999; Miller et al. 2000]. Due to the high variability in the driving cycles and related temperature profiles of a particular vehicle, it is difficult to make more precise predictions of the effectiveness of a retrofit SCR system before deployment without vehicle-specific data. For this reason, a preliminary screening of the exhaust gas composition and temperature profile during the duty cycle of the engine is recommended before implementing an SCR retrofit. This information might be required by the SCR manufacturer to customize the SCR system for that engine. A similar process for acquiring exhaust temperature profiles for the selection of a DPF aftertreatment control is discussed in detail in Section 2.2.2.2. It is important to mention that most SCR catalysts have shown reduced efficiencies at temperatures below 300°C (572°F) or temperatures higher than 500°C (932°F).

Another key point of emphasis is that the SCR catalytic activity is not selective toward NO or NO_2, and that the same reduction efficiency is attainable for both compounds. Because NO_2 plays such an important role in the SCR system, optimizing the auxiliary oxidation catalyst is crucial in order to avoid an over-production of NO_2, which can lead to an overall lower NO_X conversion [Cooper et al. 2003]. Furthermore, a reduction of carbon monoxide (CO) and hydrocarbons is expected following the implementation of SCR technology in an engine exhaust (due to the presence of the auxiliary oxidation catalyst). However, the effect of SCR on DPM output still needs further investigation.

Recently, an integrated aftertreatment system with an SCR and DPF, trademarked SCRT, has become available [Chandler et al. 2000; Rice et al. 2008]. The SCRT technology consists of a CRT system, described in Section 2.2.2.2, followed by an SCR section. This configuration combines the advantages of a DOC, a DPF, and an SCR; providing an overall reduction of CO, DPM, and NO_X. Several promising studies are currently being conducted on these systems to analyze their effects on emissions [Biswas et al. 2008].

2.2.2.6 Lean NO$_X$ Catalyst (LNC) Technology

Introduction

For some mobile applications, a lean NO$_X$ catalyst (LNC) may be an alternative aftertreatment technology to SCR (see Section 2.2.2.5) that does not suffer from the issues related to urea storage and handling. LNC systems are based on a catalyst that activates the NO$_X$ reduction via reactions with hydrocarbons (HC):

$$[HC] + NO_X + O_2 \rightarrow N_2 + H_2O + CO_2$$

For this reason, LNCs are also called hydrocarbon selective catalytic reduction (HC-SCR) systems.

In general, diesel engines emit inadequate levels of hydrocarbons for converting NO$_X$ via LNC reduction. For this reason, supplementary hydrocarbon injection (most often using diesel fuel as the source of HCs) is sometimes required to supply enough reducing agent for the LNC [Dorriah 1999]. In these cases, the systems require a dedicated metering line and a nozzle spray system. Fuel is supplied from the existing vehicle tank or, sometimes, from an additional tank.

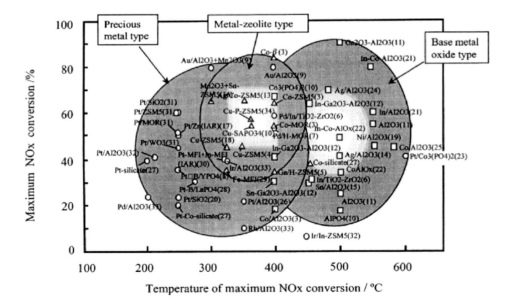

Figure 9. A map of NO$_X$ reduction performance of several lean NO$_X$ catalysts over various temperatures [adapted from Akama and Matsushita 1999]. The important information to take from this figure is that precious metal type, metal-zeolite type, and base metal oxide type catalysts are most active over different temperature ranges.

LNC Technology

In an LNC system, the reduction of NO$_X$ is achieved by reacting NO$_X$ with hydrocarbons in the presence of a catalyst. The conversion of both NO and NO$_2$ depends mostly on the

43

catalyst chemical formulation and configuration [Truex 1994; Kharas et al. 1998] as well as the temperature window at which the catalyst has the highest activity. Several catalyst options exist for use in LNC systems (see Figure 9), but three groups have shown to be most effective: (1) platinum/oxide catalysts, which are active at low temperatures (200–300°C, 392–572°F), (2) zeolite catalysts, which are active at high temperatures (350–500°C, 662–932°F), and (3) base metal oxides which are active at the highest temperatures (400–600, 752–1,112°F, an atypical range for most diesel applications).

Besides the catalyst formulation, the exhaust temperature and the hydrocarbon/NO_X ratio are the most important factors affecting the performance of LNCs. Usually, the development and choice of a catalyst for a specific application takes into account the temperature range and the gaseous composition of the exhaust. However, it is also possible to modify the reactive components, NO_X, and hydrocarbons to enhance the performance of an existing LNC system for implementation into various engine exhausts [Akama and Matsushita 1999].

One of the most attractive sources of hydrocarbons for reducing NO_X is the diesel exhaust itself. Systems using the hydrocarbons in the exhaust are referred to as "passive LNC" systems. Passive systems are often the preferred emissions control option because of their simplicity, reliability, and lower cost. However, NO_X conversion is typically very low for this type of system because exhaust hydrocarbons have a low reactivity for NO_X reduction. To help address this issue, a highly selective catalyzed DOC is usually installed to reform these hydrocarbon compounds and produce a more reactive mix.

In most cases, in order to improve the performance of LNC systems, it is crucial to increase the HC/NO_X ratio by introducing additional hydrocarbons. This can be accomplished by "active LNC" systems that either inject hydrocarbons into the exhaust stream or store hydrocarbons in the catalyst coating for later release. Hydrocarbons may either be injected directly into the exhaust system upstream of the LNC, or via a late-stage, in-cylinder injection. Both strategies involve a certain fuel economy penalty that depends on the quantity of injected fuel. They also pose the risk of overinjection of hydrocarbons, which may cause excess HC to slip through the LNC system. In such instances, an additional DOC downstream of the LNC may help to prevent increased HC emissions. Active LNC systems that store hydrocarbons in the catalyst washcoat are designed to release them at conditions that are more favorable for catalytic reactions. Such storage is realized by incorporating hydrocarbon adsorbers, also known as hydrocarbon traps, into the catalyst chemical formulation. Through this approach, the LNC efficiency can be increased without the need for hydrocarbon injection (subsequently avoiding the associated penalty in fuel economy) [Leyrer et al. 1966].

An alternative strategy to increase the performance of LNC systems is to improve the reactivity of NO_X in the exhaust stream. This can be accomplished using a precious metal catalyst to force the conversion of NO to NO_2 (because NO_2 has a higher reactivity than NO). Several studies have found that this technique can increase the overall efficiency for many LNC systems [Iwamoto et al. 1997].

Most NO_X emissions are produced by diesel engines at temperatures between 250°C and 350°C, which fall within the range of the maximum conversion capabilities of two different types of catalysts (see Figure 9). This creates a problem in selecting a catalyst with sufficient activity for conversion of NO_X. One approach to overcoming this problem has been to combine two catalysts with different maximum conversion temperature ranges. By splitting the catalyst substrates into two different locations in the engine exhaust, it is possible to extend the LNC temperature range and increase the overall NO_X conversion. For example, in light-duty applications, the first catalyst would be placed in an exhaust location where it is exposed to higher temperatures, while the second catalyst could be located after a DPM aftertreatment system and exposed to lower temperatures [Aswani et al. 2005]. As a side benefit, this type of configuration could also be useful in controlling NO_2 emissions from catalyzed DPFs (see Section 2.2.2.2), which is still an open issue for underground mine DPF applications.

The effectiveness of NO_X conversion is just one factor associated with the implementation of LNC technology. Other important issues include the durability of the system as well as the sulfur tolerance of the catalyst. The sulfur content of diesel fuels must be reduced to allow catalysts to function without poisoning. Therefore, it is recommended that ultralow-sulfur-content diesel fuel (ULSDF) should be used in vehicles outfitted with LNC aftertreatment systems.

Effects of LNC on Emissions

LNCs were not developed to provide a high level of NO_X reduction. Even though peak NO_X reductions (measured in the laboratory) are frequently reported in excess of 80% (see Figure 9), performance of these catalysts over regulatory test cycles is usually limited to 20%–30% reduction. Higher reductions can be obtained using the strategies described above, but so far, the maximum achievable NO_X conversion by LNC systems for diesel engines operated over real duty cycles has been 60% [Kharas et al. 1998].

In addition, the selectivity of the catalyst and the potential for secondary emissions are also open issues related to LNC systems. Even if the primary product of the LNC is atmospheric nitrogen, N_2, a small amount of nitrous oxide (N_2O) can be formed by this reaction. The recommended exposure limit (REL) for N_2O in underground mines is TLV-TWA 25 ppm [NIOSH 2005].

In systems containing precious metal catalysts, it has also been found that an increased reduction of NO_X is associated with increased DPM emissions, possibly related to the generation of sulfate particulates [Kawanami et al. 1995]. This is particularly true for diesel engines operating with high-sulfur-content diesel fuel.

2.3 Diesel Fuels and Lubricants

2.3.1 Diesel Fuels, Additives, and Lubricants

Introduction

Selecting adequate diesel fuels, additives, and lubricants is critical to the performance of diesel engines and has the potential to play a major role in the efforts of the underground mining industry to control emissions from diesel-powered equipment. Maintaining the quality of fuels and lubricants between refinery, terminal, and the combustion chamber is becoming more and more critical with the advancement in engine and exhaust aftertreatment technologies. The following section outlines the major emissions-related topics that pertain to diesel fuels, additives and lubricants.

Petroleum Diesel Fuel

Regulations

The U.S. Mine Safety and Health Administration (MSHA) regulates the quality of diesel fuel used in U.S. underground coal mines [66 Fed. Reg. 27864 (2001)] and metal/nonmetal mines [30 CFR 57.5065]. The current MSHA regulations require the use of low-sulfur diesel (LSD) fuel, containing less than 0.05% (500 ppm) sulfur, in underground operations of coal and metal/nonmetal mines. Pennsylvania [PADEP 2009] and West Virginia [WVDEC 2004] regulations require underground coal mines to use the most recently approved EPA highway diesel fuel. EPA regulations for onroad [66 Fed. Reg. 5001 (2001a)] and nonroad [69 Fed. Reg. 38957 (2004)] diesel engines and fuel require the use of ultralow-sulfur diesel (ULSD). ULSD, or diesel fuel containing no greater than 15 ppm sulfur, became widely available in 2006 [66 Fed. Reg. 5001 (2001)]. As of June 2010, use of ULSD is mandated for nonroad applications [69 Fed. Reg. 38957 (2004)]. Although the benefits of replacing LSD with ULSD petroleum diesel on DPM and EC emissions are relatively minor, the use of ULSD is critical to successfully implementing advanced catalyzed exhaust aftertreatment systems. ULSD is needed to avoid excessive sulfate production and poisoning of the catalyst in these systems. In addition, using ULSD and low-ash lubricating oils should minimize ash accumulation in DPF systems and extend cleaning intervals.

The quality of diesel fuels in the U.S is specified in the ASTM D-975 standard by ASTM International, formerly known as the American Society of Testing and Materials [ASTM 2009a]. Middle distillate No. 2-D is the primary grade of fuel commercially available in the U.S. However, light middle grade No. 1-D, with higher volatility and better cold weather properties, is also in commercial use. Heavy middle grade No. 4-D is primarily used for stationary and marine applications.

Petroleum diesel for nonroad use, including mining, is not subject to federal excise taxes. As a result, the IRS requires all tax-exempt fuel to be dyed red using Solvent Red 164. However, in an effort to prevent high-sulfur diesel fuel use in on-highway vehicles, the EPA requires all high-sulfur diesel fuel to be dyed. Therefore, diesel fuel with a red color may indicate either a nonroad fuel or a high-sulfur diesel fuel.

Effects of Diesel Fuel Properties on Emissions

The effects of diesel fuel properties on regulated and nonregulated emissions have been extensively studied over many years. Several were found to have only subtle effects on emissions from heavy-duty diesel engines [Nikanjam 1993; Ulmann et al. 1994; Zannis et al. 2008], although the most substantial effects were observed for sulfur content, cetane number, density, aromatic content, and oxygen content [EPA 2001b; DieselNet 2002; Maly et al. 2007]. The extent of these effects depends on engine design and engine operating conditions [Kwon et al. 2001; EPA 2001b]. In many instances, the changes in emissions due to certain fuel properties are difficult to quantify because those effects are often smaller than the differences in emissions between engines [EPA 2001b].

Sulfur content is one fuel property with a well-defined effect on emissions. A higher sulfur content in fuel results in higher emissions of SO_2 and particulate sulfate, and increases total DPM emissions [Kwon et al 2001]. Switching from LSD to ULSD has a minor potential for reducing exposures of underground miners to elemental and total carbon [NIOSH 2006b]. However, reducing the amount of sulfur and sulfuric compounds in the vehicle exhaust will help prevent irreversible degradation of aftertreatment catalysts [Stroia et al. 2008]. Therefore, the introduction of ULSD is a critical step toward the implementation of catalyzed diesel particulate filters, NO_X control technologies, and other catalyzed aftertreatment systems.

Additional Information

The availability of ULSD is one of the limiting factors preventing widespread use of engines equipped with advanced exhaust aftertreatment systems. ULSD is currently available in the U.S., Western Europe, Japan, and Canada, but it will not be available in a number of other markets for a decade or more. Maintaining combustion and emissions quality of diesel engines operated in markets with widely differing fuel poses special challenges for engine manufacturers. The unavailability of ULSD fuel in these markets will most probably force engine manufacturers to produce Tier 3 engines for a prolonged period of time. This may extend the availability of Tier 3 engines to the mining industry.

Biodiesel Fuel

Introduction

Biodiesel is a generic term for various types of diesel fuels produced from biomass. The most common sources of biomass used for biodiesel production are virgin vegetable oils from soy beans, rapeseed (canola), corn, cottonseed, sunflower seeds, and oil palms. Other important sources are animal fats such as beef tallow, pork lard, and processed waste cooking oil.

The most widely used biodiesel fuels are made of long-chain fatty-acid methyl esters (FAME) obtained from vegetable oils and animal fats [Graboski and McCormick 1998]. Soy-based FAME biodiesel is most popular in the U.S., although rapeseed-based (rapeseed methyl ester, RME) FAME biodiesel is most popular in the European Union. The properties of FAME fuels vary widely depending on feedstock and processes used in their production [NREL 2009]. The Cetane number of FAME fuels vary with feedstock, but generally have higher Cetane numbers than ULSD sold in the U.S. FAME is an oxygenated fuel; the typical oxygen content of these fuels is approximately 11%. The sulfur content of typical neat FAME is substantially lower than that of LSD, but is similar to that of ULSD.

Biodiesel fuels can easily be mixed (or blended) with conventional diesel fuels. The majority of biodiesel is used in this form. These blends are labeled using a letter "B" followed by the volume percentage of biodiesel in the blend. For example, 100% biodiesel, known as neat biodiesel, is referred to as B100. At concentrations of up to 5% (B5) in the petroleum diesel, the blend typically meets the diesel fuel specifications for the ASTM D-975 standard [ASTM 2011]. Blends with up to 20% biodiesel (B20) can be used in most diesel equipment with little or no modifications to the equipment [NREL 2009]. However, the National Renewable Energy Laboratory (NREL) and the U.S. Department of Energy (DOE) do not recommend the use of high-level biodiesel blends, except where human exposure to DPM is elevated and health concerns merit the additional attention to equipment and fuel handling [NREL 2009].

Regulations

In the U.S., the EPA recognizes biodiesel as a registered fuel and fuel additive. Neat biodiesel fuels must meet the specifications of ASTM D6751 [ASTM 2009b]. Blends with 6% to 20% biodiesel must meet ASTM D7467 [ASTM 2009c]. Blends below B5 typically meet ASTM D975 diesel fuel specifications [ASTM 2009a].

Although they are being used in a number of underground mines, biodiesel fuels are not specifically mentioned in MSHA regulations.

Effects of FAME Biodiesel Fuel on Emissions

The effects of biodiesel blends on diesel emissions are not consistent over the range of possible applications, and they are also somewhat unpredictable. Some engine technologies are more responsive to biodiesel blends than others [EPA 2002b; Durbin et al. 2007]. In addition, engine operating conditions play a major role in defining the characteristics of the emissions when using FAME fuels as a control strategy. A summary of relevant research is presented in this section.

Biodiesel is currently recognized by the U.S. EPA as a retrofit technology [EPA 2009]. In a review and analysis of the scientific literature, the U.S. EPA concluded that dramatic reductions in DPM, CO, and HC emissions, with a slight increase in NO_X emissions, are possible when neat and blended biodiesel are used in place of petroleum diesel on heavy-duty engines operated under transient conditions [EPA 2002a]. The statistical model developed in this study also predicted that further reductions would occur with increased biodiesel content. The model projects the reductions in DPM, CO, and HC emissions with neat FAME to be approximately 47% for DPM, 47% for CO, and 67% for HC (with an associated increase in NO_x of 7%). However, the values predicted by the analysis may not be reproducible for all engine types, engine operating conditions, and FAME types.

A number of studies have shown that FAME blends reduce emissions of total DPM and nonvolatile fractions of DPM [Purcell et al. 1996; Williams et al. 2006a,b; Yuan et al. 2007; Sappok and Wong 2008; Bugarski et al. 2010] and increase the particle-bound volatile organic fraction of DPM [McDonald et al. 1995; Purcell et al. 1996; Boehman et al. 2003; Stackpole 2009; MSHA 2009f; Bugarski et al. 2010]. It is generally accepted that the low-particulate-mass emissions when using FAME are a result of the fuel-bound oxygen content, higher Cetane number, and higher flame temperatures [Schönborn et al. 2009]. Similarly, some studies have shown reduced CO and HC emissions with the use of FAME fuels [Purcell et al. 1996; Monyem and Van Gerpen 2001; Yuan et al. 2007], which have also been attributed to the presence of fuel-bound oxygen [Schönborn et al. 2009].

In-mine studies have shown the potential for neat and blended FAME biodiesel fuels to reduce the exposure of underground miners to EC, TC, and DPM [McDonald et al. 1997; Watts et al. 1998; Schultz et al. 2004; NIOSH 2006a,b; Bugarski et al. 2010]. However, substantial increases in the OC fraction of TC have been observed under certain conditions [Stackpole 2009; MSHA 2009f; Bugarski et al. 2010; Schönborn et al. 2009]. DOCs are commonly deployed to counteract this potential increase in OC emissions [Watts et al. 1998; Bagley and Gratz 1998; Bagley et al. 1998; Stackpole 2009; MSHA 2009f]. However, the effects of DOCs on OC emissions depend upon the fuel formulation and the engine operating conditions [Bugarski et al. 2010]. Additionally, one drawback of using DOCs to control organic emissions is the potential for an increase in NO_2 emissions, particularly at high-load conditions [Watts et al. 1998; Bagley and Gratz 1998; Stackpole 2009; Bugarski et al. 2010].

An increase in NO_X emissions associated with biodiesel use has also been found in a number of studies [Monyem and Van Gerpen 2001; McCormick 2005; Tsolakis 2006; Durbin et al. 2007; Kawano et al. 2007; Vanbeek et al. 2009]. This NO_X increase has been attributed to an inadvertent advance in fuel injection timing, suggesting that these emissions might be controlled by increasing the exhaust gas recirculation (EGR) rate (see Section 2.2.1) in certain engines [Boehman et al. 2003; Kawano et al. 2007; Schönborn et al. 2009].

Despite the overall reductions in particulate mass, number, and EC emissions generally associated with using biodiesel, there are still concerns over the increased toxicity of these emissions [Verbeek et al. 2009; Liu et al. 2009a]. Limited information is available on the effects of FAME emissions on health and, therefore, more research is needed on this topic [McCormick 2007; Swanson et al. 2007].

Implementation of Biodiesel in Underground Mining

Changing the fuel supply from petroleum diesel to neat or blended FAME biodiesel is considered by a number of underground metal/nonmetal mine operators to be a viable method for controlling DPM emissions [Schultz et al. 2004; Tomko et al. 2010]. Some important factors to consider when implementing a biodiesel control strategy are:

- FAME fuels are more easily oxidized and, therefore, degrade more rapidly than petroleum diesel fuels [Moneyem and Van Gerpen 2001; Ogawa et al. 2008].

Oxidative degradation (as well as biological growth) can be suppressed by using additives such as 2,6-di-t-butyl-p-cresol (BTH).

- The metal ash and other impurities in biodiesel fuel can be a concern if FAME is used in engines equipped with DPF systems. Accumulation of solid impurities in the DPF may significantly shorten the ash-cleaning interval.

- A survey conducted in 2005 and 2006 [Alleman et al. 2007] discovered significant inconsistencies in the quality of FAME biodiesel fuels in the U.S. at both the production and delivery level. When possible, biodiesel fuels should be obtained from producers with (voluntary) BQ-9000™ accreditation. This is a quality accreditation assigned by the National Biodiesel Accreditation Commission (NBAC) [NBAC 2011]. This accreditation combines the ASTM standard for biodiesel (ASTM D6751) with an all-encompassing fuel quality systems program standard.

- At cold temperatures, FAME fuels crystallize and begin to gel. This gel will clog fuel filters and resist pumping from the fuel tank to the engine. The cold flow properties of FAME fuels depend strongly on feedstock (e.g., soy methyl ester has a cloud point of 0°C (32°F)), and edible tallow methyl ester has a cloud point of 19°C (66°F) [NREL 2009]. The critical properties for identifying the low-temperature operability of FAME fuels are cloud point, pour point, cold filter plugging point, and low-temperature flow test. Cloud point is the most widely used and provides the most conservative estimate of cold-weather operability. The low-temperature operability of the biodiesel blends can be improved if biodiesel is blended for use during cold-weather periods with a specially formulated cold-weather petroleum diesel (No. 1-D has substantially better cold properties than No. 2-D) or with specially formulated low-flow-temperature additives. The typical diesel cold flow additives have limited effectiveness on B100, but work with varying degrees of effectiveness with B20 [NREL 2009].

- Because neat FAME fuel gels at temperatures ranging from -11 to 17°C (12 to 63°F) (higher than petroleum diesel), the handling of neat and blended FAME fuels during cold temperatures is a major issue. Storing biodiesel in underground or heated fuel tanks can help mitigate issues with operability during periods of cold weather. Likewise, the transportation and transfer of biodiesel on and from the surface tanks to the underground tanks should be managed adequately to prevent issues with gelling or contamination of the fuel. Mines should discuss low-temperature operability with their suppliers.

- High levels of biodiesel present in the engine oil may result in serious engine oil sludge problems. Therefore, when high blends of biodiesel are used, engine-oil-change intervals should be significantly shortened.

- The implementation of biodiesel may increase sediment formation in the fueling system. The most likely impact of increased sediment formation is fuel filter plugging and varnish deposits in fuel system components.

- Neoprene and natural rubber are noncompatible with biodiesel, but Teflon™ (DuPont®), fluorocarbons, and nylon are compatible [NREL 2009]. Gaskets on some equipment may need to be replaced when implementing biofuels.

- End users should always consult the engine or combustion equipment manufacturer for further information about equipment preparation procedures before using biodiesel blends. [NREL 2009].

- FAME fuels in the U.S. contain, on average, 8% less energy per gallon than typical ULSD [NREL 2009]. Therefore, neat FAME fuel has a higher brake-specific fuel consumption (BSFC) than petroleum diesel [Monyem and Van Gerpen 2001; EPA 2002b; Williams et al. 2006a,b; NREL 2009]. However, depending on the application, the use of FAME fuel does not necessarily correspond to a loss in performance or higher fuel usage over the actual duty cycle.

- The temperature of FAME biodiesel can rise during decomposition [Shibata et al. 2008]. According to the National Biodiesel Board (NBB) [NBB 2009], in some environments, a pile of oil-soaked rags can develop enough heat to result in a spontaneous fire. Therefore, biodiesel-soaked rags should be stored in a safety can or dried individually to avoid the potential for spontaneous combustion.

Fuel Additives

Introduction

Fuel additives are added to diesel fuel for a wide variety of purposes [Bach et al. 1998; Jelles et al. 2001; Richards et al. 2006; Chevron 2007; D'Urbano and Mayer 2007; Gerlofs-Nijland et al. 2008], including:

- Improvement in the fuel delivery system performance (injector cleaners, lubricity additives),
- Improvement in the combustion process (Cetane number improvers, smoke suppressants),
- Fuel handling (antifoam, de-icing, low-temperature operability additives),
- Fuel stability (antioxidants, stabilizers, metal deactivators, dispersant),
- Contaminant control (biocides, demulsifiers, corrosion inhibitors),
- Emissions control (oxygenated compounds, biodiesel, diesel/water emulsions), and
- Enhancement of the regeneration of DPF systems.

Some additives are added to diesel fuel at the refinery or terminal [Chevron 2007]. The concentration of these additives is typically low, on the order of a few parts per million to parts per trillion. Other "aftermarket additives" are added to the fuel after the fuel leaves the terminal. The most significant aftermarket additives are those containing fuel-borne catalysts (FBCs), biodiesel, and water.

FBCs are a group of significant aftermarket additives used to lower the regeneration temperature of DPFs in advanced exhaust aftertreatment systems (see Section 2.2.2). The most widely used FBCs are based on platinum (Pt), cerium (Ce), and iron (Fe) [Bach et al 1998; Seguelong and Quigley 2002; Majewski 2003; D'Urbano and Mayer 2007; Naschke et al. 2008; Lemaire 1999]. FBC additives are added to fuel by doping the bulk fuel supply dedicated to the vehicles equipped with DPFs [McGinn et al. 2004] or via onboard dosing systems [Lemaire 1999; Seguelong and Quigley 2002; Naschke at al. 2008]. These additives should meet the following criteria [Lemaire 1999]: (1) have good stability, (2) not modify the physical and chemical properties of the fuel, (3) be compatible with the materials used in the engine systems such as fuel supply, fuel injection system, valves, piston rings, and turbocharger components, (4) be compatible with DPF materials as well as any other aftertreatment devices, and (5) not promote the formation of secondary emissions [Lemaire 1999; D'Urbano and Mayer 2007].

The potential of adding water to diesel fuel (water/diesel emulsions) to reduce diesel emissions has been extensively explored [EPA 2002c; EPA 2008a; NIOSH 2006b]. This type of fuel was marketed in the U.S. for several years, but is not currently commercially available.

Biodiesel fuel is also considered an additive by the U.S. EPA [EPA 2008b; EPA 2009]. Because of its significance, a detailed discussion on biodiesel as a fuel and fuel additive is provided earlier in this section.

Regulations

According to current federal regulations, only fuel additives registered with the EPA should be used in underground mines in the U.S. [66 Fed. Reg. 27864 (2001); 71 Fed. Reg. 28924 (2006)]. EPA registration is also required by some underground mining state regulations [PADEP 2009; WVDEC 2004]. The EPA [66 Fed. Reg. 5001 (2001a); 69 Fed. Reg. 38957 (2004)] registration process requires that manufacturers prove, through a three-tier process, that the fuel additives are safe and do not change or create new or harmful emissions species. Other regulatory agencies also use a similar process [CARB 2004; CARB 2008]. There is currently only one additive registered with the EPA under its fuel and fuel-additive registration program that meets both Tier 3 requirements [66 Fed. Reg. 5001 (2001); 69 Fed. Reg. 38957 (2004)] and is also verified as a retrofit technology [EPA 2009].

Additives containing transitional metals, such as FBCs, have received special attention from the health community and regulators due to their potential to increase the concentration of nanometer sized metallic aerosols in the air. Only a few metallic additives are currently registered with the EPA, primarily under a small business exception. FBCs containing Pt are currently under EPA scrutiny [EPA 2008c]. The use of FBCs has been more extensively explored in Europe, particularly under the auspices of the VERT program (*Verminderung der Emissionen von Real-Dieselmotoren im Tunnelbau*, or Curtailing Emissions from Diesel Engines in Tunnel Construction). A list of metallic fuel additives approved for use with DPF systems by VERT is available in D'Urbano and Mayer [2007].

Effects of Fuel Additives on Emissions

When added in small concentrations and effectively combusted, additive packages containing organic, nonmetallic compounds should have a minuscule effect on the characteristics and toxicity of diesel emissions. However, when added in high concentrations, several types of additives have been shown to have measurable effects on emissions characteristics [Ullman et al. 1994; Maricq et al. 1998].

The effects of additives containing organometallic compounds (such as FBCs) are a major concern [EPA 2008c]. The main problem with using these additives is that the majority of the metals supplied to the combustion chamber with the fuel are emitted in aerosol form [Ulrich and Wichser 2003; Farfaletti et al. 2005; Richards et al. 2006,]. The emission rates of metals from engines fueled with FBCs are primarily a result of the catalyst dosing rate and type of exhaust aftertreatment. Other factors such as engine operating conditions, engine design, and engine maintenance condition also affect these emission rates. However, FBCs have also been found to positively affect other diesel engine emissions. For example, one study showed that the total mass of DPM emitted by LD diesel engines could be reduced by 13% when a mixture of organometallic compounds, based mainly on Ce was added to the fuel [Farfaletti et al. 2005]. In some instances, Ce-based FBCs have also shown to reduce total carbon [Lee and Song 2007] and organic carbon [Skillas et al. 2000] fractions of DPM emitted by HD diesels.

The majority of DPF systems (Section 2.2.2.2) are highly efficient in trapping metallic aerosols generated by the use of FBCs [Ulrich and Wichser 2003; Richards et al. 2006]. The mass emissions of metals from diesel engines using FBC-treated fuel and equipped with DPF systems have been found to be between 3% and 18% of the total mass of emitted particles [HEI 2001]. Partial filter (PF) systems (Section 2.2.2.4) can remove some, but not all, of the metallic aerosols caused by the use of FBCs [Mayer et al. 2009]. Therefore, the use of FBCs is not recommended in engines equipped with PF systems.

Several laboratory studies on water/diesel emulsions [EPA 2002c; Farfaletti et al. 2005] have shown that the effects of these emulsions on engine emissions depend on engine technology. Warm-weather water/diesel emulsions (approximately 20% water) were shown to reduce DPM and NO_X emissions from HD diesel engines up to 59% and 20%, respectively [EPA 2002c]. Similar reductions in emissions from Euro-3 HD diesel engine were achieved with water/diesel emulsions containing 12% water [Farfaletti et al. 2005]. These laboratory evaluations also showed slight [Farfaletti et al. 2005] to substantial [EPA 2002c] increases in HC emissions. The effects of water/diesel emulsions on CO emissions were found to be engine-type dependent, providing in some cases average reductions as high as 13% and in the other cases increases as high as 35% [EPA 2002c]. The additional CO and HC emissions can potentially be reduced by a DOC.

Cold-weather (10% water) and warm-weather (20% water) water/diesel emulsions were also field-evaluated in underground mines using an isolated zone approach [NIOSH 2006b]. In this case, the cold- and warm-weather water/diesel emulsions were found to reduce EC concentrations by 67% and 85%, respectively, and for total DPM concentrations by 45% and 58%, respectively. Additionally, these additives were also evaluated in a production environment in an underground stone mine that operated an entire diesel-powered vehicle fleet using this emulsified fuel [Noll et al. 2006]. The evaluation showed that EC was reduced by cold-weather water/diesel emulsions by 44% and by warm-weather water/diesel emulsions by 57%.

Engine Lubricating Oils

Introduction

Engine lubricants act to reduce friction within the engine, protect against corrosion and wear, seal rings and liners, and control undesirable byproducts [Plumley 2005]. The base oils used for engine lubricants are distilled in processes similar to those that produce gasoline and diesel, although yielding heavier fractions. Engine lubricants are combustible and may play a significant role in the formation of diesel emissions. Even though the consumption rate of lube oil is minor compared to that of fuel (in some cases, as little as 0.2%, comparatively [Jung et al. 2003]), this consumption process contributes disproportionately to harmful emissions due to the low efficiency of oil combustion, metallic compounds within the formulation, and comparatively higher sulfur content of oil to fuel in modern systems. To combat these issues, recent manufacturing developments have placed more emphasis on reducing oil consumption in diesel engines and producing oil formulations that promote decreased oil-related emissions.

Implementation

In the U.S., engine manufacturers recommend specific oils based on the Society of Automotive Engineers' (SAE) viscosity grades and the American Petroleum Institute's (API) classifications. SAE ratings determine the viscosity of the oil at a standard operating temperature of 100°C (210°F) as well as in cold conditions. API service categories represent a series of laboratory and engine tests that specific oil brands must pass before achieving certification. Engine manufacturers often provide updated lists of recommended lubrication oil brands/formulations based on engine model. For a specific engine, recommended viscosity ratings will hold over the operating life of the unit, while recommended API categories are often updated with the release of new oil formulations. Because the efficiency and operational life of both the engine and exhaust system components are affected by oil properties and composition, it is important to adhere to the manufacturers' recommendations when selecting an oil brand and formulation. Failure to do so could result in a violation of the engine warranty and/or MSHA certification.

Due to increased engine demand as well as heightened environmental and health concerns, oil refiners are producing cleaner and more efficient oil formulations. The API has released intermittent oil standards that reflect the demand of current engines. Most recently, EPA Tier 4 emissions regulations have prompted the development of CJ-4, the API's highest-quality classification for diesel lubrication oils yet. Released in 2006, lube oils that meet this standard are designed to help modern, four-stroke, directly-injected engines meet EPA Tier 4 emissions requirements while maintaining or enhancing lubrication qualities. Table 1 summarizes the incremental change in oil composition over CI-4, the previous standard [Lubrizol 2011].

Table 1. A comparison of the composition of CI-4 rated oils with newer CJ-4 rated oils.

	API CI-4 limits	API CJ-4 limits
Ash	1.2%–1.5%	1.0%
Sulfur	No limit	0.4%
Phosphorous	0.14%	0.12%
Volatility	15.0%	13.0%

Although it is always best to follow the manufacturer's recommendations, CJ-4 oils can, generally, be used on both modern and aged diesel engines. However, it is important to note that the API service categories are usually "backwards compatible." This means that, for oils complying with a given API specification, engines manufactured before the release date of that specification will often be compatible. However, caution must be used when using older oil formulations in newer engines. Most modern engines are not compatible with older standards due to fouling of the exhaust system components and other issues mentioned previously. Engines produced after 2007 should only run on CJ-4 oils and ultralow sulfur diesel fuel. The oil change intervals cannot be lengthened simply by upgrading to an oil that meets newer API standards. Caution should also be exercised when employing CJ-4 oil with engines operating on biodiesel blended fuels because increases in acidity and viscosity are possible [Watson and Wong 2008]. More information is available on the API CJ-4 website (http://www.apicj-4.org/faqs.html).

Effects on Emissions and Performance of Aftertreatment Systems

Although the process of oil consumption is still not clearly understood, it is suggested that lubrication oil may enter the combustion chamber through reverse blowby (i.e., flow from crankcase gases past piston rings), vaporization from the cylinder walls, leaks in the valve stem seals, the turbocharger lubrication system, and other pathways [Froelund and Yilmaz 2004; Yilmaz 2003; Jung et al. 2003]. Some products resulting from the combustion of lubricating oil are increased organic emissions of DPM, gaseous sulfuric emissions, and noncombustible DPM known as ash [Plumley 2005; Miller et al. 1997; Aravelli and Heibel 2007; Kittelson et al. 2008].

Engine lube oil is composed of a base oil and an additive package. The base oil is formed from petroleum-derived mineral oils and provides the lubrication qualities of the liquid. The additive package is a combination of various chemicals and metal compounds that act as detergents, dispersants, acid neutralizers, antioxidants, corrosion and rust inhibitors, and anti-wear additives [Whitacre et al. 2010; Jung et al. 2003; Aravelli and Heibel 2007]. Most of these metals contribute to the formation of ash or solid, noncombustible byproducts that can accumulate within DPFs [Miller et al. 2007a; Vouitsis et al. 2007]. Over time, ash buildup on particulate filters leads to decreased soot collection capacity, shortened time periods between regeneration and/or service events, increased backpressure, and losses in fuel economy [Aravelli and Heibel 2007]. The rate of ash collection on a DPF can be correlated with oil consumption, but DPF service cycles cannot be reliably predicted based on this value [Macián et al. 2003; Aravelli and Heibel 2007; Jung et al. 2003].

The sulfuric and ash content of newer fuel and lube oil blends have been reduced considerably in recent years. Also, engine manufacturers emphasize the improved design of engine components (such as piston rings and crankcase filtration systems) for reducing the amount of oil consumption during combustion. If lube-oil-derived emissions are known issues, some options available to mines are: (1) upgrading to CJ-4 oils, (2) reducing contaminates in the lubrication and fuel systems through proper handling, (3) using engine manufacturer-approved lube oils with decreased volatility to reduce consumption, and (4) properly servicing engines to ensure the integrity of piston rings and other seals.

2.3.2 Handling of Fuels and Lubricants

Introduction

From an emissions standpoint, best practices for handling of diesel fuels and lubricants is largely aimed at preventing contamination and sustaining the physical and chemical properties of these fluids during storage so that they can perform effectively during the combustion process. This section discusses the proper handling of fuels and lubricants as they pertain to diesel emissions. In addition to the information provided, it is important to remember that diesel fuels and lubricants should always be purchased from reliable suppliers who maintain strict control over the quality of their product.

Sources of Fluid Contamination and Effects on Emissions

Water Contamination

Although fuel that has been emulsified with clean water has sometimes been used as a NO_X control for older, mechanically controlled diesels [EPA 2002c; EPA 2008; NIOSH 2006b; Noll et al. 2006; Nadeem et al. 2006; Armas et al. 2005; Samec et al. 2002], modern diesels rely on strict control over the charge volume and injection timing events and, therefore, any disruption that water may cause to these systems can negatively impact emissions of NO_X, PM, and HC. Additionally, water contamination of the fuel supply chain may introduce biological contaminants such as fungi or bacteria, which can lower the shelf life of fuel, clog filters, and foul fuel-delivery components [Bento and Gaylarde 2001; Owen and Coley 1995a; Flippin et al. 1964; Chung et al. 2000].

Water contamination in stationary storage tanks is often the result of rusted and/or leaky containers, residual water from tank cleaning, and precontaminated fluid passed on from the supplier. In addition, water condensate can form in the empty volume between the top of the fluid and the ceiling of the fuel storage container (or "headspace") and eventually settle at the bottom of storage containers.

Dirt, Dust, and Sediment Contamination

Dirt, dust, and other particles entering combustion systems can cause lowered efficiency or failures of key components, which both may lead to increases in harmful emissions after prolonged use [Argueyrolles et al. 2007]. The introduction of abrasive particles to the combustion process may increase engine wear and ash formation, promote increased HC emissions (through coking of injector nozzles), and accelerate sludge buildup within the crankcase. Sediment contamination may also clog fuel filters and harm critical exhaust aftertreatment components.

Common sources of contamination include dirty storage tanks and/or facilities, dusty parts or service areas during engine maintenance, and dirty fluid transfer components (containers, pumps, hoses, dispenser nozzles, funnels, siphons, etc). Rust formation in storage containers as well as the waxing of diesel fuel (when temperatures drop below the fuel's cloud point) and biological growth can cause additional sediment contamination.

Cross Contamination

Cross contamination of fuels occurs when diesel fuel is accidentally or intentionally doped with other types of fuel, when containers are not thoroughly cleaned and dried before switching to new fuels, when storage units are inappropriately labeled, or when transfer components are used for more than one type of fuel/oil. Doping diesel fuel with gasoline, whether intentionally or unintentionally, has the effect of raising combustion temperatures, thereby causing overheating of the injection nozzles, which can lead to coking of the nozzle tips [Argueyrolles et al. 2007]. Overall, cross contamination of fluids is almost never beneficial to emissions or engine performance [Argueyrolles et al. 2007; Aravelli and Heibel 2007; Miller et al. 2007b; Jung et al. 2003; Miller et al. 1997].

Regulations Pertaining to Storage and Handling of Fluids in Underground Mines

Table 2 below provides a noncomprehensive listing of relevant rules and guidelines related to the safe storage and handling of fluids. It is important to note that fire, explosion, and other safety-related recommendations should always trump suggestions that are made for controlling fluid quality if discrepancies should occur (for example, a recommendation to store fuel in low humidity environments could contradict fire safety regulations in some scenarios).

Table 2. A noncomprehensive listing of relevant rules and guidelines related to the safe storage and handling of fuels and lubricating oils in underground mines

Description of Operation Type	Code of Federal Regulatons	CFR Subparts
Underground Coal Mines	30 CFR § 75	1104, 1901–1906, 1911–1915
Surface work areas of underground coal mines	30 CFR § 77	208, 404, 1100–1105, 1711, 1915
Underground metal and nonmetal mines	30 CFR § 57	4100–4104, 4130–4131, 4160–4161, 4400–4402, 4430–4431, 4460–4463, 4500–4501, 4504–4505, 4531, 4533, 4561, 5065–5066, 14204, 16001–16004, 16012

Other rules or recommendations to consider

MSDS of fluid(s)
30 CFR § 47
29 CFR §1910.106, § 1910.110
40 CFR § 266;
49 CFR § 100185
NFPA 30, 30A, 52, 58, 120–123, 329, 385–386

Storage and Handling of Diesel Fuels

Bulk Storage of Diesel Fuels

The typical shelf life for well-maintained diesel fuel is approximately six months [BP Australia 2005a]. However, a number of factors will accelerate the aging process. The first is normal oxidation from air, which will begin to form slight sediments and gum within the fuel. Also, exposures to zinc, copper, and similar alloys such as brass, can cause reactions that will degrade fuel composition [Doyle et al. 2006]. In addition, fungal growth resulting from water contamination can raise the acidity of fuel [Bento and Gaylarde 2001; Flippin et al. 1964; Chung et al. 2000]. Dirt, dust, and rust infiltration will also degrade flow properties and destabilize the fuel. For these reasons, it is important to enforce good storage and handling procedures, particularly if long-term storage is anticipated.

Ideally, bulk diesel storage tanks should be kept in clean, cool areas. Storage facilities should be well ventilated, with concrete floors to prevent spills from permeating the ground, and located away from maintenance or other working areas. This will minimize any risks associated with long-term exposure to diesel fuel vapors [Owen and Coley 1995b]. For fuel quality purposes, low humidity is usually desirable, though fire safety recommendations may contradict this recommendation. Containers should be free from copper, zinc, and similar alloys. If fuel exposure to these metals cannot be avoided, however, additives can be used to minimize their damaging effects. These containers should be equipped with slanted or conical bottoms with a drain valve at the low point to allow for periodic drainage of contaminated water and other sediments [BP Australia 2002]. In addition, tanks should be outfitted with filtered breather systems that allow air to circulate through the headspace and limit the amount of water that will condense within the tank. Similarly, when storing above ground, fuel levels should be as high as possible to limit the amount of condensate formed. However, if storing underground, the total volume of stored fuel should be kept at a minimum for fire safety purposes. If possible, desiccating filters should be used in breather systems to further assist in removing water condensate. In order to remove sediments and gums from the tank, systems that automatically recirculate fuel through filters can also be installed. Tanks should also be drained and cleaned regularly (being allowed to dry thoroughly before refilling) to remove sediment. Periodically, the tanks should be examined for leaks and rust. Repairs should be made immediately because corruptions in the tanks may allow dirt and dust to enter the fuel supply.

Transferring Diesel Fuel

When transferring fuel between containers, dispenser nozzles should be wiped down with a clean, dry, lint-free rag, if needed. When possible, quick-connect fill systems should be implemented on storage and transfer hoses to minimize dirt infiltration [McGinn et al. 2010]. Similarly, transfer components should be cleaned before each use and stored in sealable containers. In-line filters with filtration efficiencies that meet or exceed those of onboard fuel systems should be used to minimize the transfer of particulates and sedimentation. Water-separating filters should always be used when transporting fuel to and from storage tanks; in addition, the sight bowls of these filters should be checked beforehand to ensure that they are not already filled with water. Transfer equipment should not be intermixed between different fluids.

Onboard Handling of Diesel Fuel

In most diesel fuels, the infiltration of dirt, dust, and other particles is controlled by the engine's fuel filtering system. Regular filter changes should be performed based on the recommended schedule outlined in the mine's fuel handling procedures. If premature filter plugging occurs, the overall fuel handling practices should be thoroughly evaluated for sources of contamination. When replacing filters, be cautious of dirt and debris entering the fueling system. When possible, do not prefill the new filters as this increases the likelihood of contamination [Caterpillar 1997; McGinn et al. 2010]. In addition, it is best practice to maintain fuel levels as high as possible to limit both the formation of condensation within the fuel tank and the transfer of sediments out of the tank. Periodically, the integrity of the fueling system should be examined for leaks and rust. Repairs should be made immediately because corruption in the system may allow dirt, dust, and other sediments to enter the fueling system.

Vehicles typically have engineering strategies that prevent moisture intrusion into the fuel-injection system and combustion chamber. Such designs often include onboard water separating systems. These systems should be inspected regularly to ensure that they are functioning properly and are not filled with water and/or clogged with debris. If moisture problems are excessive, it may be necessary to drain settled water from onboard tanks before starting engines. In addition, physical designs to direct moisture away from the fueling system components may be implemented to provide some degree of protection from rainwater, hose downs, splashes etc. Mechanics should periodically inspect the body surrounding the fuel systems and the plumbing from tank to manifold (including the fuel cap and tank vent) to locate and fix leaks or areas of possible water penetration.

A Special Note on Biodiesel Fuels

Biodiesel fuels typically have higher gel temperatures than other fuels (see Section 2.3.1). This can be a nuisance for cold weather mines and may lead to sludge buildup within the fuel system over time [Strong et al. 2004]. In general, it is a good practice to locate biodiesel storage tanks (as well as biodiesel-fueled vehicles) underground when possible. This will help maintain fuel temperatures above the gel point during cold months.

In addition, some diesel equipment may need servicing after switching to biodiesel fuels. Biodiesel is a mild solvent and may help remove particulate deposits in storage tanks and vehicle fueling systems. This can "clean" engines and fuel storage equipment, but it may quickly clog fuel filters [Strong et al. 2004]. To prevent this problem, fuel tanks and storage equipment should be thoroughly cleaned before introducing biodiesel-blended fuels. The first fuel filter replacements on vehicles may be necessary after only 30 hours of operation, after which the system should return to normal. In addition, the solvency of biodiesel-blended fuels has prompted improvements in gasket and seal designs in newer engines. For older diesels, it is best practice to monitor and/or upgrade fuel lines, hoses, gaskets, and fuel pump diaphragms to prevent leaks within the system [DOE 2009].

Storage and Handling of Engine Lubricants

Bulk Storage of Lubricants

Lubricant storage facilities should be clean, dry, and particle-free. Ideally, these facilities should provide filtered, climate-controlled environments (that allow bulk oil temperatures to remain near room temperature and not to exceed 21°C (70°F) [Caines et al. 2004]) with the lowest attainable humidity level that still complies with fire safety recommendations. Even though these conditions may be difficult to achieve in mining environments, it should not deter mines from attempting to maintain storage facilities as close to these ideal conditions as possible. Because of the detrimental effects lube oil contamination can have on machinery, it may make sense to use keys or access cards to limit the admission to lubrication storage areas only to those individuals who are trained in the proper handling of lube oils.

Bulk storage tanks are usually made from stainless steel, mild steel plate, anodized aluminum, or plastic. Although stainless steel and anodized aluminum may have high initial costs, their maintenance requirements are lower compared to other metals. Plastic tanks are desirable because there are no rust issues and because they can be manufactured in clear form so that oil levels can easily be seen. At a minimum, tanks should have a visual sight glass or level gauge to indicate oil levels and enable visual inspection of the condition of the oil. Catch basins should be employed to retain oil in the event of leaks, and a periodic inspection of seals and valves should be performed to limit this prospect. In cold climates, the heating of lubricants can assist in lowering the viscosity of fluids so they can be extracted from the tank [Caines et al. 2004]. In bulk storage, the watt density of heaters should not exceed 15 watts per square inch for circulating fluids and 10 watts per square inch for static fluids. This will prevent thermal breakdown of the oil, which often results from sludge and volatile formation within the oil [Fitch 2004; Noria Corporation 2004].

As with fuel tanks, lube oil storage tanks have a "headspace" (i.e., area between the oil level and roof of the tank). Controlling the moisture and particle content of this headspace can affect the properties of the extracted lube oil. Breather systems should be employed to filter contaminants from this area because a large fraction of the moisture and solid particles that enter lube oils passes through this headspace [Fitch 2004]. These breather systems should be equipped with filters whose particle filtration efficiencies match or exceed the efficiency of the filters used on fleet engines. In addition, when water vapor content within the headspace is limited, water within the oil will transfer to the headspace in an effort to maintain equilibrium. The following arrangements can help reduce headspace humidity and remove moisture content from the oil:

- The use of desiccating-type filters in breather systems,
- The use of vapor extraction fans to purge volatile hydrocarbons and water vapor from the headspace, and
- The use of metered, dry instrument air to purge headspace volume.

Even with effective headspace metering, water can build up at the bottom of storage tanks over time. This water level should always remain below the oil extraction point and can be monitored with water-phase floaters, which float on the boundary between the water and oil. Care must be taken to prevent disruption of the storage tank and limit the mixing of oil and water. Storage containers should have sloped bases with drains to allow for water and tank sludge removal. Periodically, this waste should be purged from the tank and handled as a hazardous material.

Transferring Diesel Lubricants

When transferring oil from bulk storage containers, in-line particle capture and/or super-absorbent filters should be used to prevent contaminant transmission. In particular, the particle capture filters should meet or exceed the ratings of recommended oil filters for the engine. Transfer hardware, such as pumps and valves, as well as hose ends, should be sealed from contamination when not in use. If contamination does occur, components should be flushed and cleaned thoroughly. Transfer equipment should not be intermixed between different fluids.

Visual Analyses for Contamination

Visual analyses of all stored fluids should be performed by extracting a sample and/or by inspecting through sight glasses. Visual inspections should also be performed on used fluid filters. The following may help to identify contaminants [BP Australia 2005b]:

- Water
  - "Haziness" or loss of clarity in fuel due to suspended water droplets
- Dirt and rust
  - Brown or red particle suspensions within fuel samples
  - Greasy black deposits on filters
- Fungus
  - Blackish brown buildup in filters
- Wax/gel
  - Yellow suspension in fuel
  - Yellow wax deposits on filters

Used Oil Analysis Programs

During its service life, oil becomes oxidized and contaminated with fuel, water, particulate matter, other combustion residues, and possibly coolant [Caines et al. 2004]. With time, the physical and chemical characteristics of the oil can degrade to a point where damage to the engine, as well as increases in harmful emissions, can occur. In response, a well-executed used oil analysis program can be implemented to monitor these changes over time [Macián et al. 2003]. This information may be useful in the early detection of mechanical failures, recognition of inadequate lubrication, determination of oil-change intervals, and emissions-related issues connected to oil consumption, water infiltration, and ash content.

Because the impact of these analyses rely heavily on recognizing changes to data trends over time, consistency in the handling of oils over their life cycle is critical and cannot be overemphasized. Even the most precise laboratory testing will yield unusable data unless a well-organized lubrication recording and handling plan is implemented. This means that strict control over the following areas must be maintained:

- Oil storage, handling, and sampling procedures
- Detailed recording of engine maintenance information, including engine ID, description of problems and/or repairs, date of servicing, and name of technician, etc.
- Detailed recording of oil-use information, including engine ID, oil brand/product, "top-off" dates and volume, oil-change intervals, names of servicing technician(s), etc.

Oil Sampling Procedures

Used-oil-analysis programs require dependable sampling procedures to prevent flawed laboratory results. The keys to eliminating sampling errors are maintaining proper technique and to achieve consistency from sample to sample. It is suggested that the following guidelines be followed [Jenson 2011; Fitch and Troyer 2011; Analysts Inc. 2011]:

- Sample while the machine is idling to ensure complete mixing of the oil. If this is not possible, sample just after shutdown.
- Maintain consistent and appropriate sampling points.
  - Never draw samples downstream of an oil filter.

- Avoid areas where contaminants tend to settle, these will flaw the results.
- If possible, install a dedicated sampling valve between the oil pump and oil filter, prior to the filter.
- Never sample directly from a drain port unless a drain-port sampling valve has been installed.
- Avoid vacuum sampling whenever possible. Maintaining consistency from test to test through vacuum extraction (such as through an oil dipstick tube) is difficult.
- Drain a small amount of oil from the engine through the sampling apparatus into a clean container before collecting an oil sample. If a dedicated sampling valve is installed, open and close it at least five times to loosen any particles. This will help clean the sampling train before extracting a sample.
- Without touching the sampling tubing, draw an amount of oil (in the quantity required by the analysis lab) into a lint-free, glass container. Immediately seal the container.
- Replace the volume of oil removed from the crankcase according to procedures outlined in the mine's oil analysis policy (either top off with new oil or refill with old oil).
- Record all appropriate information, including:
  - Date and engine ID #
  - Hours/miles on engine (operational hours since new or since last overhaul)
  - Hours/miles on oil (operational hours since new or since oil change)
  - Oil information (brand, product name, and grade, SAE or ISO)
  - Oil consumption or makeup oil added
    - This is equal to the amount of oil that was added to maintain proper level since last oil change or last sampling interval.
  - Notes on latest engine conditions such as recent maintenance, changes in performance, changes in operational cycles, etc.
  - Notes on sampling conditions such as sampling apparatus used, temperature, engine mode (idle), name of technician, spills, etc.
- Sample regularly and frequently.

Laboratory Testing of Used Engine Oil

There are many laboratory tests that are used to quantify the integrity of used engine oil. Typically, these tests will fall into the categories listed below. When implementing a used engine-oil testing program, it is important for mines to become familiar with the types of measurements available and to customize testing regimens to fit their needs. Often, laboratories will offer groups of tests that are specifically geared toward the monitoring of diesel engine lubricants. It is advisable that mines use independent laboratories that are ISO-9000 or ISO-17025 certified [ISO 2005a,b]. This will ensure the tests are performed without bias and according to ASTM methods. Some common tests are described as follows [Caines et al. 2004; Mayer 2011; Analysts Inc. 2011; Petroleum Technologies Group 2011; Shell 2011]:

Viscosity -Viscosity is the measure of an oil's internal resistance to flow and is considered the most important property of the lubricant. Testing the viscosity of the oil involves physical measurements that may be performed at various temperatures depending on the specific laboratory practices. Changes in viscosity are expected over oil life; however, changes from test to test can indicate improper servicing of the engine or contamination/dilution of the oil. Increases in viscosity may indicate oxidation of the base oil, buildup of suspended insoluble matter, and/or buildup of dissolved resinous matter. Decreases in viscosity may indicate that fuel dilution of the oil and/or shear breakdown of the viscosity modifier has occurred.

Base Number - Detergents in the oil act as bases to neutralize acid that is formed during combustion. Over time, the concentration of available detergents decreases as acids and bases are neutralized. The base number is, therefore, a measurement of the amount of detergency left within the oil and is reported as milligrams of potassium hydroxide per gram (mg KOH/g). This value can be a key indicator of the life remaining in a given oil and can be used for setting appropriate oil-change intervals. However, quantifying the base number depends on the measurement method used, necessitating the consistency of the analysis technique from test to test.

Contaminants - Contaminants are substances that infiltrate the lube system either from outside sources or from the engine blowby. These tests detect for water contamination, fuel dilution, antifreeze and soot contamination, as well as sulfation, oxidation, and nitration. These values are reported either in percentage of oil by volume or absorption units per centimeter. An important item to mention is that the measurement of these contaminants often involves mutual interferences with one another as well as other substances, such as wear metals. Therefore, it is advisable to consider the detection of these contaminants only as an indicator of their presence, rather than a measurement of their actual quantity.

Additives and Wear Metals - Chemical and spectrometric analyses can be used to measure the amount of wear metals and additives in the used oil. Wear metals are particles that are formed during friction-related shearing of metallic components and then deposited in the oil. Additives are substances added to the oil formulation by manufacturers during the oil development process to enhance the lubricating and cleaning properties of the oil. Usually, these substances are reported in parts per million by weight. Increases in the measurement results for these substances may indicate problems with engine wear and/or increased consumption of the base oil. Decreases may indicate increased consumption of the additive package which may correspond with increased ash collection within the exhaust system.

2.4 Maintenance of Engines and Emissions Control Technologies

2.4.1 Emissions-assisted Maintenance

Introduction

Emissions-assisted maintenance of diesel engines is based on two beliefs: (1) an improperly maintained diesel engine can emit undesirable concentrations of exhaust emissions compared to a well-maintained diesel engine and (2) onsite emission tests may be employed to determine if and where there is a need for engine maintenance [Spears 1997]. A number of studies have been performed since 1980 to move these ideas from philosophy and into working practice [Waytulonis 1987; Spears 1997; McGinn 2000], the basis of which revolves around a four-step procedure:

1. Routine measurements of diesel particulate matter (DPM) and gases emitted from the exhaust stream
2. Diagnosis of mechanical issues that may exist
3. Actions to remove the failures
4. Confirmation emissions measurement to evaluate the effectiveness of the actions

With the use of electronically controlled diesel engines, it is increasingly more difficult to standardize the diagnosis of mechanical problems for all engine makes and models based on emissions measurements. Nevertheless, changes in emissions measurements with respect to historic recorded data of any engine should always be of concern and should lead to a thorough inspection of the equipment.

Additionally, contemporary diesels introduce a number of exhaust aftertreatment control packages that, in addition to engine components, must be tested and maintained. Measuring and maintaining the engine alone is not enough to control unwanted pollutants from modern diesel engines.

Regulations

The Mine Safety and Health Administration (MSHA) regulations require that underground coal mine operators perform weekly loaded-engine, undiluted emissions tests on all engines in diesel-powered equipment approved under Part 36 as well as heavy-duty nonpermissible diesel-powered equipment [30 CFR 75.1908; 30 CFR 75.1914]. Metal/nonmetal mines do not have the requirement to perform periodic emission tests on diesel-powered equipment, but precise maintenance standards are set by MSHA in 30 CFR 57.5066. This rule states that any approved diesel-engine-powered piece of equipment must be maintained in approved condition, and any nonapproved engine must be maintained to manufacturer specifications. Although no periodic emissions tests are required, MSHA, in their Best Practice Guide, encourages metal/nonmetal mine operators to perform weekly CO measurements [MSHA 2010].

Tools

Proper tools are absolutely essential for effectively maintaining diesel engines. A report for the Diesel Emissions Evaluation Program (DEEP) [McGinn 1999] provides a list of tools for performing emissions-assisted maintenance:

Fundamental Tools
- A clean and organized work environment
- A set of pressure gauges for measuring intake, oil, and fuel pressures
- A manometer for measuring exhaust backpressure
- An infrared hand-held temperature probe
- A hand-held digital photo tachometer
- A coolant system pressure test kit
- A cylinder compression test kit

Advanced Technology Tools
- An exhaust gas analysis system
- Diagnostic software that communicates to the engine
- An electronic tool for timing mechanically fuel-injected engines

Tools for Measuring Gases

An analyzer must be used to measure gas-phase diesel exhaust components during the engine tests. The analyzer must be capable of detecting CO in the 0 to ~3000-ppm range and CO_2 in the 5 to 15 percent range. Ideally, the accuracy of the instrument would be reasonably close to that of similar laboratory-grade instruments, which are typically within ± 2%. NO_X (NO + NO_2) levels should also be measured. The concentration of NO can vary from 10–1,000 ppm. The concentration of NO_2 in untreated exhaust does not exceed 100 ppm. However, the use of a DOC can increase its concentration up to 1,000 ppm; for this reason, the latter value should be considered when selecting an instrument.

The instrument should also have a sampling probe and sample line suitable for sampling undiluted diesel exhaust. A sample conditioner should be included in the analyzer package to remove water vapor and DPM particles (using filters, water scrubbers, or Peltier coolers) ahead of the analyzer. The instrument must be capable of surviving rugged mine environments, and the probe itself must be capable of withstanding 650°C (1,202°F) exhaust temperatures.

A number of commercially available emissions analyzers meet these requirements. These instruments typically use nondispersive infrared (NDIR), Fourier transform infrared (FTIR), or electrochemical gas sensor (EGS) technologies. NDIR and FTIR are highly accurate gas sensing techniques, but they are usually more expensive and complex than needed for routine day-to-day operation in underground mines. EGS modules are available in several portable, rugged instruments, and their performance has been verified in laboratory tests. Due to the compact design of the sensors, EGS technology allows the monitoring of NO, NO_2, CO, CO_2, and O_2 using a single instrument.

For the measurement of NO_2 in undiluted exhaust, the use of a heated sampling system is always recommended. The sampling system must be heated up to 100°C (212°F) so the gas temperature remains above the dew points of water and hydrocarbons. If the sample line temperature falls below 100°C (212°F), NO_2 concentrations may be underestimated [Czerwinski et al. 2007].

Tools for Measuring DPM

Direct sampling of DPM in engine exhaust is not routinely performed in mining mainly because it is not required in U.S. underground coal and metal/nonmetal mines. In addition, this type of sampling involves complex equipment and procedures to yield accurate results. Nevertheless, even a rough tailpipe measurement of DPM can be valuable information when assessing the health of an engine and the need for maintenance. It can also be useful information to have when evaluating the initial and continued performance of certain exhaust aftertreatment technologies, such as high efficiency DPF filters.

Over the last few decades, several technologies have been developed to measure DPM concentrations emitted by diesel engines in underground mines. The goal of each technique is to provide immediate results about the DPM emissions of a specific diesel-powered vehicle. The most common example is an opacity meter. Opacity meters measure particles suspended in the exhaust and are a quick and easy-to-use tool to evaluate the condition of an engine or gross malfunctions of DPM control technologies. Opacity is defined as the percentage of light transmitted from a source and passing through a medium that is prevented from reaching a light detector. In diesel exhaust, high opacity may indicate a high concentration of unburned hydrocarbons (emitted as aerosols) and DPM particles [Williams et al. 1973], which may signify engine or aftertreatment package malfunction [Ullman and Hare 1984]. Unfortunately, the measured value of opacity is highly dependent upon test conditions—including ambient conditions, engine operating mode, measurement configuration, and instrumentation used. For example, the altitude at which the diesel engine operates can increase both engine DPM emissions [Chaffin and Ullman 1994; Graboski and McCormick 1996] and the measured value of induced smoke opacity [Chaffin and Ullman 1994]. For this reason, the Society of Automotive Engineers (SAE) has recommended that a correction factor be applied to smoke opacity measurements for tests conducted at high altitude [SAE 1996].

In general, two types of opacity meters (sometimes called "smoke meters") are available: full-flow type and partial flow sampling type. Full-flow smoke meters are clamped onto the diesel equipment tailpipe and measure the opacity across the entire exhaust gas stream. The reading from this type of smoke meter can be affected by ambient conditions such as wind, humidity, and bright light. The sampling-type smoke meters draw a portion of exhaust gas into a measurement chamber. The smoke sample must fill this chamber quickly and completely before the measurement can begin. For both types of smoke meters, a beam of light travels through the sample medium, and the signal is processed by a photocell receiver on the other end. The resulting opacity reading is then calculated based on the attenuation of light by suspended particles. The opacity can vary from 0% in a clean exhaust stream to 100% if no light is transmitted because of heavy particulate concentration.

Some sampling-type smoke meters employ a filter to collect the DPM and then compare the blackness of the filter to a Bosch or Bacharach smoke number. This number is obtained by visually comparing the blackness of the DPM spot on the filter paper to a scale that ranges from white (smoke number=0) to black (smoke number=9) in unit steps. The filter spot can be obtained either by using a hand-operated pump designed for this purpose or by using the smoke number function included in some combustion analyzers.

Some alternative techniques for measuring the level of DPM emitted by diesel engines have also been evaluated and tested—some of which remain prototypes. Recently, NIOSH developed a low-cost method that entails drawing a sample of diesel exhaust through a small filter and monitoring the pressure drop across the filter as DPM particles build up on its surface [Mischler and Volkwein 2005]. A study on the emission reduction benefits of diesel maintenance provided test data demonstrating a good correlation between this method and laboratory results for total carbon DPM concentrations [Davies and McGinn 2004]. Additionally, measurements with photometers have been shown to correlate with DPM levels, but are subject to error if humidity is high [Miller et al. 2007b]. A similar technique, based on laser light scattering photometry (LLSP), has also shown promise because the short monochromatic wavelength utilized improves performance compared to devices based on visible light [Anyon 2008]. However, more research is still needed in this field.

Procedures

Because emissions at full load are most likely to indicate a need for maintenance, full-load and maximum fuel rate are the best conditions at which to test an engine. In a laboratory setting, the engine speed and load can be precisely controlled using a dynamometer and a fuel metering system. In the field, however, the fuel rate is adjusted with the throttle pedal, and the engine is loaded via the transmission, making the engine speed and load much more difficult to control. For this reason, carbon dioxide concentration measurements should be used as an index of repeatability. This value correlates with loading during the test and should not vary much over subsequent testing of the same engine. However, carbon dioxide concentrations obtained at full-load conditions will vary for different engines because this parameter is also a function of fuel and lube-oil composition, type of engine, ambient conditions and the aftertreatment package installed. Therefore, no comparison can be made between different engines, even of the same make and model.

Diesel equipment with torque converter transmissions can be loaded along the lug curve at rated speed using a "torque converter stall" technique [Spears 1997]. A torque converter is a system that transfers power from the engine to the transmission using an enclosed hydraulic fluid. It consists of three main parts: a pump impeller, turbine, and fixed reactor. The pump impeller is connected to the engine shaft and the turbine is connected to the transmission shaft. Hydraulic fluid moves from the pump to the turbine and then the fixed reactor. Circulation of the pump drives the transmission by causing the turbine to rotate in the same direction as the pump. It is possible to block the transmission and to prevent the turbine from rotating with the pump. This condition, where the impeller moves but the turbine does not, is called stall. The greatest amount of stall happens when the pump impeller is driven at the maximum speed (i.e., the maximum fueling rate) without moving the turbine. The engine speed at which this occurs is called torque converter stall speed. Under this condition, all the engine power is dissipated through the pump in the form of heat to the hydraulic fluid. A heat exchanger is necessary to dissipate the engine power which is transferred to the fluid. In any case, the torque converter stall condition can be dangerous for the torque converter and heat exchanger and continuous operation at this condition should be limited. A detailed procedure for loading an engine with the torque converter stall method is outlined elsewhere [Spears 1997].

Some machines equipped with hydrostatic transmissions can be loaded against the transmission, a technique known as "hydrostatic stall" [Spears 1997]. A hydrostatic transmission consists of a variable-displacement hydraulic pump coupled to the engine. The pump delivers high-pressure fluid to one or more hydraulic motors, which drive the equipment wheels. The stall condition is achieved by blocking the wheels of the vehicle while the fuel pedal is fully depressed. The pressure at the outlet of the pump will increase and the pump will resist the engine rotation. This will increase the load to a stall condition. If the engine speed at the stall condition is stable, the test can be carried out. However, engine speed is more difficult to control with this method than with the torque converter stall method. Furthermore, the hydrostatic loading method may damage the equipment, and some hydrostatic equipment may not have an independent braking system, which is required to load the engine. A detailed procedure for loading an engine with a hydrostatic transmission is outlined elsewhere [Spears 1997].

An alternative to load tests is the snap acceleration cycle, a test adopted by the Society of Automotive Engineers (SAE) for testing the smoke opacity of diesel-powered commercial motor vehicles (known as the SAE J1667 Recommend Practice Test) [SAE 1996]. This involves accelerating the engine in neutral without any external load to the maximum governed speed. This test includes three snap-acceleration test cycles to determine the average smoke condition.

It is important to note that testing an engine using any of the methods mentioned in this section should only be conducted with the vehicle facing a rib and by trained personnel. No personnel should ever be between the front or rear of the vehicle and any ribs during these tests.

Diagnostics

Early diagnosis of a malfunctioning engine is the foundation of a good maintenance program. A set of recommendations for understanding and diagnosing six primary engine systems has been extensively described in a report from the DEEP project [McGinn 1999]. Readers are referred to this comprehensive report for further interpretation of emissions measurements for mechanically controlled diesels. However, it is important to note that, due to the increasing complexity of electronically controlled engine systems, it is no longer possible to directly link changes in gaseous or particulate-matter-emissions concentration with a specific fault in the diesel-power package encompassing all engine makes and models. The event of an increased concentration of one of the pollutants should, instead, be considered an alert to perform further diagnostic testing on the engine. A good preventive maintenance program will maintain near-original performance of an engine and maximize the equipment's productivity and engine life, while keeping exhaust emissions at, or near, baseline levels.

2.4.2 Maintenance for Support of Emissions Controls

The concept of emissions-assisted maintenance (see Section 2.4.1) is based on the idea that a diagnosis of engine malfunctions can be obtained by regularly measuring tailpipe emissions. Contemporary diesels have not only made these diagnoses more complex and engine specific, but they have also introduced new maintenance issues related to emissions control technologies of which mechanics must be aware. Maintenance for supporting emissions control technologies is, therefore, a practice that emphasizes the importance of sustaining the onboard emissions control systems of the engine and aftertreatment devices. The goal is to maintain near-original performance of the engine and associated technologies throughout the life of the device. The following section summarizes some of the basic practices related to maintaining the proper function of emissions control technologies. However, a comprehensive discussion in this area is beyond the scope of this document. The reader should defer to manuals provided by the manufacturer for proper and more detailed maintenance practices.

Basic Servicing of Engine Components

Section 2.3.2 discusses the detrimental effects that contaminants can have on engine performance and emissions. When performing engine service, precautions should be taken to prevent dust from entering into the engine fuel and lubrication systems. Some procedures to follow include [Caterpillar 1997]:

- Maintain a clean service area. Keep dust to a minimum.
- When possible, use a high-pressure wash to clean the engine before servicing.
- Plug all openings to the engine during the repair process.
- Keep new parts in their original packaging until needed.
- Never place components directly on the ground.
- Clean and dry reusable parts (using proper solvents) during servicing.
- Do not reuse seals.
- When possible, do not prefill fuel and oil filters because this may increase the likelihood of dust intrusion.

Key Maintenance Issues in Supporting Charge Compression Systems

Section 2.2.1 discusses the role that compressors have on engine performance and emissions.
The following practices can be used to help maintain the efficiency of charge compression systems:

- Recommended oil change intervals should be strictly followed [Dempsey 1995; Bughardt 1984].

- Boost pressures should be monitored at regular intervals and at prescribed loads and speeds. This can be accomplished by installing pressure measurement ports after the compressor and prior to the intake manifold [McGinn et al. 2010]. Common causes for low boost may include: clogging of the air filter element and fouling of the intercooler, restriction of the air intake, increased exhaust backpressure (often due to a clogged aftertreatment device), leaks in the boost system, and fouling or damage to the boost system components [McGinn et al. 2010; Dempsey 1995]. A mechanic's maintenance manual should be consulted for a detailed diagnosis of charge compression systems.

- Intake air restrictions should be checked at regular intervals. Replacement of intake air filters and other intake components should be done immediately.

- The entire air induction system should be checked at regular intervals for leaks, using low-pressure, compressed air (less than 25 psi) [McGinn et al. 2010; Dempsey 1995]. Intake air filters should be plugged during this process. Leaks should be addressed immediately.

Key Maintenance Issues in Supporting Charge Cooling Systems

Section 2.2.1 discusses the role that aftercoolers have on engine performance and emissions.
The following practices can be used to help maintain the efficiency of intake cooling systems.

- The temperature differentials of intake air across aftercoolers should be monitored at regular intervals and at prescribed loads and speeds. A likely performance inhibitor is the fouling of the internal or external heat exchanger surface.

- The surface of air-cooled heat exchangers should be kept clean and dust-free to maintain effectiveness [Dempsey 1995].

- In liquid-cooled aftercoolers, cooling systems should be flushed and cleaned according to recommended maintenance procedures for the engine. For the purposes of emissions management, the removal of fouling between the cooling liquid and the internal heat exchanger surface is important.

- It is a good practice to periodically remove and clean air-induction systems with a degreasing agent to remove fouling [Dempsey 1995]. This is particularly important in engines with low-pressure loop EGR systems.

Key Maintenance Issues in Supporting External Exhaust Gas Recirculation (EGR) Systems

Section 2.2.1 discusses the role that EGR systems play in engine performance and emissions. Because EGR systems reintroduce exhaust particulate contaminants back into the intake system, fouling from particulate matter is a major concern. The following practices can be used to help maintain the efficiency of external EGR systems:

- Turbo-boost pressures should be monitored at scheduled service intervals in EGR-equipped engines. This can be accomplished by installing pressure measurement ports after the compressor and before the intake manifold [McGinn et al. 2010].

- Periodic maintenance of intake components may be needed to remove fouling from external EGR systems that are routed upstream of the compressor.

- For external EGR systems equipped with an EGR cooler, periodic maintenance of the cooler may be needed to remove fouling from particulate matter, as it will reduce cooling capacity, which may reduce overall NO_X reduction capabilities.

- Sensors related to EGR systems should be kept free from particulate fouling.

- For external EGR, steady-state EGR flow checks should be performed periodically to monitor changes to the system over time. Alternatively, the proportion of EGR flow can be calculated by measuring carbon dioxide concentration at the intake manifold (downstream of the recirculated gas), at the exhaust manifold (upstream of the recirculation-T) and in the ambient air (intake system, upstream of the compressor or in the surroundings, upwind of the engine) and substituting into Equation 1 [Agrawal et al. 2004]. The following equation shows the calculation of the percentage of EGR flow using CO_2 measurements:

$$\text{EGR } (\%) = \frac{(CO_2)_{INTAKE\ MANIFOLD} - (CO_2)_{EXHAUST\ MANIFOLD}}{(CO_2)_{EXHAUST\ MANIFOLD} - (CO_2)_{AMBIENT}} \times 100 \tag{1}$$

where EGR = percentage of exhaust gas recirculation
CO_2 = measurement of CO_2 gas in parts per million

Key Maintenance Issues in Supporting Fuel Delivery and Injection Systems

Section 2.2.1 discusses the role that fuel delivery and injection systems have on engine emissions. Injection events are highly controlled in contemporary diesels. They coordinate closely with loading parameters in order to limit the formation of emissions at a given load. For this reason, it is very important for these systems to sustain their original performance levels throughout the life of the engine. The following practices can be used to help maintain the efficiency of fuel injection and delivery systems [BHB Billiton 2005; McGinn et al. 2010; Argueyrolles et al. 2007; Dempsey 1995]:

- Because fuel injection systems are highly sensitive, have a potentially large impact on engine performance and emissions, and typically require little maintenance, adjustments and repairs should be avoided by field mechanics when possible. Instead, consultation with the manufacturer is encouraged.

- Use only high-quality fuels and high-efficiency OEM-supplied fuel filters on all engines.

- When possible, fuel injectors with designs that minimize fuel leakage into the cylinder should be used. Injectors with reduced sac volume, or space between injector needle and nozzle holes, are a good example of this.

- Replace fuel filters regularly as a part of scheduled maintenance.

- Avoid dirt infiltration, especially during fuel transfer. Maintain clean transfer equipment. This will help prevent coking of injector nozzles.

- Ensure that all engines are equipped with a water separator located upstream of the fuel filter. Engine operators should drain traps daily.

- Use filtered breather systems on all fuel tanks to prevent dust infiltration.

- Maintain engine cooling systems and minimize high throttle conditions to limit temperature strains on fuel injection components. High temperatures can accelerate the coking process of injector nozzles.

- Use administrative controls to ensure that fuel tank levels are maintained above 50% (never to fall below 20%). This will help sink heat and prevent water from condensing on the inside of the fuel tank.

- For more detailed information, refer to Sections 2.2.2 and 2.3.

Key Maintenance Issues in Supporting Crankcase Filtration Systems

Section 2.2.1 discusses the role crankcase filtration systems have regarding engine emissions. The following practices can be used to help maintain proper performance of crankcase ventilation systems [BHB Billiton 2005; McGinn et al. 2010; Argueyrolles et al. 2007; Dempsey 1995]:

- When possible, closed crankcase ventilation (CCV) systems should be installed to minimize crankcase emissions.
- Coalescing filters are recommended. These filters should be checked and replaced according to the manufacturer's recommended maintenance schedule.

Key Maintenance Issues in Supporting Diesel Oxidation Catalyst (DOC) Systems

Section 2.2.2.1 discusses the role of DOC systems in regard to engine emissions. Because the DOC is often installed as an aftertreatment control technology, its effects on the performance of the exhaust system and on engine emissions need to be monitored. The following practices can be used to help maintain proper performance of a DOC:

- The performance of a DOC can be checked by taking regular measurements of the concentration of carbon monoxide both before and after the DOC at predetermined engine loadings. A single measurement of the carbon monoxide concentration at the outlet of the device is insufficient because, with such methodology, it is difficult to determine whether increases in CO over time are related to decreased DOC performance or an increase of carbon monoxide at the engine level.

- The concentration of nitrogen dioxide should also be monitored before and after the DOC. A history of this data should be stored to assess the activity of the DOC in increasing the concentration of this compound.

- The pressure drop across the DOC should be monitored. A failure in the DOC structure or the displacement of the device within the canister can cause an increase in backpressure.

- For more detailed information, refer to Section 2.2.2.1.

Key Maintenance Issues in Supporting Diesel Particulate Filter (DPF) Systems

Section 2.2.2.2 discusses the role that DPF systems have on engine emissions. The following practices can be used to help maintain proper performance of this system:

- The presence of DPM on the inner walls of the exhaust system downstream of the DPF should be constantly monitored because this may indicate filtration issues with the DPF.

- A decrease in pressure drop across the DPF and diminished filtration efficiency are strong indicators of DPF failure [Kim et al. 2008; Dabhoiwala et al. 2008].

- When possible, a periodic check of emissions upstream and downstream of the system using a portable gas/DPM analyzer is recommended. [Stachulak et al. 2005, 2006]. The smoke number results can be used to verify DPF failure. If applicable, CO and NO_2 results can be used to verify catalyst activity.

- The accumulation of ash in the inlet channels of DPF should be avoided because it results in a gradual increase in exhaust backpressure and a loss of engine efficiency, potentially leading to engine damage. The cleaning of ash can be performed onsite using an automated cleaning station or an off-site professional cleaning service.

- The removal of ash from a sintered metal DPF (SM-DPF) can be performed easily and quickly by using a jet of cold water. This procedure takes much less time than similar procedures for cleaning wall-flow monoliths [Weltens and Vogel 2008; Eberwein 2008].

- As a rule of thumb, DPF systems should not be installed on engines that consume oil at a rate higher than 1% of fuel consumption [Mayer 2008a].

- For more detailed information, refer to Section 2.2.2.2.

3 Control of Exposure to Airborne Diesel Pollutants

3.1 Mine Ventilation for Control of Diesel Emissions

Introduction

Ventilation is the life support system for underground mining. It can be the key control for providing adequate oxygen to working areas in underground mines [Hardcastle and Kocsis 2004; Hartman and Mutmansky 2002] and reducing dust concentrations, radiation exposures, and hazardous gas concentrations from the ore body and from blasting [Haney et al. 2005; Loring 2008; Gherghel and De Souza 2008; Chekan et al. 2002]. In addition, ventilation plays a vital role in controlling diesel-generated gas and particulate concentrations. This section describes the role of ventilation in a mine's diesel emissions control strategy and presents methods used for improving ventilation.

Regulations

A diesel engine that is to be used in a coal mine in the United States must be approved by the Mine Safety and Health Administration (MSHA) and is assigned a gaseous ventilation rate [66 Fed. Reg. 27864 (2001)]. The gaseous ventilation rate is the airflow needed to dilute gases emitted by the engine to or below 5,000 parts per million (ppm) carbon dioxide, 50 ppm carbon monoxide, 25 ppm nitrogen monoxide, and 5 ppm nitrogen dioxide [Adu-Acheampong et al. 2008; Haney et al. 2005]. Regulations in U.S. coal mines [30 CFR 75.325] require that the ventilation supplied to a working section or an area where mechanized mining equipment is being installed or removed be at least equal to the sum of the gaseous ventilation rates of each vehicle operating in that area. Therefore, in coal mines, the ventilation system is used to meet these regulations and control the gas concentrations from diesel engines. In many cases, the ventilation quantity used for controlling other hazardous gases, such as methane, supplies enough air to comply with these diesel regulations.

However, while ventilation systems in U.S. coal mines can adequately control diesel gaseous concentrations, they are not commonly designed to lower diesel particulate matter (DPM) exposures. Although MSHA-approved engines each have an assigned particulate index (PI, defined as the ventilation needed to dilute the DPM emitted from the engine to 1 mg/m^3), the MSHA diesel rule for coal mines does not require ventilation to meet these PI quantities. MSHA also does not regulate the concentration of DPM in the coal mine atmosphere, but instead, limits the tailpipe particulate emissions of vehicles [66 Fed. Reg. 27864 (2001)]. Therefore, ambient DPM is not usually measured in U.S. coal mines, and ventilation is not specifically used to control ambient DPM concentrations.

In metal/nonmetal mines, the ventilation does not have to meet the specific gaseous ventilation rates or PIs for each of the MSHA-approved engines used in these mines. Instead, the regulations specify limits for airborne gases and particles and allow the mine operators to meet the requirements in any way they choose, often through design of specified ventilation systems. The regulatory concentrations for gases are specified by the 1973 American Conference of Industrial Hygienists (ACGIH) threshold limit values (TLVs) [71 Fed. Reg. 28924 (2006)]. For DPM, a permissible exposure limit (PEL) of 160 $\mu g/m^3$ total carbon is specified in the U.S. diesel rule for metal/nonmetal mines [71 Fed. Reg. 28924 (2006)]. Many mines choose to control DPM using ventilation and in these cases, the ventilation required to reduce DPM to the final PEL often exceeds the airflow needed for controlling other contaminants. Therefore, ventilation improvements have been applied in many metal/nonmetal mines to minimize DPM levels.

Optimizing Ventilation Systems

Optimizing the ventilation system can be an essential step for complying with both federal and state regulations. In order to make the most of the optimization process, mines should first perform the following steps [Adu-Acheampong et al. 2008; Duckworth et al. 2009; Grau and Krog 2008; Hardcastle et al. 2008; Hopperstead 2008; Martikainen 2006; Ponce 2006; Pritchard 2010; Wallace et al. 2006; Rawlins 2006]:

1. Determine the required airflow and evaluate the present ventilation system.
2. Investigate steps to improve ventilation at the working areas.
3. Identify the costs of these improvements.

Once the mine operator collects all necessary information, the amount of ventilation that is technically and economically practical can be determined. Once a feasible ventilation rate is determined, additional control technologies can be chosen to further reduce DPM concentrations below the final limit, if needed.

Determining Required Airflow

The air quantity needed to dilute gaseous emissions below the TLVs can be calculated by adding together the MSHA gaseous ventilation airflows for each operating piece of diesel equipment. For DPM, PIs can be used to determine the quantity of air needed to dilute DPM to the final PEL, assuming ventilation is the only control being used. Summing the PIs for each piece of operating equipment will provide an estimate of the air required to reduce DPM to 1 mg/m^3 [Adu-Acheampong et al. 2008]. In order to calculate the airflow required to dilute DPM below a specific level, multiply the sum of the PIs by [(1,000 µg/m^3) / (desired DPM concentration in µg/m^3)]. This formula is given as Equation 2:

$$\text{Required Dilutant Air} = (PI_1 + PI_2 + PI_j) \times \left(\frac{1,000}{\text{PDM desired}} \right) \qquad (2)$$

where PI = particle index
$DPM\ desired$ = the desired DPM concentration in µg/m^3.

For example, the total air needed to dilute DPM to a concentration of 160 µg/m^3 can be calculated by multiplying the sum of the PIs by [(1,000 µg/m^3) / (160 µg/m^3)]. For MSHA-approved engines, the PIs have already been determined.

The Air Quality Estimator (AQE), developed by the National Institute for Occupational Safety and Health (NIOSH) and MSHA [Robertson et al. 2004], can also be used to determine the airflow needed to dilute DPM to a desired concentration. AQE is a computer program that estimates the total air quantity needed to dilute DPM to the final PEL using the manufacturer's engine test data and the efficiency of the control technologies being used. The AQE can also be used to determine ventilation rates needed to dilute DPM to the final PEL using different control scenarios. This software can be found on the MSHA website. In addition, a case study is covered in Grau et al. 2004b.

An alternative "rule of thumb" method has also been developed for determining the required ventilation rate [Hardcastle et al. 2008; Ontario Ministry of Labour 1994; Mine Safety Operations Division 2008]. The concept is that a value of 100 cfm/hp will provide enough air to ensure safe levels of gaseous emissions from diesel engines [Hardcastle et al. 2008]. This ventilation rate alone probably will not provide enough air to comply with the MSHA final DPM rule for metal/nonmetal mines. However, it may provide enough air to help a mine comply with the rule if used in combination with other control technologies, such as DPFs (see Section 2.2.2.2). A case study of this is highlighted in Schnakenberg [2001].

Evaluating the ventilation system

Quantifying the present airflow at the working areas with the current ventilation system is needed to determine areas where losses in airflow are occurring and the extent of necessary improvements. This is usually done by performing ventilation surveys, measuring *in situ* rock properties, and software modeling [Wallace et al. 2006; Brake 2008; Hardcastle et al. 2008; Hopperstead 2008; Ponce 2006]. It can also be advantageous in this step to measure the concentration of contaminants to determine how well the current ventilation system is minimizing their concentrations.

It is also helpful to measure the concentrations of gases and DPM while evaluating and improving ventilation systems. One way of performing this task is to measure the real-time carbon dioxide concentration. The carbon dioxide concentration in the mine is proportional to the fuel used by the diesel equipment, after subtracting the background atmospheric concentration [Bugarski et al. 2005; Schnakenberg et al. 1986; Johnson and Carlson 1986]. The ambient carbon dioxide concentration around a diesel engine is a function of load applied to the engine, ventilation, and the number of vehicles in the area. Therefore, under similar operating conditions (and without changes to the exhaust aftertreatment technologies), the effects of ventilation changes can be estimated by monitoring the carbon dioxide concentration in that area. Elevated concentrations of carbon dioxide may provide a warning that the area's ventilation is low.

Additionally, other instruments are available to assist in evaluating ventilation controls (see Section 4). For example, one metal/nonmetal mine used a real-time elemental carbon monitor to determine problem areas in ventilation [Lethbridge and Good 2010].

Improving Ventilation

The next step for optimizing the ventilation system is to determine methods for improving the current ventilation. These methods include: (1) increasing the airflow, (2) improving the efficiency of the ventilation, and (3) other specific strategies.

1. **Increasing airflow**. One of the primary methods for improving ventilation is increasing airflow, which can be done in mechanically ventilated mines by using fans with more

horsepower or adding fans in parallel with existing ones. In some cases, this requires adding new ventilation shafts or airways. For example, two case studies highlight a salt mine that increased its main airflow from 127,000 cfm to 160,000 cfm by installing a new fan, and a metal mine that increased its intake air by 100,000 cfm by adding a fan and two raised boreholes [Manos 2010; Lethbridge and Good 2010].

In mines using natural ventilation, airflow depends on the differences between the densities of the air inside and outside of the mine [Grau et al. 2004a; Head 2001]. Natural ventilation is affected by temperature and can change drastically in magnitude and direction with time of day and season. Therefore, natural ventilation is not a reliable control for reducing DPM [Head 2001]. In mines using natural ventilation, fans can be installed to increase the airflow.

Some large-opening mines (openings greater than about 1,000 ft^2) can increase airflow by using a propeller fan instead of a vane-axial fan to supply outside air. These fans need to overcome the mine resistance to airflow to provide the desired quantity of air. Vane-axial fans, which use short rigid blades enclosed in a tubular housing, are most commonly used in underground mines because they are economical and can overcome static air pressure of up to 20 inches of water gauge [Head 2001; Grau et al. 2004a; Grau et al. 2006]. However, in large-opening mines (openings greater than about 1,000 ft^2) such as stone and salt mines, resistances can be very low, and a propeller-type fan, which uses long slender blades twisted to provide some angle of push on the air, may also be used [Krog and Grau 2006; Head 2001; Grau et al. 2004a]. The propeller fan has an advantage over the vane axial fan because it can provide higher air volumes at lower operational costs [Krog and Grau 2006; Grau et al. 2006; Grau et al. 2004a]. In one example, a stone mine was able to increase airflow by about 190% by replacing a vane axial exhaust fan with two propeller fans for the same operational cost [Krog and Grau 2006]. In cases where mine resistances are high (such as deep hard-rock mines with ventilation operating pressures over 20 inches of water gauge), centrifugal (squirrel cage) fans may be used. Although more expensive, they are also more robust and can handle difficult operating conditions such as shaft water, restricted shafts, and blasting pressures.

A mine may also increase airflow by reusing underground shop air, as discussed by Pritchard (2010). In this example, the ventilation system was initially designed so that some intake air was provided only to the shop area and then directed to the returns. After evaluating the air to ensure it was not contaminated, the air ventilating the shop was redirected to the working face (production areas), allowing for an extra 40,000 cfm of air to be supplied to the face areas.

2. **Improving the efficiency of ventilation.** Increasing the efficiency of the ventilation system is another way of improving airflow in a mine. The ventilation efficiency is the ratio of the total air quantity flowing to all working areas and the total quantity of supplied air [Grau and Krog 2009]. Increasing the efficiency, therefore, entails either reducing the air that goes to nonessential areas of the mine or delivering more of the fresh (intake) air to the working areas. The following methods describe techniques used by some mines to increase ventilation efficiency in these ways.

Use and maintenance of stoppings - A common way to reduce the air going to nonessential areas of the mine is to use stoppings, including durable stoppings such as walls or panels and less rigid means such as curtains or brattices. When using curtains, maintenance is a major concern, because these stoppings can easily become damaged. Therefore, routine repair of curtains, or any other components of the ventilation system are required to ensure adequate ventilation.

Brattices or curtains often develop leaks due to flapping, damage from excess blast pressures, and other in-mine hazards [Grau et al. 2004a; Grau and Meighen 2006]. To provide relief from blast pressures, some mines use VELCRO® fasteners on curtains or place sandbags on the bottom of the curtains [Timko and Thimons 1987; Grau and Meighen 2006]. An alternative "EZ-Up curtain" was tested by NIOSH as a temporary or portable stopping. This type of stopping uses a fabric that is laced onto tubing and raised to the mine roof with a strap-and-ratchet mechanism. In tests, sandbags were used on the bottom to hold the curtain in place without leaking during normal mining operations, but provided the ability to release the curtain in the case of excessive pressures from blasting to avoid damage. In NIOSH tests, the overall integrity of the stopping was maintained after being exposed to blast pressures up to 2.5 psig [Grau and Meighen 2006].

To reduce leakage, one salt mine constructed some of their stoppings from a plastic grid material with a nonwoven felt glued on the grid (to prevent leaks), and then sprayed the perimeter with a sealant foam [Manos 2010]. If the stopping needed to withstand the shock from blasting, a yellow brattice material placed within a metal frame system was used and again sprayed with a sealant foam [Manos 2010]. This mine was able to reduce its DPM concentrations from approximately 900 $\mu g/m^3$ to below 500 $\mu g/m^3$ by using these types of stoppings to help increase the airflow into the mine from 127,000 to 160,000 cfm.

Durable stoppings are sometimes used to increase the ventilation system efficiency by reducing the number of portable ventilation structures (such as curtains). This, in turn, minimized the leakage from these structures. More durable stopping material is especially effective in large-opening mines where curtains can be difficult to construct and maintain and can have a high capital cost [Grau et al. 2004a; Grau and Meighen 2006].

One method akin to providing durable stoppings is lengthening the size of the pillars [Grau and Krog 2008; Pritchard 2010]. In one case, a mine was able to reduce leakage by 4,000 cfm per panel by increasing the size of the pillars from 100 to 120 feet [Pritchard 2010]. Stone from the ore body can also be an effective durable stopping material and, if available, can be used to create a wall to direct airflow [Grau and Krog 2008, 2009]. Figure 10 shows an example of how one mine used this technique (a long unmined pillar without connections to minimize leakage) to direct ventilation to the face area [Noll et al. 2008]. In another mine, a combination of this technique and curtain stoppings allowed more than 70% of the air produced by the main fans to reach the face area [Grau and Krog 2008, 2009].

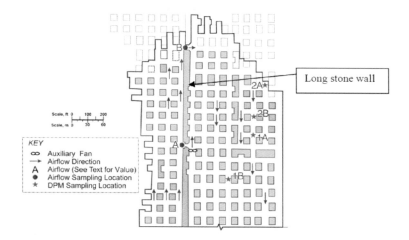

Long stone wall

Figure 10. Ventilation map of a stone mine that used a stone wall for a stopping and a perimeter ventilation plan.

Another option is to use oversized Omega block walls (see Figure 11), which have been shown to both increase ventilation efficiency and remain undamaged when exposed to blast pressures up to 2.5 psig [Grau et al. 2004a; Grau and Meighen 2006]. However, although Omega block walls are an effective stopping material, they are also permanent, which makes them impractical in some situations.

Figure 11. Omega Blocks used as a stopping for directing airflow. Picture courtesy of Grau and Meighen [2006].

In addition, dedicating entries as either intake or return airways can also improve ventilation efficiency. This method minimizes the amount of stopping material employed and, therefore, the amount of leakage [Pritchard 2010].

Use and location of auxiliary fans - In addition to minimizing air leakage, efficiency of the ventilation system can be increased by improving the delivery of air to working areas. Mines have demonstrated improved ventilation by adding auxiliary fans (portable fans used to direct air to areas not ventilated by the normal air current, such as a tunnel or slope) [Grau and Krog 2008, 2009; NIOSH 2007a; Kissell. and Volkwein 2002]. In one case study, the percentage of air reaching the face was increased from 10% to 57% by using auxiliary fans placed in targeted locations [Grau and Krog 2008]. In another mine, auxiliary fans allowed for an increased airflow at the face from 4,500 to 14,000 cfm. [Kissell and Volkwein 2002].

Both vane-axial and propeller fans have been shown to be effective in enhancing airflow to working areas [Krog and Grau 2006; Chekan et al. 2004, 2006]. Researchers from NIOSH have asserted that free-standing propeller fans work best for ventilating large regions, and vane axial fans work best for ventilating the working face and dead-end areas that do not have a connection to other ventilation entries or drifts of smaller dimensions.

The placement of auxiliary fans can be very important for improving ventilation. In one study, 57% of the available airflow reached the face when auxiliary fans were located by the last open crosscut and in the furthest upstream entry. However, less than 10% of the air reached the face when the auxiliary fan was too far from the face or from the last crosscut [Grau and Krog 2008]. In addition, auxiliary fans must be placed in fresh-air locations to avoid air recirculation and to ensure fresh air is delivered to the face.

Use of ventilation designs for large-opening mines - Researchers from NIOSH have designed several different ventilation methods to improve ventilation for large-opening mines, including split-mine, perimeter, and unit ventilation designs [Krog et al. 2004; Grau and Krog 2008].

Split–mine ventilation is a mine-wide system designed to deliver most of the air to the last open crosscut near the working faces. It uses a continuous stopping line from the intake portal to the working face, which is parallel to the mining direction and behind the active working faces by three to four breaks to reduce blast damage. Auxiliary ventilation provides airflow to face areas. This has been shown to be an effective ventilation design for new, large-opening mines.

Perimeter ventilation is a system designed for mature mines. A stopping line, perpendicular to the mining direction, is developed by leaving unmined ore or using curtains. The stopping line allows continuous airflow across the face area by bypassing the bulk of the old workings. Figure 12 shows a mine that uses perimeter ventilation and curtains (brattices) for stoppings. In this mine, over 100,000 cfm of total air was provided to locations A through C [Noll et al. 2008].

Researchers have also identified unit ventilation as a design that can improve air quantity at the working face. In unit ventilation, the section to be mined is surrounded by in-place stone stoppings and auxiliary fans, and curtains are used to direct the air from the preexisting ventilation system to the working face. In this blocked-off section, the stone is mined diagonally, forming a wedge-shaped block of pillars. Figure 12 shows a mine that uses perimeter and some unit ventilation in certain areas, as well as curtains and stone walls as stoppings. In this mine, more than 200,000 cfm of total air was supplied to locations A and B.

The NIOSH website [NIOSH 2011] has several publications that provide more detail on the different types of large opening mine ventilation [Krog et al. 2004; Grau et al. 2004a,b; Grau et al. 2006; Grau and Krog 2008].

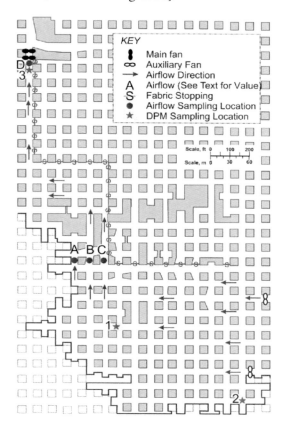

Figure 12. Ventilation map of a stone mine that uses brattice stoppings and a perimeter ventilation plan.

3. **Improving ventilation using other methods.** In addition to the methods discussed above, several other systems can be used for improving the ventilation of a mine. In some mines, adding an intake shaft closer to the working faces and exhaust fans may give support to the current system [Martikainen 2006]. In some cases, the location of the intake of fresh air into the mine can be far from the exhaust fan and the working face, which can cause high air pressure and require more energy/fan power to direct adequate

airflows to the face. The air at the face also can become contaminated with diesel emissions as it passes over other vehicles working in the mine. The addition of an intake shaft closer to the exhaust fan and working face could result in providing cleaner air to the working area and less pressure in the ventilation system because the air is moved for a shorter distance. Careful modeling and monitoring is needed to avoid unventilated "dead" zones in a mine using this option.

Several studies also reported improved ventilation through frequent evaluation and redirection of airflow to the working areas [Hardcastle et al. 2008; Hardcastle and Kocsis 2004; Pritchard 2010]. In one example, at the end of each week, mine personnel determined mining activities for the following week and entered them into a spreadsheet that calculated the required ventilation for each activity, based upon the required diesel equipment [Hardcastle et al. 2008]. Inactive sites were shaded in gray, and the distribution of ventilation was implemented using the results of the spreadsheet.

3.2 Enclosed Cabins

Introduction

Enclosed or environmental cabins are one of the mainstay engineering controls for reducing mobile equipment operators' exposures to airborne dust at surface and underground mines [NIOSH 2008a], and they are commonly used for protecting miners from harmful noise levels [Suter 2002; NIOSH 2009]. Figure 13 shows an effective design for a filtration and pressurization system of an enclosed cab that protects miners from dust. The cab contains a nonporous barrier that totally surrounds the operator and provides a safe, clean environment for the operator by drawing air through an intake filter to capture toxic substances and produce a positive pressure inside the cab. The cab can also be heated and air-conditioned to provide a comfortable atmosphere for the operator.

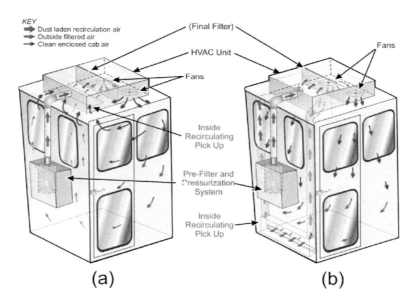

Figure 13. Typical designs of environmental cab with filtration, pressurization, and air-conditioning systems used to protect miners from dust and diesel aerosols: (a) intake and return at the roof flow design, and (b) unidirectional flow design [adapted from Cecala et al. 2009].

Many metal/nonmetal mines are now using this control technology for protecting miners not only from dust, but also from diesel particulate matter (DPM). Enclosed cabs can be very effective in reducing DPM exposures and helping mines comply with diesel regulations that limit the DPM exposure of miners to a permissible exposure limit (PEL) of 160 µg/m^3 total carbon (eight-hour time-weighted average) [MSHA 2008]. This chapter describes the expected efficiency and some optimal methods for reducing DPM exposures when using enclosed cabs.

84

Efficiency of Enclosed Cabins

Properly functioning enclosed cabs have been shown to be more than 90% efficient in protecting miners from dust and DPM [Noll et al. 2008; Cecala et al. 2001, 2002, 2004, 2005, 2009; Organiscak and Page 1999; Organiscak et al. 2003; Chekan and Colinet 2003]. However, the same studies have reported efficiencies below 40% when certain factors are not optimized [Cecala et al. 2009; Organiscak and Page 1999; NIOSH 2001b; Organiscak et al. 2003; Cecala et al. 2004; Cecala et al. 2009, Chekan and Colinet 2002, 2003; Duckworth et al. 2009; NIOSH 2008b; NIOSH 2001a; NIOSH 2007b]. Some of these factors include the use of a recirculation filter, intake filter efficiency, cab integrity (e.g. leaks in the system and sustained pressurization), and open windows [Cecala et al. 2004, 2007, 2009; Organiscak and Page 1999; Organiscak et al. 2003; Chekan and Colinet 2002, 2003; NIOSH 2008b; Noll et al. 2008; Duckworth et al. 2009; NIOSH 2003]. The recirculation filter is necessary for maximizing the reduction of dust in some cab systems because the dust from the miner's clothes and on the floor of the cab can re-entrain into the atmosphere and can be inhaled by the miner. A recirculation system causes air in the cab to flow through a recirculation filter so that dust particles are not reaerosolized in the miner's breathing zone. The quality of the intake filter, cab integrity, and open windows can also have an effect on the efficiency of enclosed cabs.

Filters

Two of the main components influencing cab system performance are the specifications and condition of the intake or main filter, which captures the contaminants in the air before the air enters the cab [Cecala et al. 2004, 2005, 2009; Organiscak and Page 1999; Organiscak et al. 2003; Chekan and Colinet 2003]. Filters are given a minimum efficiency reporting value (MERV) rating by American Society of Heating, Refrigerating and Air-Conditioning Engineers (ASHRAE) that signifies the ability of the filter to remove particles at different size ranges [Cecala et al. 2004]. The higher the rating number, the more efficient the filter is at capturing submicron particles, which are in the size range of DPM.

In one laboratory study, MERV 8 filters were not efficient for removing DPM, but a high-efficiency particulate air (HEPA) filter, rated at over 99% for capturing particles down to 0.3 microns, was more than 99% efficient [Noll et al. 2010]. In the same study, a MERV-16-rated filter was able to capture DPM with a 95% efficiency, a level of protection that may be sufficient in many cases. In addition, a MERV 16 filter has cost benefits as well as a lower restriction on airflow through the cab. NIOSH is continuing research to determine the best filter for DPM exposure reduction as well as filter life.

Cab Integrity

The structural condition and integrity of the cab is another important factor to consider when implementing enclosed cabs. Studies have shown a direct correlation between cab integrity and cab efficiency [Cecala et al. 2004, 2005, 2009; Organiscak and Page 1999; Organiscak et al. 2003; Chekan and Colinet 2003]. The cab integrity can be determined by measuring the pressurization of the cab, because leaks and structural damage of the cab will cause the pressurization to decrease. The sustained pressure should be at least 0.1 inches of water, but it is common for pressures to be higher. If the pressure is below 0.1 inches of water or lower than usual, the cab needs better sealing. A detailed procedure for measuring pressurization is presented in papers by Cecala et al. [2005, 2009]. Higher cab pressures, in most cases, can be achieved by installing new door gaskets and seals and by filling any minor holes or openings with silicon caulking or other sealing material [Chekan and Colinet 2002]. Compromised cab integrity can be immediately detected by installing a pressure meter inside the cab.

Two studies have shown that opening cab doors and windows can also significantly decrease the ability of the cab to reduce DPM exposure over an entire shift [Noll et al. 2008; Duckworth et al. 2009]. In one study, the reduction went from over 90% to below 40% on the same cab depending on the time and extent that the window and/or door were kept open [Noll et al. 2008]. The studies reported that in order to maximize the performance of the cab system, cab windows and doors must be closed for as long as possible.

Cab Filtration Efficiency

Cab filtration efficiency refers to the percentage of DPM outside the cab that is prevented from entering the cab. Because cab filtration efficiency can be affected by many parameters, it is important to measure the efficiency of the cab system for each vehicle in the mine. A simultaneous measurement of the inside and outside of the cab is the best and most accurate method for determining cab efficiency of a vehicle. This entails placing instruments that measure DPM inside and outside of the cab while the vehicle is operating in the mine. The percentage efficiency of the cab can then be determined using Equation 3 which follows:

$$\text{Efficiency}(\%) = \frac{DPM_{OUTSIDE} - DPM_{INSIDE}}{DPM_{OUTSIDE}} \times 100 \tag{3}$$

where DPM = measurement of DPM mass concentration [ug/m^3].

The concentration of DPM can be measured by using the setup described in Section 4.1 for performing ambient NIOSH method 5040 sampling. Elemental carbon (EC) would be the best surrogate because EC is selective to DPM and can be measured precisely and accurately [Noll et al. 2006]. Real-time EC monitors (see Section 4.1), combined with a pressure sensor to monitor pressure loss within the cab, make an ideal setup for measuring cab DPM filtration efficiency. The EC monitors record DPM concentrations inside and outside of the cab, and the pressure monitor indicates when the door or window is open (loss of pressure within the cab). Such a direct measurement technique is desirable because the whole system is tested under actual conditions, and the work practices of the miner are taken into account. The efficiency of cabs can vary from day to day depending upon environment and work practices. Therefore, multiple tests will provide the best results.

Another method of measuring cab efficiency is by placing portable particle counters inside and outside of the cab while the cab is sealed. It is best to complete this testing outside of the mine, because the number of particles inside a mine can overload these instruments. One-minute samples should be taken for 30 minutes. For more details on this process and mathematical equations, refer to articles by Organiscak and Cecala [2009], Cecala et al. [2005], and Cecala et al. [2009].

Implementation

Enclosed cabs are most commonly used in large-opening mines because the equipment is larger and often comes with a cab. Smaller equipment, such as what is typically used in metal mines, can sometimes be retrofitted with a cab (unless they are too small, and the cab hinders visibility). However, because all miners cannot work within cabs, enclosed cabs are usually not an all-encompassing solution. In these cases, enclosed cabs should be used, when possible, to protect miners in the vehicles at the face area (where the highest concentrations of DPM can exist). Other controls, such as ventilation, biodiesel, maintenance, or administrative practices, should be used for those miners who do not work inside vehicles. In some mines, enclosed cabs may also be useful where other controls are not effective. For example, in a metal mine that uses biodiesel, ventilation, and diesel particulate filters, the ambient DPM concentrations may still be above the PEL in areas where ventilation is inadequate and where several vehicles operate [Noll et al. 2010]. Enclosed cabs can provide the needed additional protection to keep a miner's exposure below the PEL in these areas (if the option of having that miner work within an enclosed cab for the majority of his or her shift is available).

3.3 Personal Protective Equipment (PPE)

Introduction

Personal protective equipment (PPE) is often used to protect miners against hazards. When protective equipment is required, MSHA regulations ensure that such equipment offers adequate protection for workers. In the case of exposure to diesel contaminants in underground mines, a respirator is the major PPE control used for reducing worker exposure.

Respirator Basic Concepts

A respirator is a personal protective device that is worn on the face, covers at least the nose and mouth, and is used to reduce the wearer's risk of inhaling hazardous airborne particles (including dust particles and infectious agents), gases, or vapors. Many miners in the United States need to wear a respirator to perform some of their work tasks. Therefore, a written respirator program that addresses such issues as selection, fitting, use, and maintenance of respirators is essential for ensuring that workers are properly and effectively using the equipment. The following outlines the basic concepts in establishing an effective respirator program.

Respirators should only be used as a "last line of defense" in a hierarchy of control. This hierarchy of control is a sequence of options that offer a number of ways to approach the hazard exposure in an occupational environment. The hierarchy starts with eliminating the hazard and ends with personal protective equipment.

Respirators protect the user in two different ways: (1) by removing the contaminants from the air through air-purifying respirators (APRs) or (2) by supplying clean, pollutant-free air from another source, air-supplying respirators (ASR).

APRs can be further subdivided into three categories:

1. **Disposable particulate filtering respirators.** The entire respirator is discarded when it becomes unsuitable for further use as a result of diminished hygiene (or a situation that may increase the risk of further exposure to trapped particles or dirt) for the operator, excessive resistance due to particle loading, or physical damage.

2. **Nonpowered air-purifying respirators.** Sometimes referred to as reusable respirators because the facepiece is cleaned and reused, but the filter cartridges are discarded and replaced when they become unsuitable for further use.

3. **Powered air-purifying respirators (PAPRs).** A battery-powered blower moves the airflow through the filters.

When APRs are equipped with adequate cartridges or canisters, these respirators can provide protection from particles as well as protection from selected noxious gases (such as organic vapors, acid gases, and NO_2).

To select the correct respirator for protection against particulates, the following conditions must be known:

- The identity and concentration of the particulates in the workplace air.

- The OSHA or MSHA permissible exposure limit (PEL), the NIOSH recommended exposure limit (REL), or other relevant occupational exposure limits for the contaminant.

- The hazard ratio (HR) (i.e., the airborne particulate concentration divided by the exposure limit).

- The assigned protection factor (APF) for the class of respirator [OSHA 2008]. The APF is assigned by OSHA, and represents the minimum anticipated level of protection provided by each type of respirator worn in accordance with an adequate respiratory protection program (the APF should be significantly greater than the HR).

- Any service life information available for combination cartridges or canisters.

Multiplying the occupational exposure limit by the APF for a respirator gives the maximum workplace concentration in which that respirator can be used. For example, if the commonly accepted APF for a half-mask respirator is 10, and the PEL is 5 mg/m^3, then 50 mg/m^3 is the highest workplace concentration in which a half-mask respirator can be used against that contaminant. If the workplace concentration is greater than 50 mg/m^3, a more protective respirator (with a higher APF) should be used.

Particulate Filters

For underground mine users, the historic regulation regarding the certification of particulate respirators is 30 CFR 11 (also referred to as "Part 11"), promulgated in 1972 [30 CFR 11 1972]. However, new research, testing, and manufacturing technology made the Part 11 particulate filter certification procedures outdated. As a result, NIOSH developed a new set of certifications for testing nonpowered, air-purifying, particulate-filter respirators, which became effective on July 10, 1995. Since then, new 42 CFR 84 respirators have had to pass a more demanding certification test than the old respirators certified under Part 11.

The new effective Part 84 produced several changes [42 CFR 84]. Among them, the most notable are:

- NIOSH has exclusive authority for testing and certification of respirators with the exception of certain mine emergency devices, which will continue to be jointly certified by NIOSH and MSHA.

- All new respirators must meet the performance criteria recommended by the CDC for respiratory devices used in health-care settings for protection against *Mycobacterium tuberculosis* (Mtb), the infectious agent that causes tuberculosis (TB) [59 Fed. Reg. 54242 (1994)].

- All particulate respirators approved under Part 84 will have a certification label bearing the NIOSH and the Department of Health and Human Services (DHHS) emblems; whereas, those approved under Part 11 have the emblems of NIOSH and MSHA. This allows the user to distinguish particulate respirators certified before July 10, 1995, under Part 11, from particulate respirators certified after that date under Part 84.

- The only respirators certified by NIOSH under Part 11 that meet CDC filtration efficiency performance criteria for protection against TB are those with HEPA filters. These filters, certified under Part 11, can still be used.

- Several new classes of air-purifying, particulate respirators are less expensive than respirators with HEPA filters.

- The Part 84 regulation contains a new nine-level filter classification system.

Three levels of filter efficiency, each with three categories of resistance to filter efficiency degradation, have been created. The three levels of filter efficiency include 95, 99, and 99.97% efficiency levels. The three categories of resistance to filter efficiency degradation are labeled N-, R-, and P-series filters. The label N means "Not to be used with oils". R means "Resistant to oils" and P means "Oil proof." Therefore, R- or P-series filters can be used for protection against oil or non-oil aerosols. N-series filters should be used only for non-oil aerosols. The filter efficiency level, along with the category of resistance to filter efficient degradation, indicates the "class" of the filter. The class of filter will be clearly marked on the filter, filter package, or respirator box. For example, a filter marked N95 would mean an N-series filter that is at least 95% efficient. The minimum level of particulate filtration approved by NIOSH is 95%.

All filters should be replaced whenever they are damaged, soiled, or cause noticeably increased breathing resistance (e.g., causing discomfort to the wearer). The use and reuse of both N-series and P-series filters are subject to considerations of hygiene, damage, and increased breathing resistance. However, for dirty workplaces that could result in high filter loading, service time for N-series filters may be extended beyond eight hours of use (continuous or intermittent) by performing an evaluation in specific workplace settings that: (a) demonstrates that extended use will not degrade the filter efficiency below the efficiency level specified in Part 84, or (b) demonstrates that the total mass loading of the filter(s) is less than 200 mg [NIOSH 1996]. R-series filters should be used only for a single shift (or for eight hours of continuous or intermittent use) when oil is present, but service time can be extended using the methods described above for N-series filters. These determinations should be repeated whenever conditions change or modifications are made to processes that could change the type of particulate generated in the user's facility.

Respiratory Protection Equipment in Underground Coal Mines

General guidelines for the use of respiratory protection equipment in underground coal mines are described in the Code of Federal Regulations [30 CFR 70.300; 30 CFR 70.305; 30 CFR 72.710]. The mandatory health standards for underground coal mines require that respiratory equipment approved by NIOSH under Part 84 will be made available to all workers whenever they are exposed to concentrations of dust in excess of the levels required to be maintained. The same requirement applies to exposure for short periods to inhalation hazards of gas, dusts, fumes, or mist. Respirators will not be substituted for environmental control measures in the active workings.

The institution of a respiratory program, consistent with the guidelines of the American National Standards Institute (ANSI) [1969], is required for underground coal mines. There are no specific requirements or guidelines for underground coal mines regarding exposure to DPM.

Respiratory Protection Equipment in Underground Metal/Nonmetal Mines

MSHA requires underground metal/nonmetal mine operators to institute a respirator program governing selection, maintenance, training, fitting, supervision, cleaning, and use of respirators [30 CFR 57.5005]. To control occupational diseases resulting from exposure to air contaminated with harmful dusts, fumes, mists, gases, or vapors, the primary objective is first to prevent atmospheric contamination. MSHA's current policy, as prescribed by the regulation, is to require that this be accomplished by feasible engineering measures. When effective controls are not feasible, or while they are being instituted, or during occasional entry into hazardous atmospheres to perform maintenance or investigations, appropriate respirators are to be used in accordance with established procedures protecting the miners.

Whenever respiratory protection equipment is used, a program for selection, maintenance, training, fitting, supervision, cleaning, and use must meet the following minimum requirements:

- Respirators must be approved by NIOSH under Part 84.

- The respirator program must be consistent with the requirements of ANSI Z88.2-1969 [ANSI 1969]. These incorporated requirements mandate that miners who must wear respirators be fit-tested with the respirator to be used. In addition, the following directives should be met: (1) development of standard operating procedures governing the selection and use of respirators, (2) records of the date of issuance of the respirator, and (3) records of fit-test results. The fit-testing records are essential for determining that the worker is wearing the proper respirator [Fed. Reg. E7-20237 (2007)].

- When respiratory protection is used in atmospheres immediately harmful to life, the presence of at least one other person with backup equipment and rescue capability will be required in the event of failure of the respiratory equipment.

MSHA also provides guidance regarding which respirators can be used in the case of exposure to diesel particulate matter (DPM) in underground metal/nonmetal mines [30 CFR 57.5060]. The respiratory protection must be in accordance with the above-presented guidelines and also meet the following requirements:

Air-purifying respirators must be equipped with one of the following:

- A filter certified by NIOSH under Part 11 as a high-efficiency particulate air (HEPA) filter;

- A filter certified by NIOSH under Part 84 as 99.97% efficient; or

- A filter certified by NIOSH for DPM.

As of the publication of this document, NIOSH has not yet specifically certified any filter for DPM. Because NIOSH considers DPM as an aerosol containing oil, the N-series filters cannot be used to protect miners from this exposure. For this reason, only HEPA, R100, and P100 filters can be used for personal protection respirators against DPM exposure [Janssen and Bidwell 2006]. Currently, there are no approved R100 filtering facepieces (disposable particulate respirators), thus only P100 filtering facepieces are approved by MSHA for protection from DPM exposure. The list of approved P100 filtering facepiece respirators can be found on the National Personal Protective Technology Laboratory (NPPTL) web page [NPPTL 2010a].

NIOSH-approved, powered air-purifying respirators (PAPRs) with HEPA filters are also acceptable for DPM protection, provided the protection factor is adequate for the exposure [NPPTL 2010b]. Powered air-purifying respirators without a tight-fitting facepiece are typically assigned a protection factor of 25. Thus, the ambient DPM concentration cannot exceed 25 times the regulatory concentration for DPM ($25 \times 160 \ \mu g/m^3 = 4{,}000 \ \mu g/m^3$) if PAPRs are to be worn.

4 Monitoring of Diesel Particulate Matter and Gases

4.1 Diesel Particulate Matter (DPM)

In 2001, the Mine Safety and Health Administration (MSHA) promulgated regulations to limit the exposure of underground miners to diesel particulate matter (DPM) [MSHA 2002; 66 Fed. Reg. 27864 (2001)]. The development of measurement techniques to accurately determine the exposures of underground miners to DPM was a key part of establishing these rules. Still, the measurement of DPM in underground mines can be very complicated due to the interference of other aerosols (e.g., such as dust or oil mist) in the mining environment as well as the complex composition of DPM (a mixture of elemental carbon (EC), many different organic carbon (OC) compounds, sulfates, and metals) (see Section 2.1) [Kittelson 1998].

Gravimetric methods were not sensitive or selective enough to be used to measure DPM exposures [Marple et al. 1986; NIOSH 1990; Rubow et al. 1990; McCartney and Cantrell 1992; Cantrell et al. 1987, NIOSH 1990a; Cantrell and Rubow 1992, Cantrell and Watts 1996; Noll et al. 2006; 71 Fed. Reg. 28924 (2006); 66 Fed. Reg. 27864 (2001); Gangal et al. 1990; Gangal and Dainty 1993; Verma 1999]. Therefore, a surrogate measurement was needed. A method that measures EC and total carbon (TC, or the sum of OC and EC) as surrogates was first investigated by MSHA for DPM compliance sampling. In this method, particulate was collected onto a quartz fiber filter using a cyclone and an impactor with a 0.8 μm cutpoint to segregate the dust from the DPM. After sampling, the filter was analyzed for EC and TC using a thermal optical method (NIOSH method 5040) [Birch 2002; NIOSH 2004; Birch and Cary 1996]. This method proved to be both accurate and sensitive at low DPM concentrations [Birch 2002; NIOSH 2004; Birch and Cary 1996; Verma et al. 1999].

However, because coal dust can be composed of over 75% carbon, the small amount of coal dust that can penetrate through the impactor can potentially interfere with TC from DPM results. In addition, there was also concern about using EC as a surrogate because the amount of EC in DPM can depend upon engine load. Therefore, it was determined that a compliance standard based on these surrogates was impractical in coal mines [66 Fed. Reg. 27864 (2001)]. The interference of TC from the coal dust was later supported by additional results from a NIOSH study [Birch and Noll 2004]. As a result, MSHA does not require ambient sampling of DPM in underground coal mines, but instead limits tailpipe emissions of vehicles to 2.5 grams of DPM per hour for all heavy-duty vehicles and 5 grams per hour for light-duty vehicles [66 Fed. Reg. 27864 (2001)]. Therefore, ambient DPM concentrations in U.S. coal mines are not commonly measured.

However, there is some evidence to support the idea that DPM measurement is possible in underground coal mines. Several studies have shown that it is possible to selectively measure EC in DPM in the presence of coal dust when an impactor is used [Noll and Birch 2004; Birch and Noll 2004] and that a relatively consistent relationship between DPM and EC in coal mines may exist [Wu et al. 2009]. There is still some concern about the potential variability of the relationship between DPM and EC and, therefore, additional data is needed to determine the overall consistency of this ratio.

Unlike in coal mines, DPM is routinely measured in metal/nonmetal mines in the U.S. Dust from metal/nonmetal mines does not contain as much carbon as coal dust, and TC and EC are not significantly influenced by mineral dust from metal/nonmetal mines when an impactor with a 0.8 μm cutpoint and cyclone are used [Cantrell and Rubow 1991; McCartney and Cantrell 1992; Cash et al. 2003; Noll et al. 2005]. This characteristic, combined with the fact that TC and EC make up major components of DPM [Cantrell and Rubow 1991; McCartney and Cantrell 1992; Cash et al. 2003; Noll et al. 2005] (see Section 2.1.1), enabled MSHA to conclude that DPM can be measured reliably in underground metal/nonmetal mines using EC and TC as surrogates. Furthermore, a sampling method of this type was established for compliance measurement [MSHA 2002].

This section describes the use of TC and EC as surrogates for DPM in underground metal/nonmetal mines. The techniques for compliance sampling, apparatus and analytical methods used for measuring EC and TC, as well as technologies for real-time monitoring of DPM are also discussed in this section.

Measurement of DPM Using Total Carbon (TC) as a Surrogate

MSHA chose TC as the primary surrogate because it accounts for over 80% of DPM [71 Fed. Reg. 28924 (2006); Pierson and Brachaczek 1983; Kittelson 1998]. However, even when using an impactor, TC can be prone to interferences such as cigarette smoke and oil mist, which are organic carbon (OC) aerosols that generally belong to the same size category as diesel aerosols [Noll et al. 2006]. Unfortunately, no methods to correct for cigarette smoke or oil mist have been developed to date [Tucker and Pretty 2005].

Another interference to particulate TC is the adsorption of vapor-phase OC (see Section 2.1.1) on quartz filters. Quartz filters are used to collect DPM samples because they are highly efficient in collecting particulate matter and can withstand the temperatures required for NIOSH Method 5040 analysis. However, quartz filters can also adsorb some vapor-phase OC, which is not traditionally recognized as part of DPM. This adsorption can contribute a positive bias in DPM TC results [Eatough et al. 1995; Kirchstetter et al. 2001; Turpin et al. 1994; Noll and Birch 2008]. To account for this bias, one method places a second quartz filter behind the initial sample filter, resulting in two filters positioned in series [Eatough et al. 1995; Kirchstetter et al. 2001; Turpin et al. 1994; Noll and Birch 2008]. In theory, all of the particulate matter will collect on the first filter, and both the first and second filters will adsorb the same amount of vapor-phase OC. The results from the second filter, which is only exposed to vapor-phase OC, can then be subtracted from the results from the first filter to correct for the adsorbed vapor-phase OC. This correction is referred to as the tandem filter correction.

Studies have reported different accuracies when using the tandem filter correction. The accuracy of the correction seems to depend upon flow rate, filter size, sampling time, and concentration of vapor-phase OC [Eatough et al. 1995; Kirchstetter et al. 2001; Turpin et al. 1994; Noll and Birch 2008; McDow and Huntzicker 1990; Olson and Norris 2005; Mader et al. 2003]. Additionally, some of these studies recommended at least 200 minutes of sampling time so that both filters have enough time to adsorb the same amount of vapor-phase OC [Eatough et al. 1995].

94

When applied to occupational DPM samples, the tandem filter correction worked well for some researchers [Noll and Birch 2008]. In one study, a bias of over 30% on TC measurements (due to the adsorption of vapor-phase OC) was reported for many DPM samples that were collected in a laboratory and under simulated mining conditions. The bias decreased to below 11% when the tandem filter correction was applied. In the same study, the bias from vapor-phase OC adsorption in samples taken in an underground mine was twice the experimental error. The bias decreased below the experimental error when the tandem filter correction was applied. It is important to mention that this study did not include samples of DPM generated when using biodiesel without a diesel oxidation catalyst (DOC), and there is a possibility that a different contribution and correction of the vapor-phase OC may result when using biodiesel without a DOC. This occurrence still needs further investigation.

Some researchers have also used a denuder in front of a filter to scrub out the vapor-phase OC so that only particulate would collect onto the sampling filter [Noll and Birch 2008; Eatough et al. 1995; Mader et al. 2001; Subramanian et al. 2004]. This method is somewhat complicated, however, and under some conditions may cause some organics in the particulate phase to evaporate from the sampling filter [Noll and Birch 2008; Eatough et al. 1995; Kirchstetter et al. 2001; Subramanian et al. 2004].

Another method used to correct for the adsorption of vapor-phase OC is to use a dynamic blank collected on a quartz filter behind a Teflon filter [Noll and Birch 2008; Eatough et al. 1995; Kirchstetter et al. 2001; Turpin et al. 1994, 2000; Olson and Norris 2005]. In this method, the particulate sample is collected onto a quartz sample filter in one cassette. In another cassette, a quartz filter (the dynamic blank) is placed in series behind a Teflon filter. In this setup, the Teflon filter will collect the particulate matter in the dynamic blank, while the quartz filter is exposed only to vapor-phase OC. Theoretically, the dynamic blank and the sample filter should adsorb the same amount of vapor-phase OC, which means that the adsorbed vapor-phase OC can be corrected by subtracting the results from the dynamic blank from the actual sample filter. Some studies have shown this method to be accurate and claim that it is better than the tandem filter correction; other studies have reported that it can cause the loss of some OC particulate under certain conditions [Turpin et al. 1994; Olson and Norris 2005; Subramanian et al. 2004]. However, in a recent NIOSH study [Noll and Birch 2008], no difference in accuracy between the two correction methods was reported for occupational DPM samples. Therefore, either correction should be sufficient for DPM mining samples.

When using TC to evaluate DPM concentrations, a size selector device with a submicron cutpoint needs to be used to segregate the dust from the diesel (e.g., a cyclone and impactor combination). The sample also needs to be taken away from the influence of cigarette smoke, oil mist, and other potential submicron carbon aerosols. In order to limit error in the TC measurements, the adsorption of vapor-phase OC also needs to be corrected. The tandem filter correction is the simplest type of correction and has been successfully used in mining applications. However, when using this correction, studies have reported that about 10% of the dynamic blanks in the commercial cassettes used for DPM sampling can be contaminated [Noll et al. 2007]. The filters are determined to be contaminated when the OC on the second filter for one sample out of a set of three is higher than the OC on the first filter. Another sign that there is a problem with the blank is if the value is out of the typical range, which for the dynamic blank is usually within 0.3–5.8 $\mu g/cm^2$ [Noll et al. 2007]. Therefore, at minimum, two (duplicate) samples should be taken to ensure that there is at least one uncontaminated blank. This practice will also improve the overall accuracy of the testing.

Measurement of DPM Using Elemental Carbon (EC) as a Surrogate

Unlike TC, EC is selective to DPM and does not require a complicated sampling strategy to avoid or correct for interferences. This provides the advantages of sampling for DPM in all areas of the mine with no need for a dynamic blank.

A potential disadvantage to using EC as a surrogate is that some laboratory tests have shown that the fraction of EC in DPM may vary depending on engine load [66 Fed. Reg. 27864 (2001)]. In order to see how this affects mining samples, further studies were performed to investigate the relationship between DPM and EC in underground mines. In one set of samples, a linear relationship (r^2 of 0.98) was observed between DPM mass and EC when vehicles that were not equipped with diesel particulate filters (DPFs) were operated under simulated mining conditions (within an isolated zone) and where interferences were controlled. The EC fraction of DPM changed when DPFs were used [Noll et al. 2007]. Similarly, samples collected during actual production in four metal/nonmetal mines (where interferences were corrected for or potentially avoided) showed a strong linear relationship (e.g., r^2 of 0.99) between EC and TC [Noll et al. 2007]. The relationship between EC and TC seemed to become more variable at and below $160 \mu g/m^3$ TC. However, there was limited data at these concentrations, and the influence of interferences may not have been completely avoided. Additionally, experimental error at these low concentrations may have contributed to the variability in this range. With this data set, the relationship between EC and DPM at concentrations at and below $160 \mu g/m^3$ TC could not be reliably determined. Therefore, more data at the lower concentrations is necessary to obtain a better understanding of the EC to total DPM relationship at concentrations near $160 \mu g/m^3$ TC. It is also necessary to obtain more data because some results from a controlled study (isolated zone) described above showed the potential for DPFs to alter the relationship between EC and DPM [Noll et al. 2007]. However, this data was limited, and no results from field tests in mines using DPFs in production scenarios were collected.

Compliance sampling for DPM

Although using EC as a surrogate provides a selective, measurable, and simple method to determine DPM concentration, the fraction of TC in DPM is not as dependent upon engine load as the fraction of EC. Therefore, TC is considered by MSHA to be more representative of total DPM [66 Fed. Reg. 27864 (2001)]. As a result, the final eight-hour time-weighted average (TWA) PEL for metal/nonmetal mines is a TC value ($160 \mu g/m^3$ TC) that, in order to avoid the influence of interferences associated with TC, is determined in two ways [MSHA 2008].

In the first method, a full-shift personal sample using a cyclone and an impactor (described in more detail below) is collected and sent to an MSHA analytical laboratory for analysis of EC and TC using NIOSH method 5040. If the TC from the personal sample is above $160 \mu g/m^3$, the TC result for compliance is determined using the second method as well, because the personal TC value can be prone to interferences.

In the second method, the EC concentration of the personal sample is multiplied by a TC:EC ratio (obtained from an area sample) to calculate the TC value for compliance. The conversion factor is the ratio of the TC value (dynamic blank corrected) to the EC value. The area sample is collected at the same time as the personal sample, downstream of the miner and at least 500 feet away from oil mist and 25 feet away from cigarette smoke. The exact location of this area sample is determined by the inspector. The inspector should avoid these interferences when selecting the sampling location, but still collect a sample that has a TC:EC ratio that is representative of the air in the miner's breathing zone. This will ensure that the multiplication of the ratio value with the EC value would represent the TC concentration from the DPM exposure of the miner.

When a mine is evaluating compliance to the DPM rule, both personal and area samples should be collected. When taking an area sample to determine the conversion factor, the practices mentioned previously for TC sampling should be used. When determining the location of the area sample, it is important to note that taking a sample downstream from cigarette smoke and oil mist does not necessarily avoid their influence. In order for the interference to be negligible, the contaminated air needs to be mixed with adequate interference-free air. A main exhaust, at times, provides the best dilution. Because the area sample is collected in a diluted air stream, it is also important to note that there should be a high enough concentration to ensure accurate TC and EC values. A minimal value of 40 $\mu g/m^3$ eight-hour TWA TC, after applying the tandem filter correction, has been used in other studies [Noll et al. 2007]. In order to confirm that the TC is from DPM and not interferences, a minimal value of 30 $\mu g/m^3$ eight-hour TWA EC may be used instead. In order not to collect an area sample each time, mines may also be able to determine a relatively consistent TC:EC ratio for their mine after evaluating many area samples.

Sampling Apparatuses for Measuring EC and TC

For taking personal samples, the following items are typically used: a personal constant-flow sampling pump, a nylon 10-mm Dorr-Oliver cyclone, a submicron impactor, and two quartz filters placed in tandem (in series) (see Figure 14). This usually entails using the DPM cassette made by SKC, Inc., which includes a built-in impactor and two quartz fiber filters. The pump is operated at 1.7 lpm and is usually attached to the miner's belt. The cassette is installed into a lapel holder that is usually attached to the miner's lapel within the breathing zone. This apparatus can also be used to collect area samples.

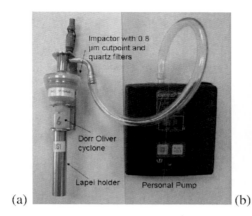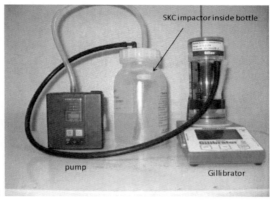

(a)   (b)

Figure 14. (a) Sampling apparatus for NIOSH 5040 samples in underground mines and (b) flow calibration apparatus—an SKC impactor with cyclone is placed into a bottle. The SKC cassette with an internal impactor is attached to tubing that extends out of the bottle to a pump. Another piece of tubing extends out of the jar to a Gilibrator™ (from Gilian®) where the flow is measured. This apparatus measures the flow through the inlet of the cyclone.

After a sample is collected, it is sent to a laboratory and analyzed for EC and TC using NIOSH Method 5040 [NIOSH 2004]. The flow rate of the pump should be checked or calibrated before and after sampling. It should be attached to an apparatus similar to the sampling setup, and the flow should be measured at the inlet of the apparatus because the impactor can cause a pressure drop resulting in a difference between the flow rate at the inlet of the sampling apparatus and the inlet of the pump. One common method is to place a separate cassette (with impactor and cyclone) in a bottle as shown in Figure 14. Tubing is attached to the outlet of the impactor inside the bottle, run out of the bottle, and attached to a pump. The bottle is sealed except for an inlet hole where the flow is measured with a Gilibrator or similar flow calibrator (as shown in Figure 14). The pump should be running for several minutes before checking the flow, and flow results should be measured five to six times. The flow should be taken at the same altitude as where the sampling has occurred because volumetric flow measurements vary with air density.

NIOSH Method 5040 Analysis

NIOSH Method 5040 is a thermal optical method for OC and EC analysis. A sample is first heated in four temperature steps, ending at about 870°C (1,598°F), in a pure helium (He) atmosphere. The evolved OC is oxidized to carbon dioxide (CO_2), reduced to methane (CH_4), and finally measured using a flame ionization detector (FID). At this temperature, the EC does not evolve because there is no oxygen (O_2) available with which it can react. After these temperature stages, the EC is measured by reducing the temperature to about 600°C and then again raising the temperature to about 900°C (1,652°F) in an He/O_2 atmosphere (O_2 is now present to react with the EC to form CO_2). The EC is then measured in the same way as the OC. TC is the sum of OC and EC. NIOSH method 5040 has been shown to meet the NIOSH accuracy criteria and has provided good results for interlaboratory testing [Birch 2002; NIOSH 2004].

OC standards usually made from sucrose are used to calibrate the instruments, but there are currently no reliable EC standards (EC standards are a topic of research by several laboratories). Some normal quality assurance procedures are the analysis of blanks and OC standards, periodic duplication of analysis, and periodic interlaboratory comparisons of EC and TC samples [Birch 2002].

Real-Time Measurement

NIOSH Method 5040 is an accurate method for determining EC, but it only provides the average concentration for an entire work shift. Another disadvantage of NIOSH Method 5040 is that it can take weeks to obtain results, causing a huge shortcoming when evaluating DPM control strategies. By the time the data is analyzed, conditions within the mine have often changed.

Because of these liabilities, real-time measurement of DPM has been an area of recent research. Real-time measurements, even if not as accurate as laboratory methods, can provide valuable information on the trends of DPM concentrations throughout the shift, giving mines a better understanding of how different control strategies are affecting DPM exposures. Additionally, the near-instantaneous availability of measurement data can make the implementation of these controls much easier and more effective.

Some mines have attempted to expand the use of light-scattering instruments to measure real-time DPM by using an impactor in front of the instrument to segregate the dust from the diesel [Zhu et al. 2005; Miller et al. 2007; Stephenson et al. 2006; Arnott et al. 2008]. However, the results were highly variable and limited [Noll and Janisko 2007]. Even when using an impactor, light scattering instruments are often prone to interferences from dust, cigarette smoke, and oil mist. Also, they respond differently according to particle sizes, and are affected by relative humidity greater than 60%. [NIOSH 2010; Chekan et al. 2006; Williams and Timko 1984; Chakrabarti et al. 2004; Quintana et al. 2000]. For these reasons, data collected using light scattering devices should be carefully scrutinized when measuring DPM in underground mines.

Photoacoustic instruments have also been tested in an underground metal/nonmetal mine to measure DPM concentrations in real time [Arnott et al. 1999, 2008; Hamasha and Arnott 2009]. Very limited field data has been collected with this type of instrument, and these results were shown to be 50% different from NIOSH Method 5040 samples [Arnott et al. 2008]. However, with more testing, design adjustments, and better calibration, this instrument may prove to be a viable DPM measurement device in the future.

NIOSH was able to accurately measure real-time DPM with a portable instrument that uses laser absorption to continuously measure EC concentrations in metal/nonmetal mines [Janisko and Noll 2008; Noll et al. 2007]. In this device, an impactor is first used to separate diesel particulate matter from mineral dust (based on particle size), and the DPM is then collected on a filter within the instrument, where the actual measurement takes place. This technique has been shown to be accurate in the laboratory and in some metal/nonmetal mines (within 10% of elemental carbon results measured by NIOSH method 5040 in the laboratory) [Janisko and Noll 2008; Noll et al. 2007]. A disadvantage of this technique is that it only provides EC concentrations and does not measure TC, which is the surrogate used for compliance sampling. However, if a reliable TC/EC ratio has been obtained from previous surveys (via NIOSH method 5040 tests); this value can be entered into the instrument to deliver calculated TC measurements. It is expected to be commercially available soon.

The personal dust monitor (PDM), a portable instrument designed to provide continuous mass measurements of respirable coal dust, was used in two studies to measure real-time DPM mass in coal mines. This instrument has been shown in extensive field measurements to meet the NIOSH accuracy and precision criteria for field instruments [Volkwein et al. 2004; NIOSH 2006]. When used as a DPM mass concentration measurement device, the PDM is typically outfitted with an impactor with a 0.8 μm cutpoint at 1.7 lpm to separate the DPM from the coal dust. At least one study has reported success using the PDM to measure DPM mass concentration in an underground coal mine [Gillies and Wu 2006]. However, at certain concentrations, coal dust may still cause a significant interference. A study reported a 2% to 4% respirable dust penetration through the impactor when evaluating two different coal dusts [Gilles and Wu 2008]. A 4% penetration through the impactor would result in an 80 μg/m^3 PDM reading when exposed to 2,000 μg/m^3 of dust. In this case, for an area with 200 μg/m^3 DPM and 2,000 μg/m^3 dust, the PDM would read 40% higher for the DPM concentration. The amount of dust that penetrates through the impactor depends upon the particle size, concentration, and type of dust. Cigarette smoke and oil mist can also contribute to PDM readings—even when an impactor is used.

4.2 Gases

Introduction

Monitoring the airborne concentrations of gases produced by diesel-powered vehicles is crucial for both underground coal and metal/nonmetal mines. Proper monitoring and management of recorded data is critical in determining whether or not a mine is within compliance. Monitoring is also crucial in evaluating the effectiveness of specific control technologies for curtailing emissions. In addition, accurate monitoring of regulated gases is necessary to establish a successful ventilation strategy. This is true in both coal and metal/nonmetal mines, where the exposure limits for regulated gases are based on ambient and personal exposure concentration levels.

Regulations

Atmospheric monitoring processes are outlined in 30 CFR 75.351 for underground coal mines. During onshift examinations [30 CFR 75.362], a certified person must determine the concentration of carbon monoxide (CO) and nitrogen dioxide (NO_2) in the working drift [30 CFR 70.1900]. When the CO and NO_2 concentrations exceed 50% of the threshold limit value (TLV), the mine operator must take appropriate actions to reduce these values.

For metal/nonmetal mines, regulations indicate that gas surveys should be conducted as frequently as necessary to determine the adequacy of control measures [30 CFR 57.5002]. As described in the personal protection equipment section (Section 3.3), control of employee exposure to harmful airborne contaminants should initially be managed through engineering controls and then by dilution of exhaust ventilation with uncontaminated air [30 CFR 57.5005].

Measurement Devices

Sampling Tubes

Traditional occupational and environmental monitoring approaches are based on discrete sampling methods that draw gases into a sampling device and invoke reaction with a compound to give an indication of pollutant concentration. This type of sampling is conducted in two ways: active (pumped) sampling and passive (diffusive) sampling.

In an active sampling system, the air is pulled through a sampling media by a vacuum pump. By knowing the pump flow rate, the sampling time, and the mass of the targeted compound on the sampling media, it is possible to calculate the concentration of the compound. On the other hand, passive samplers consist only of a diffusion barrier, a collection media, and a sampler case. By using the law of diffusion, the sampling time, and the mass of the targeted compound on the sampling media, it is possible to calculate the concentration of the gas. The sampling rate of a passive sampler can be controlled by manipulating the length and inner diameter of the diffusion barrier [Lee et al. 1992]. Passive sampling tubes are a popular tool for exposure assessment in workplaces because they are lightweight, have low initial cost, are easy to operate, and have low requirements for maintenance and calibration. Active sampling tubes have an increased complexity and cost due to the need for a sampling pump.

The key component of a sampling tube is the collection medium. Various types of collection media are available for sampling different gases with either active or passive sampling methods. In general, these media are classified into two types: liquid and solid reagents. The liquid media use chemical reactions for the absorption of pollutants. The solid reagent (or adsorbent) uses chemisorption and/or physisorption.

Colorimetric dosimeter tubes (Figure 15) are a passive method for measuring the time-weighted average (TWA) exposure of a worker to gases and vapors. Using this method, the mineworker's TWA exposure for a targeted compound is obtained by simply dividing the color stain indication by the number of hours in the sampling period. Alternatively, the media can also be extracted in the laboratory and analyzed via chromatographic technique [Lee et al. 1992]. Sample collection time periods can range from very short-term to full-shift measurement.

Figure 15. A photograph of colorimetric dosimeter tubes.

Bundle Tubes

In recent years, the use of bundle tubes has been proposed for monitoring gases (typically carbon monoxide, carbon dioxide, methane, and oxygen) in underground coal mines [Brady 2008]. This can also include emissions from diesel engines. Tube bundle systems draw gas samples from designated underground sampling locations to the surface through plastic tubes. These gas samples are then analyzed at the surface using infrared and paramagnetic techniques. Good analytical equipment can be housed in dedicated, air-conditioned rooms on the surface where the samples can be dried and passed through particulate filters prior to entering the analyzer(s). The sampling tubes themselves can be located anywhere in the mine, including gobs, because once the sampling tubes are positioned, there is no requirement to access the end of the tube. In addition, continued sampling can occur from any location without requiring additional underground trips to collect samples. This is particularly advantageous in emergency situations when personnel may have been withdrawn from the mine and reentry is prohibited.

Because samples need to be drawn to the surface before analysis, a lag time as long as one or more hours exists from sample collection to analysis. Also, depending on the number of tubes in the system and the programmed sampling sequence, each point may only be sampled once every thirty to sixty minutes. Therefore, this technique is better suited for evaluating long-term trends in gas concentrations than for the instantaneous detection of gases.

Real-Time Instrumentation

Real-time monitors may be more expensive and have higher upfront costs than sampling tubes, but they do not require further analysis, and they provide instantaneous or near-instantaneous measurement. Portable, lightweight monitors are the most common types of personal, real-time instruments used in underground mines to measure the concentration of toxic gases. Some desirable characteristics of a real-time monitor are:

- Accuracy within the range of interest
- Continuous monitoring and data recording
- Potential to monitor multiple gases
- Portability and communication

Accuracy within the range of interest is one of the most important parameters for any monitoring device. When determining this parameter, it is important not to confuse accuracy with precision. Accuracy is a measure of how closely the monitor is able to quantify the true concentration; precision is the degree of reproducibility of a measurement, whatever the measured value. There are devices with high accuracy and low precision or the opposite. Although the precision of an instrument is strictly connected with its design, the accuracy can be modified and improved with a proper calibration procedure.

The possibility of recording and storing the data is another important feature for a real time monitor. This capability allows for later analysis of the data set versus occurrences in the mine that may affect this data. Furthermore the ability of a monitor to measure the concentration of more than one gas compound increases the potential of the device by reducing the number of monitors to transport and the overall cost of the analysis.

The portability of the instrument is also important because it allows the sensor to be located wherever the gas needs to be measured. Effective signal communication, such as an instrument that can send data directly to the surface, is also desirable because it makes the process less laborious.

Electrochemical Cell Detectors

Several real-time and portable gas monitors used in underground mines are equipped with electrochemical cell detectors. These detectors have sensors that are selective for the gas of interest [Hanrahan et al. 2004]. When the gas of interest comes into contact with the sensor for that gas, a chemical reaction occurs, creating an electrical signal that can be measured. The strength of the electrical signal correlates with the concentration of the chemical of interest in the air. Proper calibration of this electrical signal is necessary for accurate measurement. The magnitude of the electrical signal is controlled by how much of the target gas is converted at the working electrode. Sensors are usually designed so that the amount of gas of interest supplied to the sensor is limited by diffusion, allowing for the output from the sensor to be linearly proportional to the gas concentration. This linear output is one of the advantages of electrochemical sensors because it allows for more precise measurement of low concentrations and much simpler calibration of the instrument (only a baseline point and one challenge point are needed for calibration).

103

Diffusion control offers another advantage. Changing the diffusion barrier allows the sensor manufacturer to tailor the sensor to a particular target gas concentration range. In addition, because the diffusion barrier is primarily mechanical, the calibration of electrochemical sensors tends to be more stable over time. This allows these instruments to require much less maintenance than some other detection technologies. [Warburton et al. 1998]. Other beneficial characteristics of electrochemical sensors include high sensitivity and selectivity, a wide linear range, minimal space and power requirements, and low cost. The life of the electrochemical sensor should also be considered. Typically, the cells have an operational life of several years, but it is crucial to follow the manufacturer's guidelines for this information.

In underground metal/nonmetal mines, the most common gases monitored are CO, O_2, NO, NO_2 and SO_2. Methane (CH_4) is usually added to this list when monitoring in coal mines or in other gaseous mines. At the concentration levels typical in underground mining environments, no cross sensitivities and interferences from other gases have been found when using electrochemical sensors [Austin et al. 2006]. However, at higher gas concentrations, cross sensitivities have been documented by manufacturers of various CO, hydrogen sulfide (H_2S), NO, NO_2, or SO_2 detectors [Austin et al. 2006]

Infrared Sensors

In general, individual gases absorb unique combinations of wavelengths of light, and in some cases, frequencies. Infrared (IR) sensors use these absorption properties to determine the type and amount of gas present.

The main components of infrared sensors are an infrared source (lamp), a sample chamber or light tube, a wavelength filter, and the infrared detector. The gas is pumped or diffused into the sample chamber, and the gas concentration is measured electro-optically by its absorption of a specific wavelength in the IR region of light. The amount of light energy received at the detector decreases as more of the "target" gas passes into the sensing cavity.

If only one specific compound is to be measured, it is possible to find portable infrared monitors that fulfill this need [Palassis 1999]. In contrast, larger, laboratory-grade instruments can detect many different gases simultaneously. The main drawback to all IR sensors is their cost. Because of the added complexity, IR sensors are more expensive than other instruments. However, they have the potential to last longer than electrochemical cells, which have a limited life.

Photoacoustic Infrared Sensors

The photoacoustic spectroscopy technique is based on the photoacoustic effect, or the conversion of light to sound during absorption [Harren et al. 2000]. Molecules of any gas are always in motion. As they move around inside a measurement chamber, they generate pressure. When a gas absorbs infrared light, the molecules' temperatures rise, and the molecules begin to move more rapidly. As a result, the pressure inside the measurement chamber increases. This pressure creates an audible pulse that can be detected by a sensitive microphone. This is the basis for photoacoustic instrumentation.

In recent years, photoacoustic spectroscopy has become a powerful technique for studying concentrations of gases at the part-per-billion or even part-per-trillion levels. Several photoacoustic gas sensors for detection of carbon monoxide, carbon dioxide, and other compounds (such as nitrogen oxides and hydrocarbons) have been designed and fabricated [Elia et al. 2005]. The photoacoustic signal has also been investigated as a technique for measuring the concentration of some gases flowing or emitted in underground space, such as mines or tunnels [Roczko 2010; Yutaka et al. 1999]. Although this technique is largely being used in research scenarios, there is a strong possibility that related instrumentation may be used in underground mining as the technology matures.

Calibration

The only way to guarantee that an instrument will measure a concentration of gas accurately and reliably is to test whether the sensor(s) respond accurately with a known concentration of that gas. This process is essential because instruments calculate every measurement in reference to the calibration results and have no other way to compensate for changes in the characteristics of the sensors.

In instruments based on electrochemical sensors, calibration of these instruments typically only requires two comparison points—one at zero concentration and one at the upper limit of the instrument's measurement range (a span value). This is because these sensors usually respond linearly to gas concentration within the measurement range. Other nonlinear measurement technologies may require a multiple-point calibration incorporating three or more points. It is always important to follow the manufacturer's recommended calibration process for any instrument.

Zero calibration usually occurs automatically when an instrument is switched on. However, additional zero calibration can be performed by exposing the instrument to an inert gas (nitrogen is the most common zero gas). The span calibration—a second point of the calibration curve—can only be achieved using a calibration gas of known concentration and accuracy.

For electrochemical sensors, the responsiveness may vary depending on environmental conditions. Therefore, when possible, the monitors should be calibrated at environmental conditions that are the same as or similar to actual field conditions. Calibration at locations where the equipment is to be used is always preferable.

The following are a few basic instrument calibration rules to ensure accurate measurement using portable monitors [OSHA 2004]:

- **Follow the manufacturer's guidelines for proper calibration.** The type and concentration of calibration gas, sample tubing, flow regulators, and calibration adapters are key links in the calibration chain. Using equipment provided by the original manufacturer should ensure a proper start to every calibration.

- **Only use certified calibration gas before its expiration date.** The most important tool used in calibration is the gas itself. The instrument can only be as accurate as the gas used to calibrate it. Be certain your supplier can provide a traceable certificate of analysis for every calibration gas cylinder. The concentration of calibration gas, particularly the concentration of reactive gases such as hydrogen sulfide or chlorine, will only remain stable for a finite period of time.

- **Train workers on the proper methods of calibration.** Most instruments are designed to be field calibrated with instructions detailed in user manuals, training videos, or computer-based training modules. Everyone responsible for performing instrument calibration should be trained and tested accordingly.

5 Administrative controls and practices

5.1 Administrative Controls

Introduction

Many different types of control technologies are being used to reduce DPM exposures and comply with the MSHA diesel rules [66 Fed. Reg. 27864 (2001), 71 Fed. Reg. 28924 (2006)]. This usually entails using multiple types of control technologies (as an integrated approach to DPM reduction) because rarely will a single control strategy result in compliance with this rule (see Section 1). Administrative controls are work practices that can reduce DPM exposures. Some examples include: limiting idling time of engines, limiting the number of vehicles in an area, and scheduling potentially highly exposed individuals to work during nonproduction hours.* This form of management works well with other control technologies and can play a major role in a comprehensive diesel control plan. This chapter will describe several administrative controls that are considered viable strategies for reducing DPM exposures.

It is important to note that one practice that is not a viable administrative control is job rotation, or rotating miners who perform similar tasks to reduce the exposure time for each miner. Job rotation is prohibited by law because the number of miners that are exposed to DPM can increase [71 Fed. Reg. 28924 (2006)].

Administrative Control Options

Limiting Idling

One type of administrative control is to eliminate unnecessary emissions by limiting the idling time for vehicles not in use [Haney et al. 2005]. When compounding this practice over the entire diesel fleet, the emissions reductions can add up. Additionally, limiting idling has the added benefit of saving on both fuel usage and cost (approximately one gallon of fuel used per hour of idling) [Emissions Advantage 2005].

Prohibiting Smoking in Enclosed Cabs

As described in more detail in Section 3.2, open windows in enclosed cabs can significantly decrease the ability of cabs to protect miners from exposure to DPM. Miners tend to open cab windows either to remove cigarette smoke or to reduce cigarette odor from the previous shift. A suggested administrative control solution is to prohibit smoking inside enclosed cabs, thus reducing the miners' need to open cab windows.

Installing and Maintaining Heating and Air Conditioning Systems in Enclosed Cabs

Outfitting enclosed cabs with functioning heating and air-conditioning systems will allow workers to remain comfortable while inside the cab. This will encourage them to keep windows and doors closed, which will help protect them from DPM exposure. After installation, these systems must be maintained in accordance with manufacturers' recommendations to ensure their proper function. Therefore, the maintenance of heating and air-conditioning systems should be incorporated into the mine's existing maintenance program.

Limiting the Number of Vehicles in an Area

An administrative control used in many mines is limiting the number of vehicles in an area. In some mines, vehicle operators place tags on a board at the entrance of a section to indicate that the vehicle has entered that area [Hardcastle et al. 2008, Wu and Gillies 2008]. New vehicles may enter the section only when there is a spare tag position. The number of tag positions can be limited so that the DPM and gas concentrations do not exceed a certain level. This concentration estimate is obtained using the number of vehicles, past tailpipe emission measurements (Section 2.4), and ventilation rates (Section 3.1). However, as real-time instruments become increasingly available (Section 4.1), the number of allowable vehicles in the area could be established from the results of actual measurements of DPM [Wu and Gillies 2008] and gas concentrations. Also, it is important to mention that *both* gas and DPM should be considered when administering such a control, as gas levels do not necessarily correlate with DPM concentrations for all engines and control technologies.

An alternative method to limiting the number of vehicles in an area is to set up one-way passages [Haney et al. 2005] in certain areas. This may reduce the amount of vehicle traffic through that area, which could potentially lower DPM and gas levels.

Controlling the Location of Workers

For some jobs in the mine, it may be possible to relocate workers to areas with lower DPM concentrations [Haney et al. 2005]. For example, if a limestone mine uses enclosed cabs to protect miners who are operating vehicles, blasters who work outside of cabs could work during nonproduction times and, therefore, be less exposed to DPM. If this is not possible, real-time DPM instrumentation (Section 4.1) may be an option that would allow mineworkers to identify and relocate to low-DPM concentration work areas.

Managing Vehicles from Contractors

Some outside contractors bring their own vehicles into the mine. These vehicles can introduce additional DPM into the mine atmosphere, potentially resulting in an overexposure. Mines should be aware of how contractors' vehicles will affect DPM concentrations by obtaining information on the emissions of these vehicles. Mines should require contractors' vehicles to comply with the same emissions standards and testing as the mine's own diesel fleet.

Tracking and Monitoring DPM Concentrations

At least one mine is controlling ventilation by implementing a tracking system to show the location of miners and vehicles [Meyer 2008]. This type of tracking system could lead to several administrative controls for reducing DPM and gaseous exposures, especially if the tracking system is incorporated with real-time monitoring devices. The following is a list of potential administrative controls that could be implemented when using a combined tracking and monitoring system:

1. Determine the concentration of DPM and gases in an area.
   a. Use this information to limit the number of vehicles in an area.
   b. Use this information to determine which areas need additional reductions in DPM and/or gases.
2. Provide a warning signal when a miner is at risk for an overexposure.
   a. Relocate the worker to a different section, or
   b. Perform preventive actions, such as increased ventilation.
3. Determine alternative areas of low DPM and gas concentrations where some miners (such as blasters) can be relocated.

Remote Control Loaders

In some mines, loaders that can be operated using a remote control are being used as a hazard control so that miners are not exposed to areas with questionable ground support. In such a setup, the operator is in visual contact with the vehicle and operates the loader with a remote control in an entry. This remote control technique can also help reduce the exposure of the miner to DPM. For example, it can be hard to provide good ventilation in dead-end entries, and high concentrations of DPM are often observed in these areas. The miner could use the remote-control vehicle to move the ore in the dead-end entry but the miner could be physically located in a cross entry where there is good ventilation and a lower concentration of DPM.

Another way the remote-control loader has been used to protect miners is by locating the operator in an enclosed cab in a different vehicle, from which the loader can be operated remotely (see Section 3.2) [Caterpillar 2007]. The enclosed cab could be either on a vehicle or in another location in the mine.

Some companies and mines are investigating running loaders and trucks remotely and automatically from outside of the mine or in a control room with treated air [DeGaspari 2003; Caterpillar 2007; Noort and McCarthy 2009; Larsson et al. 2010]. In either case, the miners are working away from potential health hazards. There have been some successes with drillers and some loaders in several types of situations [DeGaspari 2003; Caterpillar 2007]. In the future, more miners may be able to work remotely, thus avoiding exposure to contaminants.

5.2 Training

Introduction

In a work environment filled with immediate, life-threatening dangers, it is difficult to ensure that the hazards related to diesel combustion are not overlooked. When coupled with the fact that control and monitoring of diesel contaminants is a complex task, this makes training of both management and personnel in the subject area even more essential.

Training is a tool that allows individuals to acquire skills and knowledge of the rules, concepts, or attitudes necessary to function effectively in specific task situations. With regard to occupational safety and health, training consists of instruction in hazard recognition and control measures, safe work practices, proper use of personal protective equipment (PPE), proper measurement techniques, and emergency procedures and preventive actions. Training also provides workers with ways to obtain additional information about potential hazards and their control, allowing them to assume a more active role in implementing hazard control programs or to effect organizational changes that enhance worksite protection [NIOSH 1998].

Regarding the use of diesel engines in U.S. underground mines, training is a key element in understanding the hazards connected with the pollutants emitted by these engines, and it is recognized as an essential building block for effectively implementing exposure control practices. Training provides management, mineworkers, regulators, and researchers with a common language for effective communication. Once this gap is bridged, good practice skills and attitudes can be relayed more effectively to the end users, and valuable feedback pertinent to the understanding of hazardous issues can be returned. This type of atmosphere is essential for successfully implementing any type of diesel exposure control strategy, or maintenance and monitoring program.

Mandatory Training

For underground coal mines, MSHA requires that mineworkers be qualified before performing maintenance, repairs, examinations, and tests on diesel-powered equipment. To become qualified, a person must successfully complete a training and qualification program in accordance with [30 CFR 75.1915]. The training and tests must be carried out by a qualified instructor and cover topics related to practices for safely maintaining diesel equipment, many of which may be discussed in this guide. Similarly, mine workers conducting ventilation-related sampling or construction or repair of seals need to be trained in accordance with [30 CFR 75.338].

For underground metal/nonmetal mines, operators must provide annual training to all miners who can reasonably be expected to be exposed to diesel emissions, in accordance with [30 CFR 57.5070]. The training must cover the health risks associated with exposure to diesel particulate matter as well as the methods used in the mine to control diesel particulate matter concentration.

Training Opportunities for Continued Learning

In a subject area which is rapidly evolving, it is important to maintain pace with current issues. Table 3 that follows is a selected list of training and continuous learning opportunities related to the use of diesel engines in underground mines. This is only a partial listing of what is available.

Table 3. Selected training opportunities concerning diesel control in underground mines

Topic	Types of training
Diesel Particulate Filters	Workshops by NIOSH and MSHA
	Presentations from earlier NIOSH workshops: http://www.cdc.gov/niosh/mining/topics/diesel/metalworkshop/metal.htm
	Air Resources Board course 511: http://www.arb.ca.gov/training/courses.php?course=511
	Information: http://www.aa-academy.com/Training/Learning%20Zone/Diesel%20Particulate%20Filter%20(DPF).asp
	NIOSH website: http://www.cdc.gov/niosh/mining/
	MSHA website: http://www.msha.gov
	SAE courses such as Diesel Exhaust Emission Control: New Developments
	Annual MDEC Conference: http://www.mdec.ca
	Annual U.S./North American Mine Ventilation Symposium
	Directions in Engine-Efficiency and Emissions Research (DEER) Conference: http://www1.eere.energy.gov/vehiclesandfuels/resources/conferences/deer/index.html
Biodiesel	Workshops by NIOSH and MSHA
	Presentations from earlier NIOSH workshops: http://www.cdc.gov/niosh/mining/topics/diesel/metalworkshop/metal.htm
	National Biodiesel Board: http://www.biodiesel.org/markets/min/
	National Alternative Fuels Training Consortium courses and workshops: http://www.naftc.wvu.edu/NAFTC/training/catalogs.html
	NIOSH website: http://www.cdc.gov/niosh/mining/
	MSHA website: http://www.msha.gov
	Annual MDEC Conference: http://www.mdec.ca
	Annual U.S./North American Mine Ventilation Symposium
Enclosed Cabs	Workshops by NIOSH and MSHA
	Presentations from earlier NIOSH workshops: http://www.cdc.gov/niosh/mining/topics/diesel/metalworkshop/metal.htm
	SME Conference
	Annual U.S./North American Mine Ventilation Symposium
	NIOSH website: http://www.cdc.gov/niosh/mining/
	MSHA website: http://www.msha.gov

Topic	Types of training
Maintenance	Workshops by NIOSH and MSHA Presentations from earlier NIOSH workshop: http://www.cdc.gov/niosh/mining/topics/diesel/metalworkshop/metal.htm SME Conference
	Annual U.S./North American Mine Ventilation Symposium
	NIOSH website: http://www.cdc.gov/niosh/mining/
	MSHA website: http://www.msha.gov
	Mine Health and Safety Solutions DIESEL MAINTENANCE TRAINING http://www.mininghealthandsafety.com/page.php/services-dmt/Consulting-Services.html NIOSH website: http://www.cdc.gov/niosh/mining/
	MSHA website: http://www.msha.gov
Measurement of DPM	Workshops by NIOSH and MSHA NIOSH website: http://www.cdc.gov/niosh/mining/
	MSHA website: http://www.msha.gov
	Annual U.S./North American Mine Ventilation Symposium
PPE	NIOSH website: http://www.cdc.gov/niosh/mining/
	3M respirator training: http://www.3m.com/product/information/Respirator-Training.html, http://solutions.3m.com/wps/portal/3M/en_US/Health/Safety/Products/Two/
Fuels and Lubricants	Machinery Lubrication Magazine: http://www.machinerylubrication.com/
	Oil Doc Conference and Exhibition: http://www.oildoc.com/conference/
	ASTM Diesel Fuel Training Course: http://www.astm.org/TRAIN/courses.html Directions in Engine-Efficiency and Emissions Research (DEER) Conference: http://www1.eere.energy.gov/vehiclesandfuels/resources/conferences/deer/index.html BP Australia Fuel News Topics: http://www.bp.com/sectiongenericarticle.do?categoryId=9012403&contentId=7016829
In-Cylinder Controls	Dieselnet Technology Guide: http://www.dieselnet.com/tg.php
	SAE World Congress: http://www.sae.org/congress/
	SAE Commercial Vehicle Engineering Congress: http://www.sae.org/events/cve/
	SAE Training Seminars and Webinars: http://www.sae.org/events/training/
	Directions in Engine-Efficiency and Emissions Research (DEER) Conference: http://www1.eere.energy.gov/vehiclesandfuels/resources/conferences/deer/index.html

6 References

6.1 Section 1

61 Fed. Reg. 55411 [1996]. Mine Safety and Health Administration: 30 CFR Part 7. Approval, exhaust as monitoring, and safety requirements for the use of diesel-powered equipment in underground coal mines; final rule. Code of Federal Regulations. Washington, DC: U.S. Government Printing Office, Office of the Federal Register.

66 Fed. Reg. 27864 [2001]. Mine Safety and Health Administration: 30 CFR Part 72. Diesel particulate matter exposure of underground coal miners. Limit on concentration of diesel particulate matter. Code of Federal Regulations. Washington, DC: U.S. Government Printing Office, Office of the Federal Register.

71 Fed. Reg. 28924 [2006]. Mine Safety and Health Administration: 30 CFR 57. Diesel particulate matter exposure of underground metal and nonmetal miners. Limit on concentration of diesel particulate matter. Code of Federal Regulations. Washington, DC: U.S. Government Printing Office, Office of the Federal Register.

Conard BR, Stachulak JS, Mayer A, Schnakenberg GH Jr, Bugarski AD, Gangal M, Nault G, Mayotte R, Coppal R, Bedard G [2006]. Evaluation of diesel particulate filter systems at Stobie Mine. March. Final report of investigation to the Diesel Emissions Evaluation Program. [http://www.deep.org/reports/stobiedpf.pdf].

McGinn S, Grenier M, Gangal M, Rubeli B, Bugarski A, Schnakenberg G, Johnson R, Petrie D, Crowther G, Penney J [2004]. Noranda Inc. – Brunswick Mine diesel particulate filter field study. Final report of investigation to the Diesel Emissions Evaluation Program. October. [http://www.deep.org/reports/nordpf_final.pdf].

Mischler SE, Colinet JF [2009]. Controlling and monitoring diesel emissions in underground mines in the United States. Mine In: Proceedings for the 9th International Mine Ventilation Congress. New Delhi, India: Oxford & IBH Publishing Co. Pvt. Ltd., pp. 2:879–888.

MSHA [2008]. Enforcement of diesel particulate matter final limit at metal and nonmetal underground mines. Washington, DC: U.S. Department of Labor, Mine Safety and Health Administration, Program policy letter No. P08-IV-01. [http://www.msha.gov/regs/complian/ppls/2008/PPL08-IV-1.pdf].

Schnakenberg GH Jr [2006]. An integrated approach for managing diesel emissions controls for underground metal mines. In: Mutmansky JM, Ramani RV, eds. Proceedings of the 11th U.S./North American Mine Ventilation Symposium. London: Taylor & Francis Group, pp. 121–125.

6.2 Section 2

26 Fed. Reg. 645 [1961]. Mine Safety and Health Administration: 30 CFR Part 36. Approval requirements for permissible mobile diesel-powered transportation equipment. Code of Federal Regulations. Washington, DC: U.S. Government Printing Office, Office of the Federal Register.

30 CFR 57.5001. Safety and Health Standards. Underground metal and nonmetal mines. Exposure limit for airborne contaminants. Code of Federal Regulations. Washington, DC: U.S. Government Printing Office, Office of the Federal Register.

30 CFR 57.5065. Fueling Practices. Underground metal and nonmetal mines. Maintenance standards. Code of Federal regulations. Washington, DC: U.S. Government Printing Office, Office of the Federal Register.

30 CFR 57.5066. Safety and Health Standards. Underground metal and nonmetal mines. Maintenance standards. Code of Federal regulations. Washington, DC: U.S. Government Printing Office, Office of the Federal Register.

30 CFR 70.1900. Exhaust Gas Monitoring Mandatory Health Standards. Underground coal mines. Subpart T—diesel exhaust gas monitoring. Code of Federal Regulations. Washington, DC: U.S. Government Printing Office, Office of the Federal Register.

30 CFR 75.1908. Mandatory Safety Standards. Underground coal mines. Nonpermissible diesel-powered equipment categories. Code of Federal Regulations. Washington, DC: U.S. Government Printing Office, Office of the Federal Register.

30 CFR 75.1914. Mandatory Safety Standards. Underground coal mines. Maintenance of diesel-powered equipment. Code of Federal Regulations. Washington, DC: U.S. Government Printing Office, Office of the Federal Register.

40 CFR 89. Control of emissions from new and in-use nonroad compression-ignition engines. Code of Federal Regulations. Washington, DC: U.S. Government Printing Office, Office of the Federal Register.

61 Fed Reg. 55412 [1996]. Mine Safety and Health Administration: 30 CFR Part 7. Approval, exhaust gas monitoring, and safety requirements for the use of diesel-powered equipment in underground coal mines; final rule. Code of Federal Regulations. Washington, DC: U.S. Government Printing Office, Office of the Federal Register.

66 Fed. Reg. 27864 [2001]. Mine Safety and Health Administration: 30 CFR Part 72. Diesel particulate matter exposure of underground coal miners. Limit on concentration of diesel particulate matter; final rule. Code of Federal Regulations. Washington, DC: U.S. Government Printing Office, Office of the Federal Register.

66 Fed. Reg. 5001 [2001]. Environmental Protection Agency: 40 CFR Parts 69, 80, and 86. Clean diesel trucks, buses, and fuel: heavy-duty diesel engine and vehicle standards and highway diesel fuel sulfur control requirements; final rule. Code of Federal Regulations. Washington, DC: U.S. Government Printing Office, Office of the Federal Register.

69 Fed. Reg. 38957–39006 [2004]. Environmental Protection Agency: 40 CFR Parts 9, 69, 80, 86, 89, 94, 1039, 1048, 1051, 1065, and 1068. Control of emissions of air pollution from nonroad diesel engines and fuel; final rule. Code of Federal Regulations. Washington, DC: U.S. Government Printing Office, Office of the Federal Register.

71 Fed. Reg. 28924 [2006]. Mine Safety and Health Administration: 30 CFR 57.5060. Diesel particulate matter exposure of underground metal and nonmetal miners. Limit on concentration of diesel particulate matter; final rule. Code of Federal Regulations; Washington, DC: U.S. Government Printing Office, Office of the Federal Register.

ACGIH [1991]. Documentation of the threshold limit values and biological exposure indices. 6th ed. Cincinnati, OH: American Conference of Governmental Industrial Hygienists.

Agrawal AK, Singh SK, Sinha S, Shukla MK [2004]. Effect of EGR on the exhaust gas temperature and exhaust opacity in compression ignition engines. Sadhana 29(3):275–284. [http://www.ias.ac.in/sadhana/Pdf2004Jun/Pe1131.pdf].

Akama H, Matsushita K [1999]. Recent lean NOX catalyst technologies for automobile exhaust control. Catal Surv Jpn 3:139–146.

Ålander TJA, Leskinen AP, Raunemaa TM, Rantanen L [2004]. Characterization of diesel particles: effects of fuel formulation, exhaust aftertreatment, and engine operation on particle carbon composition and volatility. Env Sci Tech 38:2707–2714.

Allansson R, Blakeman PG, Cooper BJ, Hess H, Silcock PJ, Walker AP [2002]. Optimizing the low temperature performance and regeneration efficiency of the continuously regenerating diesel particulate filter (Cr-Dpf) system. SAE Technical Paper 2002-01-0428.

Alleman TL, McCormick RL, Deutch S [2007]. B100 Quality survey results. U.S. Department of Energy, National Renewable Energy Laboratory, Milestone Report NREL/TP-540-41549.

Ambs JL, Hilman TL [1992]. Disposable and reusable diesel exhaust filters. In: Diesels in underground mines: measurement and control of particulate emissions. U.S. Department of the Interior, Bureau of Mines. Information Circular 9324.

Ambs JL, McClure BT [1993]. The influence of oxidation catalyst on NO2 in diesel exhaust. SAE Technical Paper 932494.

Ambs JL, Setren RS [1995]. Safety evaluation of disposable diesel exhaust filters for permissible mining equipment. In: Wala AM, ed. Proceedings of the 7th U.S./North American Mine Ventilation Symposium. Littleton, CO: Society for Mining, Metallurgy, and Exploration.

Ambs JL, Cantrell BK, Watts WF, Olson KS [1994]. Evaluation of a disposable diesel exhaust filter for permissible mining machines. U.S. Department of the Interior, Bureau of Mines, Report of Investigation 9508.

Analysts Inc. [2011]. Basics of oil analysis. In: Analysts Inc. [http://www.analystsinc.com/documents/BasicsOA.pdf].

Anyon P [2008]. Managing diesel particle emissions through engine maintenance—an Australian perspective. In: Wallace K, ed. Proceedings of the 12th US/North American Mine Ventilation Symposium. Reno, NV: University of Nevada, Reno.

Aravelli K, Heibel A [2007]. Improved lifetime pressure drop management for robust cordierite (RC) filters with asymmetric cell technology (ACT). SAE Technical Paper 2007-01-0920.

Argueyrolles B, Dehoux S, Gastaldi P, Grosjean L, Levy F, Michel A, Passerel D [2007]. Influence of injector nozzle design and cavitation on coking phenomenon. SAE Technical Paper 2007-01-1896.

Armas O, Ballesterosa R, Martosb FJ, Agudeloc JR [2005]. Characterization of light duty diesel engine pollutant emissions using water-emulsified fuel. J Fuel 84(7-8):1011–1018.

Arnold S, Slupski K, Groskreutz M, Vrbas G, Cadle R, Shahed S [2001]. Advanced turbocharging technologies for heavy-duty diesel engines. SAE Technical Paper 2001-01-3260.

ASTM [2009a]. Standard specifications for diesel fuel oils. ASTM D975 – 09a. ASTM International.

ASTM [2009b]. Standard specifications for biodiesel fuel blend stock (B100) for middle distillate fuels. ASTM D6751 – 09. ASTM International.

ASTM [2009c]. Standard specification for diesel fuel oil, biodiesel blend (B6 to B20). ASTM D D7467 – 09a. ASTM International.

ASTM [2011]. Standard specification for diesel fuel oils. ASTM D975 – 11. ASTM International. [http://www.astm.org/Standards/D975.htm].

Aswani DJ, van Nieuwstadt MJ, Cook JA, Grizzle JW [2005]. Control oriented modeling of a diesel active lean NOX catalyst aftertreatment system. J Dyn Syst Meas Cont 127(1):1–12.

Babu KVR, Dias C, Waje S, Reck A, Wosnik K [2008]. PM Metalit®—a continuously regenerated particle flow particle filter—concept and experience with Korean retrofit program. SAE Technical Paper 2008-28-0008.

Bach E, Zikoridse G, Sandig R, Lemaire J, Mustel W, Naschke W, Bestenteiner GM, Brück R [1998]. Combination of different regeneration methods for diesel particulate traps. SAE Technical Paper 980541.

Bagley ST, Gratz LD [1998]. Evaluation of biodiesel fuel and oxidation catalyst in an underground mine. Part 3: biological and chemical characterization. Final report submitted to Diesel Emissions Evaluation Program (DEEP). [http://www.deep.org/reports/inco_bio_mtu.pdf].

Bagley ST, Gratz LD, Johnson JH, McDonald JF [1998]. Effects of oxidation catalytic converter and a biodiesel fuel on chemical, mutagenic, and particle size characteristics of emissions from a diesel engine. Env Sci Tech 32:1183–1191.

Bento FM, Gaylarde CC [2001]. Biodeterioration of stored diesel oil: studies in Brazil. Int Biodeter Biodegr 47(2):107–112.

BHP Billiton [2005]. Diesel emissions management. Revision 1. BHP Billiton Ltd.

Biswas S, Hu S, Verma V, Herner JD, Robertson WH, Ayala A, Sioutas C [2008]. Physical properties of particulate matter (PM) from late model heavy-duty diesel vehicles operating with advanced PM and NOX emissions control technologies. Atmos Environ 42:5622–5634.

Boehman AL, Alam M, Song J, Acharya R, Szybist J, Zallo V, Miller K [2003]. Fuel formulation effects on diesel fuel injection, combustion, emissions, and emission control. Proceedings of the 2003 Diesel Engine Emissions Reduction Conference. U.S. Department of Energy.

Boehman AL, Song J, Alam M [2005]. Impact of biodiesel blending on diesel soot and the regeneration of particulate filters. Energy Fuels 19:1857–1864.

Boger T, Rose D, Tilgner I-C, Heibel AK [2008a]. Regeneration strategies for an enhanced thermal management of oxide diesel particulate filters. SAE Technical Paper 2008-01-0328.

Boger T, Tilgner I-C, Shen M, Jiang Y [2008b]. Oxide base particulate filters for light-duty diesel applications—impact of the filter length on the regeneration and pressure drop behavior. SAE Technical Paper 2008-01-0485.

Bosch H, Janssen F [1988]. Preface. Catal Today 2(4).

Bouchez M, Dementhon JB [2000]. Strategies for the control of particulate trap regeneration. SAE Technical Paper 2000-01-0472.

BP Australia [2002]. Fuel news: a different slant on fuel storage—a case study. Publication No. ADF0705.doc. [http://www.bp.com/liveassets/bp_internet/australia/corporate_australia/STAGING/local_assets/downloads_pdfs/f/Fuel_news_different_slant_on_fuel.pdf].

BP Australia [2005a]. Fuel news: long-term storage of diesel fuel. Publication No. ADF1403.doc. [http://www.bp.com/liveassets/bp_internet/australia/corporate_australia/STAGING/local_assets/downloads_pdfs/f/Long_Term_Storage_ADF.pdf].

BP Australia [2005b]. Fuel news: Common fuel problems number 1. Publication No. ADF0908.doc. [http://www.bp.com/liveassets/bp_internet/australia/corporate_australia/STAGING/local_assets/downloads_pdfs/f/Common_ADF_Problems1.pdf].

Bugarski AD, Cauda EG, Janisko SJ, Hummer JA, Patts LD [2010]. Aerosols emitted in underground mine air by diesel engine fueled with biodiesel. J Air Waste Manage Assoc 60:237–244.

Bugarski AD, Schnakenberg GH, Patts LD [2006]. Implementation of diesel particulate filter technology in underground metal and nonmetal mines. In: Mutmansky JM, Ramani RV, eds. Proceedings of the 11th U.S./North American Mine Ventilation Symposium. London: Taylor & Francis Group, pp. 127–133.

Bugarski AD, Schnakenberg GH Jr, Hummer JA, Cauda E, Janisko SJ, Patts LD [2007]. Examination of diesel aftertreatment systems at NIOSH Lake Lynn Laboratory. Proceeding of the 13th Annual Mining Diesel Emissions Conference. Ottawa, Ontario, Canada: Mining Diesel Emissions Council.

Bugarski AD, Schnakenberg GH Jr, Hummer JA, Cauda E, Janisko SJ, Patts LD [2009]. Effects of diesel exhaust aftertreatment devices on concentrations and size distribution of aerosols in underground mine air. Env Sci Tech 43:6737–6743.

Bughardt DM [1984]. Know your diesel. Englewood Cliffs, NJ: Prentice-Hall.

Busch S, Bohac SV, Assanis DN [2007]. A study of the transition between lean conventional diesel combustion and lean, premixed, low-temperature diesel combustion. In: Proceedings of the ASME Internal Combustion Engine Division Fall Technical Conference. Charleston, SC: ASME. [http://me.engin.umich.edu/autolab/Publications/Adobe/P2007_06.pdf].

Caines JA, Haycock RF, Hillier JE [2004]. Blending, storage, purchase and use. In: Automotive lubricants reference book. 2nd rev. ed. Warrendale, PA: SAE International, pp. 347–372.

Cantrell BK, Rubow KL [1992]. Measurement of diesel aerosol in underground coal mines. In: Diesels in underground mines: measurement and control of particulate emissions. U.S. Department of the Interior, Bureau of Mines, Information Circular 9324, pp. 11–17.

Cantrell BK, Volwein JC [2001]. Mine aerosol measurement. In: Baron PA and Willeke K, eds. Aerosol measurement: principles, techniques, and applications. 2nd ed. New York: Wiley Interscience, pp. 804–805.

Cantrell BK, Rubow KL, Watts WF Jr., Carlson DH [1991]. Pollutant levels in underground coal mines using diesel equipment. Society for Mining Metallurgy, and Exploration. AIME Transactions 290:1901–1907.

CARB [2004]. The California diesel fuel regulations. State of California, California Environmental Protection Agency, California Air Resources Board, California Code of Regulations, Title 13, Section 2281-2285. August 14.

CARB [2008]. Guidance document and recommendations on the types of scientific information submitted by applicants for California fuels environmental multimedia. Evaluation. State of California, California Environmental Protection Agency, California Air Resources Board, Agreements No. 060-409, 06-410, p. 239

CARB [2009a]. Verification procedure—currently verified. California Environmental Protection Agency, California Air Resources Board. [http://www.arb.ca.gov/diesel/verdev/vt/cvt.htm].

CARB [2009b]. Verification procedure, warranty and in-use compliance requirements for in-use strategies to control emissions from diesel engines. California Code of Regulations, Title 13, Division 3. [http://www.arb.ca.gov/diesel/verdev/reg/procedure_jan1009.pdf].

CARB [2010]. Verification procedure—currently verified. California Environmental Protection Agency, California Air Resources Board. [http://www.arb.ca.gov/diesel/verdev/vt/cvt.htm].

Caterpillar [1997]. Fuel contamination control. Caterpillar Inc., Fuel Systems. Publication No. PEHP7046. [http://www.cat.com/cda/files/1386246/7/PEHJ7046-03.pdf].

Cauda E, Bugarski A, Patts L [2010]. Diesel aftertreatment control technologies in underground mines: the NO2 issue. In: Hardcastle S, McKinnon DL, eds. Proceedings of the 13th U.S./North American Mine Ventilation Symposium. Sudbury, ON, Canada: MIRARCO—Mining Innovation.

Cavataio G, Cheng Y, Montreuil C, Lambert C [2008]. Sulfur tolerance and DeSOx studies on diesel SCR catalysts. SAE Technical Paper 011023.

Chaffin C, Ullman T [1994]. Effects of increased altitude on heavy-duty diesel engine emissions. SAE Technical Paper 940669.

Chandler GR, Cooper BJ, Harris JP, Thoss JE, Uusimäki A, Walker AP, Warren JP [2000]. An integrated SCR and continuous regeneration trap system to meet future NOx and PM legislation. SAE Technical Paper 2000-01-0188.

Chevron [2007]. Diesel fuel technical review. Chevron. [http://www.chevron.com/products/ourfuels/prodserv/fuels/documents/Diesel_Fuel_Tech_Review.pdf].

Chilumukuru KP, Arasappa R, Jonson JH, Naber JD [2009]. An experimental study of particulate thermal oxidation in a catalyzed filter during active regeneration. SAE Technical Paper 2009-01-1474.

Cho SM [1994]. Properly apply selective catalytic reduction for NOX removal. Chem Eng Prog 39–45.

Chung YC, Chen HC, Shyub YT, Hua J [2000]. Temperature and water effects on the biodeterioration for marine fuel oil. J Fuel 79(12):1525–1532.

Colammusi A [2008]. Disposable filters. In: Mayer A, ed. Particle filter retrofit for all diesel engines. Brill Ulrich, Haus der Technik Fachbuch Band 97.

Conard BR, Stachulak JS, Mayer A, Schnakenberg GH Jr, Bugarski AD, Gangal M, Nault G, Mayotte R, Coppal R, Bedard G [2006]. Evaluation of diesel particulate filter systems at Stobie Mine. March. Final report of investigation to the Diesel Emissions Evaluation Program. [http://www.deep.org/reports/stobiedpf.pdf].

Cooper BJ, McDonnald AC, Walker AP, Sanchez M [2003]. The development and on-road performance and durability of the four-way emission control SCRT system. In: Proceedings of the 9th Diesel Engine Emissions Reduction Conference (DEER). U.S. Department of Energy.

Czerwinski J, Peterman J-L, Comte P, Lemaire J, Mayer A [2007]. Diesel NO/ NO2/NOX emissions—new experiences and challenges. SAE Technical Paper 2007-01-0321.

D'Urbano G, Mayer A [2007]. FOEN/Suva filterlist. Tested and approved particle filter systems for retrofitting diesel engines. Status: December 2007. The environment in practice. No. 0741. Lucerne, Switzerland: Federal Office of the Environment. Bern. 35 pp.

Dabhoiwala RH, Johnson JH, Naber JD, Bagley ST [2008]. A methodology to estimate the mass of particulate matter retained in a catalyzed particulate filter as applied to active regeneration and on-board diagnostics to detect filter failure. SAE Technical Paper 2008-01-0764.

Dabhoiwala RH, Johnson JH, Naber JD [2009]. Experimental study comparing particle size and mass concentration data for a cracked and uncracked diesel particulate filter. SAE Technical Paper 2009-01-0629.

Davies B, McGinn S [2004]. The effect of maintenance of diesel engines on particulate generation. 6th International Scientific Conference of the International Occupational Hygiene Association. Geneva, Switzerland: World Health Organization.

De Filippo A, Maricq MM [2008]. Diesel nucleation mode particles: semivolatile or solid? Env Sci Tech 42:7957–7962.

DEEP [1999]. Diesel emission control strategies available to the underground mining industry. Diesel Emissions Evaluation Program. [http://www.deep.org/reports/esi_final_report.pdf].

Dempsey P [1995]. Troubleshooting and repairing diesel engines. 3rd ed. New York: McGraw-Hill, Inc.

DePetrillo FS, Ibrahim OM, Wenghoefer HM [2007]. An actively regenerated diesel exhaust particulate filter that demonstrates significant NO2 reduction. In: Proceedings of 13th Mining Diesel Emissions Conference. Ottawa, Ontario, Canada: Mining Diesel Emissions Council.

Dickey DW, Ryan TW III, Matheaus AC [1998]. NOX control in heavy-duty diesel engines—what is the limit? SAE Technical Paper 980174.

Diesel R [1895]. Method of and apparatus for converting heat into work. U.S. Patent 542846. Washington, DC: U.S. Patent and Trademark Office.

DieselNet [1997]. Ceramic catalyst substrates. In: DieselNet Technology Guide. [http://www.dieselnet.com/tech/cat_subs_cer.html].

DieselNet [2002]. Fuel properties and emissions. In: DieselNet Technology Guide. [http://www.dieselnet.com/tech/fuel_emi.html].

DieselNet [2003]. Metallic catalyst substrates. In: DieselNet Technology Guide. [http://www.dieselnet.com/tech/cat_subs_cer.html].

DieselNet [2005a]. Catalytic coating & materials. In; DieselNet Technology Guide. [http://www.dieselnet.com/tech/cat_mat.html].

DieselNet [2005b]. Diesel Filter Systems. In: DieselNet Technology Guide. [http://www.dieselnet.com/tech/dpf_sys.html].

DieselNet [2009]. Engine and vehicle dynamometer cycles. In: DieselNet. [http://www.dieselnet.com/standards/cycles/].

DOE [2009]. Clean cities fact sheet: biodiesel clears the air in underground mines. Washington, DC: U.S. Department of Energy, Publication No. DOE/GO-102009-2824. [http://www.afdc.energy.gov/afdc/pdfs/45626.pdf].

Dorriah P [1999]. The QuadCATTM four-way catalytic converter: an integrated aftertreatment system for diesel engines. SAE Technical Paper 012924.

Doyle A, Tristao MLB, Felcman J [2006]. Study of fuel insolubles: formation conditions and characterization of copper compounds. J Fuel 85(14-15):2195–2201.

Durbin DT, Cocker DR III, Sawant AA, Johnson K, Miller JW, Holden BB, Helgeson NL, Jack JA [2007]. Regulated emissions from biodiesel fuels from on/off-road applications. Atmos Environ 41:5647–5658.

Eaton SJ, Bunting BG, Toops TJ, Nguyen K [2009]. The roles of phosphorus and soot on the deactivation of diesel oxidation catalyst. SAE Technical Paper 2009-01-0628.

Eberwein B [2008]. CRT filters: experience with road vehicles. In: Mayer A, ed. Particle filter retrofit for all diesel engines. Brill Ulrich, Haus der Technik Fachbuch Band 97.

EC 1999/96/EC [2000]. Directive 1999/96/EC of the European Parliament and the Council of 13 December 1999. The European Parliament and the Council of European Union. Official Journal of the European Union, L 044, pp. 0001–0155.

EC 595/2009 [2009]. Regulation (EC) No 595/2009 of the European Parliament and the Council of 18 June 2009. The European Parliament and the Council of European Union. Official Journal of the European Union, L 188, pp. 0001–0013.

EPA [2001a]. Nonroad diesel emission standards: staff technical paper. Washington, DC: U.S. Environmental Protection Agency, EPA420-R-01-052.

EPA [2001b]. Strategies and issues in correlating diesel fuel properties with emissions. Staff discussion document. Washington, DC: U.S. Environmental Protection Agency, EPA420-P-01-001.

EPA [2002a]. Health assessment document for diesel engine exhaust. Washington, DC: U.S. Environmental Protection Agency, EPA/600/8-90/057F.

EPA [2002b]. A comprehensive analysis of biodiesel impact on exhaust emissions. Draft technical report. Washington, DC: U.S. Environmental Protection Agency, EPA420-P-02-001.

EPA [2002c]. Impacts of Lubrizol's PuriNOx water/diesel emulsion on exhaust emissions from heavy-duty engines. Draft technical report, Washington, DC: U.S. Environmental Protection Agency, EPA420-P-02-007.

EPA [2004]. Final regulatory analysis: control of emissions from nonroad diesel engines. Washington, DC: U.S. Environmental Protection Agency, EPA420-R-04-007.

EPA [2007a]. Diesel oxidation catalysts: informational update. Washington, DC: U.S. Environmental Protection Agency, EPA420-F-07-068. [http://www.epa.gov/otaq/diesel/documents/420f07068.htm].

EPA [2007b]. Nitrogen dioxide limits from retrofit technologies. Washington, DC: U.S. Environmental Protection Agency, EPA420-B-08-005.

EPA [2008a]. Verified retrofit technologies from Lubrizol. U. S. Environmental Protection Agency. [http://www.epa.gov/oms/retrofit/techlist-lubrizol.htm].

EPA [2008b]. Verified retrofit technologies—biodiesel. U.S. Environmental Protection Agency. [http://www.epa.gov/OMS/retrofit/techlist-biodeisel.htm].

EPA [2008c]. Emissions from platinum based fuel additives. Washington, DC: U.S. Environmental Protection Agency, EPA420-B-08-014. [http://www.epa.gov/otaq/retrofit/documents/420b08014.pdf].

EPA [2009]. Verified retrofit technologies. U.S. Environmental Protection Agency. [http://www.epa.gov/otaq/retrofit/verif-list.htm].

EPA [2010]. Verified retrofit technologies. U.S. Environmental Protection Agency. [http://www.epa.gov/oms/retrofit/verif-list.htm].

Farfaletti A, Astorga C, Martini G, Manfredi U, Mueller A, Rey M, De Santi G, Krasenbrink A, Larsen BR [2005]. Effects of water/fuel emulsions and cerium-based combustion improver additive on HD and LD diesel exhaust emissions. Env Sci Tech 39:6792–6799.

Filipi Z, Wang Y, Dennis A [2001]. Effect of variable turbine (VGT) on diesel engine and vehicle system transient response. SAE Technical Paper 2001-01-1247.

Fitch J [2004]. Bulk lubricant storage and handling. In: Machinery lubrication online. [http://www.machinerylubrication.com/Read/665/bulk-oil-storage].

Fitch J, Troyer D [2011]. The basics of used oil sampling. In: Machinery lubrication online. [http://www.machinerylubrication.com/Read/650/used-oil-sampling].

Flippin RS, Smith C, Mickelson AMN [1964]. Fusarium growth supported by hydrocarbons. Appl Microbiol *12*(2):93–95. [http://www.ncbi.nlm.nih.gov/pmc/articles/PMC1058074/pdf/applmicro00352-0003.pdf].

Fritz N, Mathes W, Zuerbig J, Mueller R [1999]. On-road demonstration of NOX emission control for diesel trucks with SiNOx urea SCR system. SAE Technical Paper 1999-01-0111.

Froelund K, Yilmaz E [2004]. Impact of engine oil consumption on particulate emissions. In: Automotive Manufacturers Association. [http://www.osd.org.tr/17.pdf].

Fukuda K, Kohakura M, Shibuya M, Kaneko T, Nakamura O, Furui K, Okada M, Tsuchihashi K, Hosono K, Hasegawa T, Hirata K, Saitou K, Kawatani T, Baba H, Sugiyama G [2008]. Impact of high biodiesel blends on performance of exhaust aftertreatment systems. SAE Technical Paper 2008-01-2494.

Gabrielsson P [2004]. Urea-SCR in automotive applications. Topics Catal *28*(1-4).

Gerlofs-Nijland ME, Groenewegen L, Casee FR [2008]. Health effects of addition and combustion of fuel additives. The Netherlands National Institute for Public Health and the Environment (RIVM), Letter report 6301600001/2008.

Giechaskiel B, Munoiz-Bueno R, Rubino L, Manfredi U, Dilara P, De Santi G, Andersson J [2007]. Particle Measurement Programme (PMP): Particle size and number emissions before, during, and after regeneration events of a Euro 4 DPF equipped light-duty diesel vehicle. SAE Technical Paper 2007-01-1944.

Gieshoff J [2000]. Improved SCR system for heavy duty applications. SAE Technical Paper 010189.

Gieshoff J [2001]. Advanced urea SCR catalyst for automotive applications. SAE Technical Paper 010514.

Goo JH, Irfan MF, Kim SD, Hong SC [2007]. Effects of NO2 and SO2 on selective catalytic reduction of nitrogen oxides by ammonia. Chemosphere *67*:718–723.

Görsmann C [2008]. Catalytic coatings for diesel particulate filter regeneration. In: Mayer A, ed. Particle filter retrofit for all diesel engines. Brill Ulrich, Haus der Technik Fachbuch Band 97.

Graboski MS, McCormick RL [1998]. Combustion of fat and vegetable oils derived fuels in diesel engines. Prog Energy Combust Sci *24*; 125–164.

Graboski MS, McCormick RL [1996]. Effect of diesel fuel chemistry on regulated emissions at high altitude. SAE Technical Paper 961947.

Grose M, Sakurai H, Savstrom J, Stolzenburg MR, Watts WF, Morgan CG, Murray IP, Twigg MV, Kittelson DB, McMurry PH [2006]. Chemical and physical properties of ultrafine diesel exhaust particles sampled downstream of a catalytic trap. Env Sci Tech *40*:5502–5507.

Han Z, Uludogan A, Hampson GJ, Reitz RD [1996]. Mechanism of soot and NOX emission reduction using multiple-injection in a diesel engine. SAE Technical Paper 960633. [http://www.erc.wisc.edu/documents/SAE960633.pdf].

Haney RA, Saseen GP, Waytulonis RW. [1997]. An overview of diesel particulate exposures and control technology in the U.S. mining industry. Appl Occup Environ *12*(12):1013–1018.

Havenith C, Verbeek RP [1997]. Transient performance of a urea DeNOX catalyst for low emissions heavy-duty diesel engines. SAE Technical Paper 970185.

HEI [2001]. Evaluation of human health risk from cerium added to diesel fuel. Boston, MA: Health Effects Institute. Communication 9.

Helmantel A, Golovitchev V [2009]. Injection strategy optimization for a light duty DI diesel engine in medium load conditions with high EGR rates. SAE Technical Paper 2009-01-1441.

Herner JD, Hu S, Robertson WH, Huai T, Collins JF, Dwyer H, Ayala A [2009]. Effects of advanced aftertreatment for PM and NO_X control on heavy-duty diesel truck emissions. Env Sci Tech 43, 5928–5933.

Heywood JB [1988a]. Internal combustion engine fundamentals. New York: McGraw Hill, pp. 248–273.

Heywood JB [1988b]. Internal combustion engine fundamentals. New York: McGraw Hill, pp. 491–565.

Heywood JB [1988c]. Internal combustion engine fundamentals. New York: McGraw Hill, pp. 567–646.

Horibe N, Ishiyama T [2009]. Relations among NOx, pressure rise rate, HC and CO in LTC operation of a diesel engine. SAE Technical Paper 2009-01-1443.

Horibe N, Takahashi K, Kee S, Ishiyama T, Shioji, M [2007]. The effects of injection conditions and combustion chamber geometry on performance and emissions of DI-PCCI operation in a diesel engine. SAE Technical Paper 2007-01-1874.

Houben H, Miebach R, Sauerteig JE [1994]. The optimized Deutz Services diesel particulate filter system DPFS II. SAE Technical Paper 942264.

Howitt JS, Montierth MR [1984]. Cellular ceramic diesel particulate filter. SAE Technical Paper 810114.

Hug C [2008]. Particle filters and SCR-Denox with locomotives, ships and stationary plants. In: Mayer A, ed. Particle filter retrofit for all diesel engines. Brill Ulrich, Haus der Technik Fachbuch Band 97.

ISO [2005a]. Quality management systems. International Organization For Standardization. ISO 9000:2005. [http://www.iso.org].

ISO [2005b]. General requirements for the competence of testing and calibration laboratories. International Organization For Standardization. ISO/IEC 17025:2005. [http://www.iso.org].

Iwamoto M, Hernandez AM, Zengyo T [1997]. Oxidation of NO to NO_2 on a Pt-MFI zeolite and subsequent reduction of NOX by C2H4 on an In-MFI zeolite: a novel de-NOX strategy in excess oxygen. Chem Comm *1*:37–38.

Jacobs T, Assanis D, Filipi Z [2003]. The impact of exhaust gas recirculation on performance and emissions of a heavy-duty diesel engine. SAE Technical Paper 2003-01-1068.

Jaroszczyk T, Holm C, Fallon S, Schwandt B, Gradoń L, Steffen B, Zuroski M, Koleshwar A, Moy J [2006]. New developments in diesel engine crankcase emission reduction— requirements, design and performance. J KONES Powertrain Trans *13*(2):155–167. [http://www.ilot.edu.pl/KONES/2006/02/16.pdf].

Jaussi F [2008]. Methods to select the appropriate regeneration method for a specific application. In: Mayer A, ed. Particle filter retrofit for all diesel engines. Brill Ulrich, Haus der Technik Fachbuch Band 97.

Jelles SJ, Makkee M, Moulijn JA [2001]. Ultra low dosage of platinum and cerium fuel additives in diesel particulate control. Topics Catal *16-17*(1-4):269–273.

Jelles SJ, Makkee M, Moulijn JA, Acres GJK, Peter-Hoblyn JD [1999]. Diesel particulate control. Application of an activated particulate trap in combination with fuel additives at an ultra low dose rate. SAE Technical Paper 1999-01-0113.

Jenson CC [2011]. Clean oil guide. Svendborg, Denmark: C.C.JENSON A/S. [http://www.cjc.dk/fileadmin/user_upload/pdf/CJC_Brochures/Clean_Oil_Guide.pdf].

Johansen K, Dahl S, Mogensen G, Pehrson S, Schramm J, Ivarsson A [2007]. Novel base metal-palladium catalytic diesel filter coating with NO2 reducing properties. SAE Technical Paper 2007-01-1921.

Johnson TV [2009]. Diesel emission control in review. SAE Technical Paper 2009-01-0121.

Jung H, Kittelson DB, Zachariah MR [2003]. The influence of engine lubricating oil on diesel nanoparticle emissions and kinetics of oxidation. SAE Technical Paper 2003-01-3179.

Katare SR, Patterson JE, Laing PM [2007]. Aged DOC is a net consumer of NO_2: analysis of vehicle, engine-dynamometer, and reactor data. SAE Technical Paper 2007-01-3984.

Kawanami M, Horiuchi M, Lox E, Leyrer J, Psaras D [1995]. Advanced catalyst studies of diesel NOX reduction for on- highway truck. SAE Technical Paper 950154.

Kawano D, Ishil H, Goto Y, Noda A, Aoyagi Y [2007]. Optimization of engine system for application of biodiesel fuel. SAE Technical Paper 2007-01-2028.

Khair M, McKinnon DL [1999]. Performance evaluation of advanced emissions control technologies for diesel heavy-duty engines. SAE Technical Paper 1999-01-3564.

Khair MK, Merritt PM, Lu Q, Lemaire J, Morin J-P, Johansen K [2008]. Catalytic formulation for NO_2 suppression and control. SAE Technical Paper 2008-01-1548.

Khalek IA, Bougher TL, Merritt PM [2009]. Phase 1 of the advanced collaborative emissions study. Final report. Alpharetta, GA: Coordinating Research Council Inc. [http://www.crcao.com/reports/recentstudies2009/ACES%20Phase%201/ACES%20Phase1% 20Final%20Report%2015JUN2009.pdf].

Khalek IA, Fritz SG, Pass N [2003]. Particle size distribution and mass emissions from a mining diesel engine equipped with a dry system technologies emission control system. SAE Technical Paper 2003–01–0285.

Kharas KC, Bailey OH, Vuichard J [1998]. Improvements in intimately coupled diesel hydrocarbon adsorber/lean NOX catalysis leading to durable Euro 3 performance. SAE Technical Paper 012603.

Kim J-H, Lee J-H, Seo J-M, Bauman JL, Hornback LR, Joo H-S, Lindeman DD [2008]. Test development and understanding of filter ring-off-cracks in catalyzed silicon carbide (SiC) diesel particulate filter system design. SAE Technical Paper 2008-01-0765.

Kittelson DB [1998]. Engines and nanoparticles: a review. J Aerosol Sci *29*:575–588.

Kittelson DB, Pipho MJ, Ambs,JL, Siegla DC [1986]. Particle concentrations in a diesel cylinder: comparison of theory and experiment. SAE Technical Paper 861569.

Kittelson DB, Watts WF, Johnson JP, Rowntree C, Payne M, Goodier S, Warrens C, Preston H, Zink U, Ortiz M, Goesmann C, Twigg MV, Walker AP, Caldow R [2006]. On-road evaluation of two diesel exhaust aftertreatment devices. J Aerosol Sci 37, 1:140–1151.

Kittelson DB, Watts WF, Johnson JP, Thorne C, Higham C, Payne M, Goodier S, Warrens C, Preston H, Zink U, Pickles D, Goersmann C, Twigg MV, Walker AP, Boddy R [2008]. Effect of fuel and lube oil sulfur on the performance of a diesel exhaust gas continuously regenerating trap. Env Sci Tech 42(24):9276–9282.

Klein H, Lox E, Kreuzer T, Kawanami M, Ried T, Bächamann K [1998]. Diesel particulate emissions of passenger cars–new insights into structural changes during the process of exhaust aftertreatment using diesel oxidation catalysts. SAE Technical Paper 980196.

Koebel, M, Elsener M, Madia G [2001]. Recent advances in the development of urea-SCR for automotive applications. SAE Technical Paper 013625.

Koebel M, Madia G, Elsener M [2002]. Selective catalytic reduction of NO and NO2 at low temperatures. Catal Today 73:239–247.

Konstandopoulos AG, Papaioannou E [2008]. Update on the science and technology of diesel particulate filters. KONA Powder Part J 26:36–65.

Konstandopoulos AG, Vlachos N, Stavropoulos I, Skopa S, Schumacher U, Woiki D, Frey M [2005]. Study of a sintered metal diesel particulate trap. SAE Technical Paper 2005-01-0968.

Kook S, Bae C, Miles PC, Choi D, Picket LM [2005]. The influence of charge dilution and injection timing on low-temperature diesel combustion and emissions. SAE Technical Paper 2005-01-3837.

Kwon YK, Mann N, Rickeard DJ, Haugland R, Ulvund KA, Kvinge F, Wilson G [2001]. Fuel effects on diesel emissions—a new understanding. SAE Technical Paper 2001-01-3522.

Ladommatos N, Abdelhalim SM, Zhao H, Hu Z [1996a]. The dilution, chemical and thermal effects of exhaust gas recirculation on diesel engine emissions—part 1: effect of reducing inlet charge oxygen. SAE Technical Paper 961165.

Ladommatos N, Abdelhalim SM, Zhao H, Hu Z [1996b]. The dilution, chemical and thermal effects of exhaust gas recirculation on diesel engine emissions—part 2: effects of carbon dioxide. SAE Technical Paper 961167.

Ladommatos N, Abdelhalim SM, Zhao H, Hu Z [1997a]. The dilution, chemical and thermal effects of exhaust gas recirculation on diesel engine emissions—part 3: effects of water vapor. SAE Technical Paper 971659.

Ladommatos N, Abdelhalim SM, Zhao H, Hu Z [1997b]. The dilution, chemical and thermal effects of exhaust gas recirculation on diesel engine emissions—part 4: effects of carbon dioxide and water vapor. SAE paper 971660.

Lee KO, Song J [2007]. Morphological examination of nano-particles derived from combustion of cerium fuel-borne catalyst doped with diesel fuel. SAE Technical Paper 2007-01-1943.

Leedham A, Caprotti R, Graupner O, Klaua T [2004]. Impact of fuel additives on diesel deposits. SAE Technical Paper 2004-01-2935.

Lemaire J [1999]. Eolys™ fuel borne catalyst for diesel particulate abatement: a key component of an integrated system. In: DieselNet Technology Guide. [http://www.dieselnetl.com/papaers/9909rhodia/].

Leyrer J, Lox ES, Ostgathe K, Strehlau W, Kreuzer T, Garr G [1966]. Advanced studies on diesel aftertreatment catalysts for passenger cars. SAE Technical Paper 960133.

Liu Y-Y, Lin T-C, Wang Y-J, Ho W-L [2009a]. Carbonyl compounds and toxicity assessments of emissions from a diesel engine running on biodiesels. J Air Waste Manage Assoc 59:163–171.

Liu ZG, Berg DR, Schaurer JJ [2008]. Detailed effects of a diesel particulate filter on the reduction of chemical species emissions. SAE Technical Paper 2008-01-0333.

Liu ZG, Berg DR, Swor TA, Schauer JJ, Zielinska B [2009b]. A study of the emissions of chemical species from heavy-duty diesel engines and the effects of modern aftertreatment technology. SAE Technical Paper 2009-01-1084.

Lorentzou S, Pagkoura C, Konstandopoulos AG, Boettcher J [2008]. Advanced catalyst coatings for diesel particulate filters. SAE Technical Paper 2008-01-0483.

Lubrizol Corporation [2011]. Frequently asked questions—engine oil additives. [http://www.lubrizol.com/EngineOilAdditives/CJ4Specification/faq.html].

Macián V, Tormos B, Olmeda P, Montoro L [2003]. Analytical approach to wear rate determination for internal combustion engine condition monitoring based on oil analysis. Tribol Int 36:771–776.

Madia G, Elsener M, Koebel M, Raimondi F, Wokaun A [2002]. Thermal stability of vanadia-tungsta-titania catalysts in the SCR process. Appl Catal B - Environ 39:181–190.

Majewski AW [2003]. Filters with fuel additives. In: DieselNet Technology Guide. [http://www.dieselnetl.com/tech/dpf_add.html#peugeot].

Majewski AW [2009a]. Diesel oxidation catalyst. In: DieselNet Technology Guide. [http://www.dieselnet.com/tech/cat_doc.htm].

Majewski AW [2009b]. Filters regeneration by fuel combustion. In: DieselNet Technology Guide. [http://www.dieselnetl.com/tech/dpf_sys_fuel.html#comm].

Majewski WA, Jääskeläinen H [2010]. Engine design for low emissions. In: DieselNet Technology Guide. [http://www.dieselnet.com/tech/engine_design.html].

Majewski AW, Khair MK [2006a]. Diesel emissions and their control. Warrendale, PA: SAE International, pp. 121–145.

Majewski AW, Khair MK [2006b]. Diesel emissions and their control. Warrendale, PA: SAE International, pp. 329–353.

Majewski AW, Khair MK [2006c]. Diesel emissions and their control. Warrendale, PA: SAE International, pp. 35–50.

Majewski AW, Ambs JL, Bickel K [1995]. Nitrogen oxides reactions in diesel oxidation catalyst. SAE Technical Paper 950374.

126

Maly RR, Schaefer V, Hass H, Cahill GF, Rouveirolles P, Röj A, Wegener R, Montagne X, Di Pancrazio A, Kashdar J [2007]. Optimal diesel fuel for future clean diesel engines. SAE Technical Paper 2007-01-0035.

Maricq M, Chase RE, Podsiadlik DH, Siegel WO, Kaiser EW [1998]. The effects of dimethoxy methane additive on diesel vehicle particulate emissions. SAE Technical Paper 982572.

Mathur A, Chavan S [2008]. Exhaust filtration: fibre based solutions in diesel exhaust filtration. Filtration + Separation, June.

Mathur S, Johnson JH, Naber JD, Bagley ST, Shende AS [2008]. Experimental studies of an advanced ceramic diesel particulate filter. SAE Technical Paper 2008-01-0622.

Mayer A [1998]. Curtailing emissions of diesel engines in tunnel sites. In: DieselNet Technical Report. [http://www.dieselnet.com/papers/9804mayer/index.html].

Mayer A [2008a]. Technical objectives. In: Mayer A, ed. Particle filter retrofit for all diesel engines. Brill Ulrich, Haus der Technik Fachbuch Band 97, pp 26–48.

Mayer A [2008b]. Typical failures and their causes. In: Mayer A, ed. Particle filter retrofit for all diesel engines. Brill Ulrich, Haus der Technik Fachbuch Band 97, pp. 289–305.

Mayer A [2011]. What the tests tell us. In: Machinery Lubrication. [http://ftp.machinerylubrication.com/Read/873/oil-tests].

Mayer A, Czerwiski J, Comte P, Jaussi F [2009]. Properties of partial-flow and coarse pore deep bed filters proposed to reduce particle emissions of vehicle engines. SAE Technical Paper 2009-01-1087.

Mayer A, Evéquoz R, Wyser-Heusi M, Czerwinski J, Matter U, Graf P [2000]. Particulate traps used in city-busses in Switzerland. SAE Technical Paper 2000-01-1927.

Mayer A, Heeb N, Czerwinski J, Wyser M [2003]. Secondary emissions from catalytic active particle filter systems. SAE Technical Paper 2003-01-0291.

Mayer A, Matter U, Scheidegger G, Czerwinski J, Wyser M, Kieser D, and Weidhofer J [1999]. Particulate traps for retrofitting construction site engines. VERT: Final measurements and implementation. SAE Technical Paper 1999-01-0116.

Mayer A, Ulrich A, Heeb NV, Czerwinski J, Neubert T [2008]. Particle filter properties after 2000 hours real world operation. SAE Technical Paper 2008-01-0332.

McClure BT [1992]. Laboratory evaluation of the effectiveness of oxidation catalytic converters. U.S. Department of the Interior, Bureau of Mines, Information Circular 9324, pp. 60–66.

McClure BT, Baumgard KJ, Watts WF [1988]. Effectiveness of catalytic converters on diesel engines used in underground mining. U.S. Department of the Interior, Bureau of Mines, Information Circular 9197.

McCormick R [2005]. Effects of biodiesel on NOX emissions. Unpublished presentation at the Air Resources Board Biodiesel Workshop, National Renewable Energy Laboratory, Golden, CO. [http://www.nrel.gov/vehiclesandfuels/npbf/pdfs/38296.pdf].

McCormick RL [2007]. The impact of biodiesel on pollutant emissions and public health. Inhal Toxicol *19*:1033–1039

McDonald JF, Cantrell BK, Watts WF, Bickel KL [1997]. Evaluation of a soybean oil based diesel fuel in an underground gold mine. CIM Bulletin *91*:91–95.

McDonald JF, Purcell DL, McClure BT, Kittelson DB [1995]. Emissions characteristics of soy methyl ester fuels in an IDI compressions ignition engine. SAE Technical Paper 950400.

McGinn S [1999]. Maintenance guidelines and best practices for diesel engines. Final report. Diesel Emissions Evaluation Program (DEEP). [http://www.deep.org/research.html].

McGinn S [2000]. The relationship between diesel engine maintenance and exhaust emissions. Final report. Diesel Emissions Evaluation Program (DEEP).

McGinn S, Ellington R, Penney J, Graham C, Huzij B [2010]. Diesel emissions: mechanics' maintenance manual. In: Diesel Emissions Evaluation Program. [http://www.deep.org/reports/mechanicsman.pdf].

McGinn S, Grenier M, Gangal M, Rubeli B, Bugarski A, Schnakenberg G, Johnson R, Petrie D, Crowther G, Penney J [2004]. Noranda Inc. – Brunswick Mine diesel particulate filter field study. Final report of investigation to the diesel emissions evaluation program. October. [http://www.deep.org/reports/nordpf_final.pdf].

Miller AL, Ahlstrand GG, Kittelson DB, Zachariah MR [2007a]. The fate of metal (Fe) during diesel combustion: morphology, chemistry, and formation pathways of nanoparticles. Combust Flame *149*(1-2):129–143.

Miller AL, Habjan MC, Park K [2007b]. Real-time estimation of elemental carbon emitted from diesel engine. Env Sci Tech *41*:5783–5788.

Miller TC, Jackson MA, Brown AJ, Wong VW [1997]. Characterization and assessment of diesel engine particulate emissions reduction via lube-oil consumption control. In: Proceedings of the 1997 Diesel Engine Emissions Reduction Workshop. Office of Transportation Technologies, U.S. Department of Energy, Publication No. CONF-970799, pp. 423–432.

Miller WR, Klein J, Mueller R, Doelling W, Zuerbig J [2000]. The development of urea-SCR technology for US heavy duty trucks. SAE Technical Paper 010190.

Mischler S, Volkwein J [2005]. Differential pressure as a measure of particulate matter emissions from diesel engines. Env Sci Tech *39*(7):2255–2261.

Moneyem A, Van Gerpen JH [2001]. The effects of biodiesel oxidation on engine performance and emissions. Biomass Bioenergy *20*:317–325.

Morawska L, Hofman W, Hitchins-Loveday J, Swanson C, Mengersten K [2005]. Experimental study of the deposition of combustion aerosols in the human respiratory tract. Aerosol Sci *36*:939–957.

Morgensen G, Johansen K, Karlsson HL [2009]. Regulated and NO2 emissions from a Euro 4 passenger car with catalyzed DPFs. SAE Technical Paper 2009-01-1083.

MSHA [2002]. Potential health hazard caused by platinum-based catalyzed diesel particulate matter exhaust filters. U.S. Department of Labor, Mine Safety and Health Administration,

Program Information Bulletin No. P02-4.
[http://www.msha.gov/regs/complian/PIB/2002/pib02-04.htm].

MSHA [2005]. Regulatory economics analysis for diesel particulate matter exposure of underground metal and nonmetal miners. U.S. Department of Labor, Mine Safety and Health Administration. [http://www.msha.gov/REGS/REA/05-10276 10681(Diesel).pdf].

MSHA [2009a]. Approved permissible and nonpermissible engines. U.S. Department of Labor, Mine Safety and Health Administration.

MSHA [2009b]. Diesel particulate matter (DPM) control technologies. U.S. Department of Labor, Mine Safety and Health Administration. [http://www.msha.gov/01-995/Coal/DPM-FilterEfflist.pdf].

MSHA [2009c]. National Diesel Inventory. U.S. Department of Labor, Mine Safety and Health Administration.
[https://lakegovprod2.msha.gov/DieselInventory/ViewDieselInventoryExternal.aspx].

MSHA [2009d]. Permissible power packages approved under Part 7. U.S. Department of Labor, Mine Safety and Health Administration, Approval and Certification Center.
[http://www.msha.gov/TECHSUPP/ACC/lists/07pwrpkg.pdf].

MSHA [2009e]. Scrubber overflow port used on Atlas Copco Incorporated permissible diesel engine power packages. U.S. Department of Labor, Mine Safety and Health Administration, Program Information Bulletin (PIB) P09-29.

MSHA [2009f]. Information on use of biodiesel fuel in underground diesel-powered equipment; availability of report. U.S. Department of Labor, Mine Safety and Health Administration. Program Information bulletin No. P09-38.
[https://lakegovprod2.msha.gov/ReportView.aspx?ReportCategory=EngineAppNumbers].

MSHA [2010]. Metal and nonmetal diesel particulate filter selection guide. U.S. Department of Labor, Mine Safety and Health Administration.
[www.msha.gov/nioshmnmfilterselectionguide/dpmfilterguide.htm].

Mucha P, Gaiser G, Kuehnkle M [2008]. Corrugated cross flow catalyst with permeable walls. SAE Technical Paper 2008-01-0809.

Nadeem M, Rangkuti C, Anuar K, Haq MRU, Tan IB, Shah SS [2006]. Diesel engine performance and emission evaluation using emulsified fuels stabilized by conventional and gemini surfactants. J Fuel 85(14–15):2111–2119.

Naschke W, Seguelong T, Rocher L [2008]. Fuel borne catalyst (FBC) for particulate trap regeneration. In: Mayer A, ed. Particle filter retrofit for all diesel engines. Brill Ulrich, Haus der Technik Fachbuch Band 97.

NBAC [2011]. BQ-9000® - The National Biodiesel Accreditation Program. National Biodiesel Accreditation Commission. [http://www.bq-9000.org/].

NBB [2009]. Biodiesel usage checklist. National Biodiesel Board.
[http://www.biodiesel.org/pdf_files/fuelfactsheets/bdusage.pdf].

Nelson CR [2009]. Heavy truck engine program; final report, reporting period: July 2000–September 2006. Columbus, IN: Cummins, Inc, US DOE contract no. DE-FC26-00OR22804. [http://www.osti.gov/bridge/servlets/purl/945214-FtCsq1/945214.pdf].

Nikanjam M [1993]. Development of the first CARB certified California additive diesel fuel. SAE Technical Paper 930728.

NIOSH [2002]. Review of technologies available to the underground mining industry for control of diesel emissions. By Schnakenberg G, Bugarski A. Pittsburgh, PA: U.S. Department of Health and Human Services, Centers for Disease Control and Prevention, National Institute for Occupational Safety and Health, DHHS (NIOSH) Information Circular 9462. [http://www.cdc.gov/niosh/mining/pubs/pubreference/outputid28.htm].

NIOSH [2005]. NIOSH pocket guide to chemical hazards. In: NIOSH Occupational Safety and Health Guidelines for Chemical Hazards. Cincinnati, OH: U.S. Department of Health and Human Services, Public Health Service, Centers for Disease Control, National Institute for Occupational Safety and Health, DHHS (NIOSH) Publication No. 2005-149.

NIOSH [2006a]. Effectiveness of selected diesel particulate matter control technologies for underground mining applications: isolated zone study, 2003. By Bugarski AD, Schnakenberg GH, Noll JD, Mischler SE, Patts LD, Hummer JA, Vanderslice SE. U.S. Department of Health and Human Services, Centers for Disease Control and Prevention, National Institute for Occupational Safety and Health, DHHS (NIOSH) Publication No. 2006-126, Report of Investigations 9667.

NIOSH [2006b]. Effectiveness of selected diesel particulate matter control technologies for underground mining applications: isolated zone study, 2004. By Bugarski AD, Schnakenberg GH, Mischler SE; Noll JD, Patts LD, Hummer JA. U.S. Department of Health and Human Services, Centers for Disease Control and Prevention, National Institute for Occupational Safety and Health, DHHS (NIOSH) Pub. No. 2006-138, Report of Investigations 9668.

Noll JD, Patts L [2009]. Field evaluation of a passive diesel particulate filter at a limestone mine. Min Eng, April.

Noll JD, Bugarski AD, Patts LD, Mischler SE, McWilliams L [2007]. Relationship between elemental carbon, total carbon, and diesel particulate matter in several underground metal/nonmetal mines. Env Sci Tech 41(3):710–716.

Noll JD, Mischler SE, Patts LD, Schnakenberg GH, Bugarski AD, Timko RJ, Love G [2006]. The effects of water emulsified fuel on diesel particulate matter concentrations in underground mines. In: Mutmansky JM, Ramani RV, eds. Proceedings of the 11th U.S./North American Mine Ventilation Symposium. London: Taylor & Francis Group, pp. 159–164.

Noria Corporation [2004].Bulk lubricant storage. In: Machinery Lubrication Online. [http://www.machinerylubrication.com/Read/907/bulk-lubricant-storage].

NREL [2009]. Biodiesel handling and use guide. 4th ed. National Renewable Energy Laboratory, NREL/TP-540-43672.

O'Sullivan R, Stevenson J, Walker A, Werth P [2004]. Low NO2 CRT particulate filter systems for diesel engine exhaust in mining applications. Proceeding of the 10th Mining Diesel Emissions Conference. Ottawa, Ontario, Canada: Mining Diesel Emissions Council.

Ogawa T, Kajiya S, Tajima I, Yamamoto M, Okada M [2008]. Analysis of oxidative deterioration of biodiesel fuel. SAE Technical Paper 2008-01-2502.

Owen K, Coley T [1995a]. Future trends and alternative fuels. In: Automotive fuels reference book. 2nd rev. ed. of Automotive fuels handbook [1990]. Warrendale, PA: Society of Automotive Engineers, pp. 529–549.

Owen K, Coley T [1995b]. Other diesel specification and non-specification properties. In: Automotive fuels reference book. 2nd rev. ed. of Automotive fuels handbook [1990]. Warrendale, PA: Society of Automotive Engineers, pp. 473–501.

PADEP [2009]. Safety laws of Pennsylvania for underground bituminous coal mines. PA Department of Environmental Protection, Act 55, Sb 949 Session of 2008.

Park JH, Park HJ, Baik JH, Nam IS, Shin CH, Lee JH, Cho BK, Oh SH [2006]. Hydrothermal stability of CuZSM5 catalyst in reducing NO by NH3 for the urea selective catalytic reduction process. J Catal *240*:47–57.

Paterson C, Van Dyne E, Stanglmaier R [2007]. Development of a diesel particulate filter burner control system for active trap regeneration. SAE Technical Paper 2007-01-1064.

Petroleum Technologies Group [2011]. How to read your Oil Analysis Report. Grand Rapids, MI: Petroleum Technologies Group. [http://www.oil-lab.com/downloads/ How_to_Read_Oil_Analysis_Reports.pdf].

Pierson WR, Brachaczek WW [1983] Particulate matter associated with vehicles on the road. Aerosol Sci Tech *2*:1–40.

Pietikäinen M, Oravisjäri K, Rautio A, Voutilainen A, Ruuskanen J, Keiski RL [2009]. Exposure assessment of particles of diesel and natural gas fuelled buses in silicon. Sci Total Environ *408*:163–168.

Plumley MJ [2005]. Lubricant oil consumption effects on diesel exhaust ash emissions using a sulfur dioxide trace technique and thermogravimetry [Thesis]. Cambridge, MA: Massachusetts Institute of Technology, Department of Ocean Engineering, Department of Mechanical Engineering. [http://dspace.mit.edu/handle/1721.1/33574].

Purcell DJ, McClure BT, McDonald J, Basu HN [1996]. Transient testing of soy methyl ester fuels in an indirect injection, compression ignition engine. J Am Oil Chem Soc *73*:381–388.

Rembor H-J [2007]. Diesel particle filters with active regeneration in mining—practical experiences from different mines. In: Proceedings of the 13th Mining Diesel Emissions Conference (MDEC), Ottawa, Ontario, Canada: Mining Diesel Emissions Council.

Rembor H-J [2008]. Regeneration with burner system. In: Mayer A, ed. Particle filter retrofit for all diesel engines. Brill Ulrich, Haus der Technik Fachbuch Band 97.

Rice M, Kramer J, Muller R, Muller-Hass K [2008]. Development of an integrated NOX and PM reduction aftertreatment system: SCR for advanced diesel engines. SAE Technical Paper 2008-01-1321.

Richards P, Chadderton J [2003]. Significant reduction in NO_2 and PM emissions through the careful design of DPF system. In: Proceedings of the 9th Mining Diesel Emissions Conference. Ottawa, Ontario, Canada: Mining Diesel Emissions Council.

Richards P, Vincent MW, Johansen K, Mogensen G [2006]. Metal emissions, NO2, and HC reductions from a base metal catalyzed DPF/FBC system. SAE Technical Paper 2006-01-0420.

Roels P, Sledsens Y, Verhelst S, Sierens R [2009]. Reducing engine-out emissions for medium high speed diesel engines: influence of injection parameters. SAE Technical Paper 2009-01-1437.

Rubeli B, Gangal M, Butler K, Alder W [2004]. Evaluation of the concentration of light-duty vehicle to the underground atmosphere diesel emissions burden. In: Ganguli R, Bandopadhyay S, eds. Proceedings of the 10th U.S./North American Mine Ventilation Symposium. Leiden, Netherlands: Balkema.

SAE [1996]. J1667 Recommended practice, snap acceleration smoke test procedure for heavy-duty powered vehicles. Society of Automotive Engineers (SAE).

Saelhoff GR [2010]. Implementing the new EU emission regulations: the challenge facing mining equipment manufacturers. Mining Reporter *1*: 11–16.

Samec N, Kegl B, Dibble RW [2002]. Numerical and experimental study of water/oil emulsified fuel combustion in a diesel engine. J Fuel *81*(16):2035–2044.

Sappok AG, Wong VW [2008]. Impact of biodiesel on ash emissions and lubricant properties affecting fuel economy and engine wear: comparison with conventional diesel fuel. SAE Technical Paper 2008-01-1395.

Schaefer M, Hofmann L, Girot P, Rohe R [2009]. Investigation of NOX – and PM-reduction by a combination of SCR-catalyst and diesel particulate filter for heavy-duty diesel engine. SAE Technical Paper 2009-01-0912.

Schmidt N, Root T, Wirojsakunchai E, Schroeder E, Kolodziej C, Foster DE, Suga T, Kawai T [2007]. Detailed diesel exhaust particulate characterization and DPF regeneration behavior measurements for two different regeneration systems. SAE Technical Paper 2007-01-1063.

Schnakenberg GH Jr. [2003]. Diesel particulate filter selection guide or diesel-powered equipment in metal and nonmetal mines. In: Mine Safety and Health Administration. [http://www.msha.gov/nioshmnmfilterselectionguide/MNM_DPF_Questions.htm].

Schönborn A, Ladommatos N, Williams J, Allan R, Rogerson J [2009]. The influence of molecular structure of fatty acid monoalkyl esters on diesel combustion. Combust Flame *156*:1396–1412.

Schrewe K [2008]. Electrical heating and ignition procedure. In: Mayer A, ed. Particle filter retrofit for all diesel engines. Brill Ulrich, Haus der Technik Fachbuch Band 97, pp. 176–185.

Schrewe K, Belcour C, Richards PJ [2008]. A study of the parameters ensuring reliable regeneration of a sintered metal particulate filter using a fuel borne catalyst. SAE Technical Paper 2008-01-2485.

Schultz MJ, Fields KG, Atchison DJ, Gerbec EJ, Haney RA, Tomko DM, Love G, Kuhnhein G [2004]. Using bio-diesel fuels to reduce DPM concentrations; DPM results using various blends of bio-diesel fuel mixtures in a stone mine. In: Ganguli R, Bandopadhyay S, eds. Proceedings of the 10th U.S./North American Mine Ventilation Symposium. Leiden, Netherlands: Balkema.

Seguelong T, Quigley M [2002]. Series application of a diesel particulate filter with a ceria-based, fuel-borne catalyst: preliminary conclusions after one year of service. SAE Technical Paper 2002-01-0436.

Seiler V, Boeckmann E, Eilts P [2008]. Performance of undamaged and damaged diesel particulate filters. SAE Technical Paper 2008-01-0335.

Setten van BAAL, Makkee M, Moulijn JA. [2001]. Science and technology of catalytic diesel particulate filter. Catal Rev *43*(4):489–564.

Shah SD, Cocker DR III, Johnson KC, Lee JM, Soriano BL, Miller JW [2006]. Emissions of regulated pollutants from in-use diesel back-up generators. Atmos Environ *40*:4199–4209.

Shah SD, Cocker DR III, Johnson KC, Lee JM, Soriano BL, Miller JW [2007]. Reduction of particulate matter emissions from diesel backup generators equipped with four different aftertreatment devices. Env Sci Tech *41*:5070–5076.

Shell [2011]. Oil condition monitoring report. [http://www-static.shell.com/static/can-en/downloads/shell_for_businesses/oils_lubricants/8-08.pdf].

Shibata Y, Koseki H, Shimizu O [2008]. Spontaneous ignition of biodiesel: a potential fire risk. Therm Sci *12*(2):159–158.

Skillas G, Qian Z, Baltensperger U, Matter U, Burtscher H [2000]. The influence of additives on the size distribution and composition of particles produced by diesel engines. Combust Sci Tech *154*:259–273.

Spears, MW [1997]. An emissions-assisted maintenance procedure for diesel-powered equipment. Minneapolis, MN: University of Minnesota, Center for Diesel Research. National Institute for Occupational Safety and Health (NIOSH), Contract No. USDI/1432 CO369004 [www.cdc.gov/niosh/mining/topics/diesel/eamp/eamp.htm].

Stachulak JS, Conard BR, Bugarski AD, Schnakenberg GH Jr [2005]. Long-term evaluation of diesel particulate filter systems at Inco's Stobie Mine. In: Gillies ADS, ed. Proceedings of the 8th International Mine Ventilation Congress. Carlton, Victoria, Australia: Australian Institute of Mining and Metallurgy.

Stachulak JS, Conard BR, Bugarski AD, Schnakenberg GH Jr [2006]. DEEP project on evaluation of diesel particulate filters at Inco's Stobie Mine. In: Mutmansky JM, Ramani RV, eds. Proceedings of the 11th U.S./North American Mine Ventilation Symposium. London: Taylor & Francis Group.

Stackpole RP II [2009]. Diesel fuel testing on an Isuzu 4JG1T engine with and without a diesel oxidation catalyst. U.S. Department of Labor, Mine Safety and Health Administration. Final Report. [http://www.msha.gov/REGS/COMPLIAN/Pib/2009/P09-38MSHAFuelTestReport.pdf].

Steigert S [2008]. Filter media for the retrofitting. In: Mayer A, ed. Particle filter retrofit for all diesel engines. Brill Ulrich, Haus der Technik Fachbuch Band 97.

Stirling E [2010]. Unpublished presentation at the Advanced Diesel Engine and Exhaust Technologies for Underground Coal and Metal/Nonmetal Mining Workshop. Pittsburgh, PA, April 14.

Stroia BJ, Currier NW, Li J, England RD, Bush JW, Hess H [2008]. Critical performance and durability parameters of an integrated aftertreatment system used to meet 2007 Tier II emissions standards. SAE Technical Paper 2008-01-0769.

Strong C, Erickson C, Shukla D [2004]. Evaluation of biodiesel fuel: Literature review. Report No. FHWA/MT-04-001/8117-20 for the Montana Department of Transportation. [http://thepeoplesway.com/research/docs/research_proj/biodiesel/final_report.pdf].

Sullivan JA, Doherty JA [2005]. NH3 and urea in the selective catalytic reduction of NOX over oxide-supported copper catalysts. Appl Catal B - Environ 55:185–194.

Suresh A, Yezerets A, Currier N, Clerc J [2008]. Diesel particulate filter system—effect of critical variables on regeneration strategy development and optimization. SAE Technical Paper 2008-01-0329.

Swanson KJ, Madden MC, Ghio AJ [2007]. Biodiesel exhaust: the need for health effects research. Environ Health Perspect 115(41):496–499.

Tomko DM, Stackpole RP, Findlay CD, Pomroy WH [2010]. Metal/nonmetal diesel particulate matter rule. In: Hardcastle S, McKinnon DL, eds. Proceedings of the 13th U.S./North American Mine Ventilation Symposium. Sudbury, ON, Canada: MIRARCO—Mining Innovation, pp. 143–148.

Truex, TJ [1994]. Lean NOX catalysts. SAE Catalysts and Emissions Control TOPTEC.

Tsolakis A [2006]. Effects on particle size distribution from the diesel engine operating on RME-biodiesel with EGR. Energy Fuels 20:1418–1424.

Ullman TL, Hare CT [1984]. Influence of maladjustment on emissions from two heavy-duty diesel bus engines. SAE Technical Paper 840416.

Ullman TL, Spreen KB, Mason RL [1994]. Effects of Cetane number, Cetane improver, aromatics, and oxygenates on 1994 heavy-duty diesel engine emissions. SAE Technical Paper 941020.

Ulrich A, Wichser A [2003]. Analysis of additive metals in fuel and emission aerosols of diesel vehicles with and without particle traps. Anal Bioanal Chem 377:71–81.

Vaaraslahti K, Risimäki J, Virtanen A, Keskinen J, Giechaskiel B, Solla A [2006]. Effects of oxidation catalyst on diesel soot particles. Env Sci Tech 40:4776–4781.

Vaaraslahti K, Virtanen A, Ristimaki J, Keskinen J [2004]. Nucleation mode formation in heavy-duty diesel exhaust with and without a particle filter. Env Sci Tech 38:4884–4890.

Vanegas A, Won H, Peters N [2009]. Influence of the nozzle spray angle on pollutant formation and combustion efficiency for a PCCI diesel engine. SAE Technical Paper 2009-01-1445.

Verbeek RP, Kooter IM, Houtzager MMG, van Vugt MATM, Krul CAM, Kadijk G [2009]. Health effects of biofuels and diesel particulate filter with a Euro III truck engine. Presented at the 13th ETH Conference on Combustion Generated Nanoparticles, Zurich, Switzerland, June.

Vouitsis E, Ntziachristos L, Samaras Z, Chrysikou L, Samara C, Miltsios G [2007]. Effect of lube oil on the physicochemical characteristics of particulate matter emitted from a Euro 4 light-duty diesel vehicle. SAE Technical Paper 2007-24-0110.

Walker AP, Allansson R, Blakeman PG, Cooper BJ, Hess H, Silcock PJ [2002]. Optimizing the low temperature performance and regeneration efficiency of the continuously regenerating diesel particulate filter (Cr-Dpf) system. SAE Technical Paper 2002-01-0428.

Warner JR, Johnson JH, Bagley ST, Huynh CT [2003]. Effects of catalyzed particulate filter on emissions from a diesel engine: chemical characterization data and particulate emissions measured with thermal optical and gravimetrical methods. SAE Technical Paper 2003-01-0049.

Watson SAG, Wong VW [2008]. The effects of fuel dilution with biodiesel on lubricant acidity, oxidation and corrosion—a study with CJ-4 and CI-4 PLUS lubricants. Presented at the 2008 Diesel Engine-Efficiency and Emissions Research (DEER) Conference, August 7. [http://www1.eere.energy.gov/vehiclesandfuels/pdfs/deer_2008/session10/deer08_watson.pdf].

Watts WF, Cantrell BK, Bickel KL, Olson KS, Rubow KL, Baz-Dreasch JJ, Carlson DH [1995]. In-mine evaluation of catalyzed diesel particulate filters used at two underground metal mines. U.S. Department of the Interior, Bureau of Mines, Report of Investigation 9571.

Watts WF Jr, Spears M, Johnson J [1998]. Evaluation of biodiesel fuel and oxidation catalyst in an underground mine. Revised final report. Diesel Emissions Evaluation Program (DEEP). [http://www.deep.org/reports/inco_bio.pdf].

Waytulonis, R. [1987]. An overview of the effects of diesel engine maintenance on emissions and performance. In: Diesels in underground mines; Proceedings: Bureau of Mines Technology Transfer Seminar. Minneapolis, MN: U.S. Department of the Interior, Bureau of Mines, Information Circular 9141.

Weltens H, Vogel HT [2008]. Design of diesel particulate systems for commercial vehicles and off-road applications. In: Mayer A, ed. Particle filter retrofit for all diesel engines. Brill Ulrich, Haus der Technik Fachbuch Band 97.

Whitacre S,Tsai H, Orban J [2010]. Lubricant basestock and additive effects on diesel engine emissions. In: U.S. Department of Energy. [http://www.afdc.energy.gov/afdc/pdfs/32842.pdf].

Williams G, Hartman FW, Mackey GR [1973]. Diesel smoke analysis on a chassis dynamometer. SAE Technical Paper 730660.

Williams A, McCormick RL, Hayes R, Ireland J [2006a]. Biodiesel effects on diesel particle filter performance. National Renewable Energy Laboratory, Milestone Report NREL/TP-540-39606.

Williams A, McCormick RL, Hayes R, Ireland J, Fang HL [2006b]. Effects of biodiesel on diesel particulate filter performance. SAE Technical Paper 2006-01-3280.

WRAP [2005]. Off-road diesel retrofit guidance document. In: Western Regional Air Partnership. [http://www.wrapair.org/forums/msf/projects/offroad_diesel_retrofit/V1-S1_Final_11-18-05.pdf].

135

WVDEC [2004]. Rules for operating diesel equipment in underground mines in West Virginia. West Virginia Diesel Equipment Commission, Title 196-1.

Yang J, Stewart M, Maupin G, Herling D, Zelenyuk A [2009]. Single wall diesel particulate filter (DPF) filtration efficiency studies using laboratory generated particles. Chem Eng Sci *64*:1625–1634.

Yao L, Ba G, Kim W, Reck A [2008]. Continuously regenerating particulate matter Metalit (PM MetalitTM) in LDV and HDV retrofit application. SAE Technical Paper 2008-01-1547.

Yilmaz E [2003]. Sources and characteristics of oil consumption in a spark-ignition engine [Dissertation]. Cambridge, MA: Massachusetts Institute of Technology, Department of Mechanical Engineering.

Yoon Y-H, Lee D-S, Blakeman PG, Matsuda K, Lee D-E, Park M-H [2009]. Development and in-field application of a new type PF partial filter system for diesel retrofit. SAE Technical Paper 2009-01-1264.

Yuan C-S, Lin H-Y, Lee W-J, Lin Y-C, Wu T-S, Chen K-F [2007]. A new alternative fuel for reduction of polycyclic aromatic hydrocarbon and particulate matter emissions from diesel engines. J Air Waste Manage Assoc *57*:465–471.

Zannis TC, Hountalas DT, Papagiannakis RG, Levendis YA [2008]. Effects of fuel chemical structure and properties on diesel engine performance and pollutant emissions: review of the results of four European research programs. SAE Technical Paper 2008-01-0838.

Zarling D, Waytulonis B, Kittelson D [2005]. Testing a low NO_2 CRT DPF system. Proceeding of the 11th Mining Diesel Emissions Conference. Ottawa, Ontario, Canada: Mining Diesel Emissions Council.

Zelenka P, Reczek W, Mustel W, Rouveirolles P [1998]. Towards securing the particulate trap regeneration: a system combining a sintered metal filter and cerium fuel additive. SAE Technical Paper 982598.

Zelenka P, Telford C, Pye D, Birkby N [2002]. Development of a full-flow burner DPF system for heavy-duty diesel engines. SAE Technical Paper 2002-01-2787.

6.3 Section 3

30 CFR 11. Code of Federal Regulations. Washington, DC: U.S. Government Printing Office, Office of the Federal Register.

30 CFR 57.5005 Control of exposure to airborne contaminants. Code of Federal regulations. Washington, DC: U.S. Government Printing Office, Office of the Federal Register.

30 CFR 57.5060. Limit on exposure to diesel particulate matter. Safety and health standards. Underground metal and nonmetal mines. Code of Federal Regulations. Washington, DC: U.S. Government Printing Office, Office of the Federal Register.

30 CFR 70.300. Respiratory equipment; respirable dust. Mandatory health standards. Underground coal mines. Code of Federal Regulations. Washington, DC: U.S. Government Printing Office, Office of the Federal Register.

30 CFR 70.305. Respiratory equipment; gas, dusts, fumes, or mists. Mandatory health standards. Underground coal mines. Code of Federal Regulations. Washington, DC: U.S. Government Printing Office, Office of the Federal Register.

30 CFR 72.710. Selection, fit, use, and maintenance of approved respirators. Health standards for coal mines. Code of Federal Regulations. Washington, DC: U.S. Government Printing Office, Office of the Federal Register.

30 CFR 75.325. Air quantity. Mandatory safety standards. Underground coal mines. Code of Federal Regulations. Washington, DC: U.S. Government Printing Office, Office of the Federal Register.

42 CFR 84. Approval of respiratory protective devices. Code of Federal Regulations. Washington, DC: U.S. Government Printing Office, Office of the Federal Register.

59 Fed. Reg. 54242 [1994]. Centers for Disease Control and Prevention: Guidelines for preventing the transmission of mycobacterium tuberculosis in health-care facilities. Code of Federal Regulations. Washington, DC: U.S. Government Printing Office, Office of the Federal Register.

66 Fed. Reg. 27864 [2001]. Mine Safety and Health Administration: 30 CFR Part 72. Diesel particulate matter exposure of underground coal miners. Limit on concentration of diesel particulate matter; final rule. Code of Federal Regulations. Washington, DC: U.S. Government Printing Office, Office of the Federal Register.

71 Fed. Reg. 28924 [2006]. Mine Safety and Health Administration: 30 CFR 57.5060. Diesel particulate matter exposure of underground metal and nonmetal miners. Limit on concentration of diesel particulate matter; final rule. Code of Federal Regulations. Washington, DC: U.S. Government Printing Office, Office of the Federal Register.

Adu-Acheampong A, Patton S, Dawson J, Huffman K [2008]. Old mines–new regulations: the re-opening of the Gordonsville, Elmwood, and Cumberland Mines under new DPM regulations. In: Wallace K, ed. Proceedings of the 12th US/North American Mine Ventilation Symposium. Reno, NV: University of Nevada, Reno, pp. 71–77.

ANSI [1969]. Practices for respiratory protection. New York: American National Standards Institute, Inc. ANSI Z88.2-1969.

Brake DJ [2008]. A protocol and standard for mine ventilation studies. In: Wallace K, ed. Proceedings of the 12th US/North American Mine Ventilation Symposium. Reno, NV: University of Nevada, Reno, pp. 3–10.

Bugarski A, Schnakenberg G, Noll J D, Mischler S, Crum M, Anderson M [2005]. Evaluation of diesel particulate filter systems and biodiesel blends in an underground mine. SME Transactions, *318*.

Cecala AB, Organiscak JA, Heitbrink WA [2001]. Dust underfoot—enclosed cab floor heaters can significantly increase operator's respirable dust exposure. Rock Prod *104*(4):39–44.

Cecala AB, Organiscak JA, Heitbrink WA, Zimmer JA, Fisher T, Gresh RE, Ashley JD II [2004]. Reducing enclosed cab drill operator's respirable dust exposure at surface coal operations with a retrofitted filtration and pressurization system. SME Transactions *314*:31–36.

Cecala AB, Organiscak JA, Page S, Thimons ED [2002]. Reducing silica exposure in aggregate operations. Aggregates Manager 6(10):24–28.

Cecala AB, Organiscak JA, Zimmer JA, Heitbrink WA, Moyer ES, Schmitz M, Ahrenholtz E, Coppock CC, Andrews EH [2005]. Reducing enclosed cab drill operator's respirable dust exposure with effective filtration and pressurization techniques. J Occup Environ Hyg 2:54–63.

Cecala AB, Organiscak JA, Zimmer JA, Hillis MS, Moredock D [2009]. Maximizing air quality inside enclosed cabs with uni-directional filtration and pressurization system. In: Proceedings for the SME Annual Meeting. Denver, CO: Society for Mining, Metallurgy, and Exploration, pp. 1–6.

Cecala AB, Organiscak JA, Zimmer JA, Moredock D, Hillis M [2007]. Closing the door to dust when adding drill steels. Rock Products 110(10):29–32.

Chekan GJ, Colinet JF [2002]. Silica dust sources in underground limestone mines. In: Bockosh GR, Kohler JL, Langton JF, Novak T, McCarter MK, Biviano A, eds. Proceedings of the 33rd Annual Institute on Mining Health, Safety and Research. Blacksburg, VA: Virginia Tech, pp. 55–70.

Chekan GJ, Colinet JF [2003]. Retrofit options for better dust control—cab filtration, pressurization systems prove effective in reducing silica dust exposures in older trucks. Aggregates Manager 8(9):9–12.

Chekan GJ, Colinet JF, Grau RH III [2002]. Silica dust sources in underground metal/nonmetal mines: two case studies. SME Transactions 312:187–193.

Chekan GJ, Colinet JF, Grau RH III [2004]. Evaluating ventilating air movement in underground limestone mines by monitoring respirable dust generated from production shots. In: Ganguli R, Bandopadhyay S, eds. Proceedings of the 10th U.S./North American Mine Ventilation Symposium. Leiden, Netherlands: Balkema, pp. 221–232.

Chekan GJ, Colinet JF, Kissell FN, Rider JP, Vinson RP, Volkwein JC [2006]. Performance of a light-scattering dust monitor in underground mines. Trans Soc Min Metall Explor 320:21–24.

Duckworth I, Loring D, Loomis I, Casten T [2009]. An overview of diesel emissions control at Freeport McMoran's block cave operations. In: Proceedings for the 9th International Mine Ventilation Congress. New Delhi, India: Oxford & IBH Publishing Co. Pvt. Ltd., pp. 889–898.

Fed. Reg. E7-20237 [2007]. Proposed information collection request submitted for public comment and recommendations. Respirator Program Records. Mine Safety and Health Administration. Code of Federal Regulations. Washington, DC: U.S. Government Printing Office, Office of the Federal Register.

Gherghel C, De Souza E [2008]. Ventilation requirements for uranium mines. In: Wallace K, ed. Proceedings of the 12th US/North American Mine Ventilation Symposium. Reno, NV: University of Nevada, Reno, pp. 65–69.

Grau RH III, Krog RB [2008]. Using mine planning and other techniques to improve ventilation in large-opening mines. 2008 SME Annual Meeting and Exhibit. Littleton, CO: Society for Mining, Metallurgy, and Exploration, pp. 1–4.

Grau RH III, Krog RB [2009].Ventilating large opening mines. J Mine Vent Soc S Afr 62(1):8–14.

Grau RH III, Meighen GM [2006]. Novel stopping designs for large-opening metal/nonmetal mines. In: Mutmansky JM, Ramani RV, eds. Proceedings of the 11th U.S./North American Mine Ventilation Symposium. London: Taylor & Francis Group, pp. 579–583.

Grau RH III, Krog RB, Robertson SB [2006]. Maximizing the ventilation of large-opening mines. In: Mutmansky JM, Ramani RV, eds. Proceedings of the 11th U.S./North American Mine Ventilation Symposium. London: Taylor & Francis Group, pp. 53–59.

Grau RH III, Robertson SB, Krog RB, Chekan GJ, Mucho TP [2004a]. Raising the bar of ventilation for large opening stone mines. In: Ganguli R, Bandopadhyay S, eds. Proceedings of the 10th U.S./North American Mine Ventilation Symposium. Leiden, Netherlands: Balkema, pp. 349–355.

Grau RH III, Robertson SB, Mucho TP, Garcia F, Smith AC [2004b]. NIOSH ventilation research addressing diesel emissions and other air quality issues in nonmetal mines. SME Transactions 316:449–458.

Haney RA, Schultz MJ, Rude RL, Tomko DM [2005]. Controls being used to reduce diesel particulate matter exposures in U.S. underground metal and nonmetal mines. In: Gillies ADS, ed. Proceedings of the 8th International Mine Ventilation Congress. Carlton, Victoria, Australia: Australian Institute of Mining and Metallurgy, pp. 249–254.

Hardcastle S, Kocsis C [2004]. The ventilation challenge. CIM Bulletin: 51–57.

Hardcastle S, Kocsis C, Li G [2008]. Analyzing ventilation requirements and the utilization efficiency of the Kidd Creek mine ventilation system. In: Wallace K, ed. Proceedings of the 12th US/North American Mine Ventilation Symposium. Reno, NV: University of Nevada, Reno, pp. 27–36.

Hartman HL, Mutmansky JM [2002]. Introduction to mining engineering. 2nd ed. New York: John Wiley and Sons Inc., pp. 435–436.

Head HJ [2001]. Proper ventilation for underground stone mines. Aggregates Manager, January: 20–22.

Hopperstead K [2008]. Case study—ventilation planning for Bog Zone, Lisheen Mine. In: Wallace K, ed. Proceedings of the 12th US/North American Mine Ventilation Symposium. Reno, NV: University of Nevada, Reno, pp. 51–54.

Janssen L, Bidwell J [2006]. Performance of four class 95 electret filters against diesel particulate matter. J Int Soc Respir Protect 23:21–29.

Johnson JG, Carlson DH [1986]. The application of advanced measurement and control technology to diesel-powered vehicles in an underground salt mine. In: Mitchell EW, ed. Heavy-duty diesel emission control: a review of technology. CIM Special Volume 36. Montreal, Quebec, Canada: Canadian Institute of Mining and Metallurgy, pp. 206–237.

Kissell FN, Volkwein JC [2002]. Improving ventilation in underground stone mines. Aggregates Manager 1(1):20–25.

Krog RB, Grau RH III [2006]. Fan selection for large-opening mines: vane-axial or propeller fans—which to choose? In: Mutmansky JM, Ramani RV, eds. Proceedings of the 11th

U.S./North American Mine Ventilation Symposium. London: Taylor & Francis Group, pp. 535–542.

Krog RB, Grau RH III, Mucho TP, Robertson SB [2004]. Ventilation planning layouts for large-opening mines. Society for Mining, Metallurgy, and Exploration, SME Preprint 04–187, pp. 1–9.

Lethbridge T, Good M [2010]. A multi-focus approach to DPM reduction at the Greens Creek Mine. In: Hardcastle S, McKinnon DL, eds. Proceedings of the 13th U.S./North American Mine Ventilation Symposium. Sudbury, ON, Canada: MIRARCO—Mining Innovation, pp. 65–71.

Loring DM [2008]. A study of radon regulation and pathology as it relates to underground hardrock mining. In: Wallace K, ed. Proceedings of the 12th US/North American Mine Ventilation Symposium. Reno, NV: University of Nevada, Reno, pp. 59–64.

Manos EZ [2010]. Continuation of DPM control strategy at the Detroit Salt Mine using Rypos HDPF/c filters on diesel equipment. In: Hardcastle S, McKinnon DL, eds. Proceedings of the 13th U.S./North American Mine Ventilation Symposium. Sudbury, ON, Canada: MIRARCO—Mining Innovation, pp. 79–82.

Martikainen A L [2006]. Ventilation planning for mining of the Sarvisuo Lode in the Orivesi mine. In: Mutmansky JM, Ramani RV, eds. Proceedings of the 11th U.S./North American Mine Ventilation Symposium. London: Taylor & Francis Group, pp. 29–34.

Mine Safety Operations Division, New South Wales Department of Primary Industries. [2008]. Guideline for the management of diesel engine pollutants in underground environments. NSW Department of Primary Industries. [http://www.dpi.nsw.gov.au/__data/assets/pdf_file/0018/225513/MDG-29-Guideline-for-the-management-of-diesel-engine-pollutants-in-underground-environments.pdf].

MSHA [2008]. Enforcement of diesel particulate matter final limit at metal and nonmetal underground mines. Washington, DC: U.S. Department of Labor, Mine Safety and Health Administration, Program policy letter No. P08-IV-01. [http://www.msha.gov/regs/complian/ppls/2008/PPL08-IV-1.pdf].

NIOSH [1996]. NIOSH guide to the selection and use of Pparticulate respirators. Cincinnati, OH: U.S. Department of Health and Human Services, Centers for Disease Control and Prevention, National Institute for Occupational Safety and Health, DHHS (NIOSH) Publication No. 96-101.

NIOSH [2001a]. Improved cab air inlet location reduces dust levels and air filter loading rates. By Organiscak JA, Page SA. U.S. Department of Health and Human Services, Centers for Disease Control and Prevention, National Institute for Occupational Safety and Health, DHHS (NIOSH) TN-485.

NIOSH [2001b]. Sweeping compound application reduces dust from soiled floors within enclosed operator cabs. By Organiscak JA, Page SA, Cecala AB. U.S. Department of Health and Human Services, Centers for Disease Control and Prevention, National Institute for Occupational Safety and Health, DHHS (NIOSH) TN-487.

NIOSH [2003]. Handbook for dust control in mining. By Kissell FN. Pittsburgh, PA: U.S. Department of Health and Human Services, Centers for Disease Control and Prevention,

National Institute for Occupational Safety and Health, DHHS (NIOSH) Publication No. 2003-147, Information Circular 9465.

NIOSH [2007a]. Handbook for methane control in mining. By Kissell FN. Pittsburgh, PA: Department of Health and Human Services, Centers for Disease Control and Prevention, National Institute for Occupational Safety and Health, DHHS (NIOSH) Publication No. 2006-127, Information Circular 9486.

NIOSH [2007b]. Recirculation filter is key to improving dust control in enclosed cabs. By Organiscak JA, Cecala AB. U.S. Department of Health and Human Services, Centers for Disease Control and Prevention, National Institute for Occupational Safety and Health, DHHS (NIOSH) Publication No. 2008-100, TN-528.

NIOSH [2008a]. Key design factors of enclosed cab dust filtration systems. By Organiscak JA, Cecala AB. U.S. Department of Health and Human Services, Centers for Disease Control and Prevention, National Institute for Occupational Safety and Health, DHHS (NIOSH) Publication No. 2009-103, Report of Investigation 9677.

NIOSH [2008b]. Minimizing respirable dust exposure in enclosed cabs by maintaining cab integrity. By Cecala AB, Organiscak JA. U.S. Department of Health and Human Services, Centers for Disease Control and Prevention, National Institute for Occupational Safety and Health, DHHS (NIOSH) TN-533.

NIOSH [2009]. Noise control in underground metal mining. By Efrem R, Randolph RF, Yantek DS, Peterson JS. Pittsburgh, PA: U.S. Department of Health and Human Services, Centers for Disease Control and Prevention, National Institute for Occupational Safety and Health, DHHS (NIOSH) Publication No. 2010-111, Information Circular 9518, pp. 1–62.

NIOSH [2011]. NIOSH Mining: Diesel Exhaust Topic Page. In: CDC/NIOSH. [http://www.cdc.gov/niosh/mining/topics/topicpage2.htm].

Noll JD, Mischler S, Cauda E, Patts L, Janisko S, Grau R [2010]. The effects of passive diesel particulate filters on diesel particulate matter concentrations in two underground metal/nonmetal mines. In: Hardcastle S, McKinnon DL, eds. Proceedings of the 13th U.S./North American Mine Ventilation Symposium. Sudbury, ON, Canada: MIRARCO—Mining Innovation, pp. 83–89.

Noll JD, Mischler S, Schnakenberg GH, Bugarski A [2006]. Measuring diesel particulate 11553 matter in underground mines using sub micron elemental carbon as a surrogate. In: Mutmansky JM, Ramani RV, eds. Proceedings of the 11th U.S./North American Mine Ventilation Symposium. London: Taylor & Francis Group, pp. 105–110.

Noll JD, Patts L, Grau R [2008]. The effects of ventilation controls and environmental cabs on diesel particulate matter concentrations in some limestone mines. In: Wallace K, ed. Proceedings of the 12th US/North American Mine Ventilation Symposium. Reno, NV: University of Nevada, Reno, pp. 463–468.

NPPTL [2010a]. NIOSH-approved P100 particulate filtering facepiece respirators. U.S. Department of Health and Human Services, Centers for Disease Control and Prevention, National Institute for Occupational Safety and Health, National Personal Protective Technology Laboratory. [http://www.cdc.gov/niosh/npptl/topics/respirators/disp_part/p100list1.html].

NPPTL [2010b]. Certified Equipment List. U.S. Department of Health and Human Services. Public Health Service, Centers for Disease Control, National Institute for Occupational Safety and Health. National Personal Protective Technology Laboratory. [http://www.cdc.gov/niosh/npptl/topics/respirators/cel/default.html].

Ontario Ministry of Labour [1994]. Mines and mining plants. Reg. 854, Section 183.1 (3), O. Reg. 779/94. S. 7.

Organiscak JA, Cecala AB [2009]. Doing the math: the effectiveness of enclosed-cab air-cleaning methods can be spelled out in mathematical equations. Rock Products: 20.

Organiscak JA, Page SA [1999]. Field assessment of control techniques and long-term dust variability for surface coal mine rock drills and bulldozers. Int J Surf Min Reclam Env *13*:165–172.

Organiscak JA, Cecala AB, Thimons ED, Heitbrink WA, Schmitz M, Ahrenholtz E [2003]. NIOSH/Industry collaborative efforts show improved mining equipment cab dust protection. SME Transactions *314*:145–152.

OSHA [2009]. Assigned protection factors for the revised respiratory protection standard. Occupational Safety and Health Administration. OSHA 3352-02 2009. [http://www.osha.gov/Publications/3352-APF-respirators.pdf].

Ponce Aguirre JR [2006]. Ventilation upgrade of Minerales Monclova's Mine 6. In: Mutmansky JM, Ramani RV, eds. Proceedings of the 11th U.S./North American Mine Ventilation Symposium. London: Taylor & Francis Group, pp. 35–40.

Pritchard CJ [2010]. Methods to improve efficiency of mine ventilation systems. Trans Soc Min Metal Explor *326*:34–38.

Rawlins CA [2006]. Underground mine ventilation planning, heat loads, and diesel equipment. In: Mutmansky J, Ramani R, eds. Proceedings of the 11th U.S./North American Mine Ventilation Symposium. London: Taylor & Francis Group, pp. 75–80.

Robertson SB, Grau RH, Dolgos J, Mucho TP [2004]. A computer software program that estimates air quantity requirements in large opening stone mines. In: Ganguli R, Bandopadhyay S, eds. Proceedings of the 10th U.S./North American Mine Ventilation Symposium. Leiden, Netherlands: Balkema, pp. 363–369.

Schnakenberg GH Jr [2001]. Estimate of technically feasible DPM levels for underground metal and nonmetal mines. Min Eng *53*(9):45–51.

Schnakenberg GH, Johnson JH, Schaefer P [1986]. Use of CO_2 measurements in monitoring air quality in dead-end drifts. In: Mitchell EW, ed. Heavy-duty diesel emission control: a review of technology. CIM Special Volume 36. Montreal, Quebec, Canada: Canadian Institute of Mining and Metallurgy, pp. 291–297.

Suter AH [2002]. Construction noise: exposure, effects and the potential for remediation: a review and analysis. Am Ind Hyg Assoc J *63*:768–789.

Timko RJ, Thimons ED [1987]. Damage resistant brattice stoppings in mines with large entries. Eng Min J *188*(5):34–36.

Wallace KG Jr, Tessier M, Pahkala M, Sletmoen L [2006]. Optimization of the Red Lake Mine ventilation system. In: Mutmansky JM, Ramani RV, eds. Proceedings of the 11th

U.S./North American Mine Ventilation Symposium. London: Taylor & Francis Group, pp. 61–66.

6.4 Section 4

30 CFR 57.5002. Safety and Health Standards. Underground metal and nonmetal mines. Exposure monitoring. Mine Safety and Health Administration, Department of Labor. Code of Federal Regulations. Washington, DC: U.S. Government Printing Office, Office of the Federal Register.

30 CFR 57.5005 Safety and Health Standards. Underground metal and nonmetal mines. Control of exposure to airborne contaminants. Mine Safety and Health Administration, Department of Labor. Code of Federal Regulations. Washington, DC: U.S. Government Printing Office, Office of the Federal Register.

30 CFR 70.1900 Mandatory Health Standards. Underground coal mines. Exhaust Gas Monitoring. Mine Safety and Health Administration, Department of Labor. Code of Federal Regulations. Washington, DC: U.S. Government Printing Office, Office of the Federal Register.

30 CFR 75.351 Atmospheric monitoring systems. Mine Safety and Health Administration, Department of Labor. Code of Federal Regulations. Washington, DC: U.S. Government Printing Office, Office of the Federal Register.

30 CFR 75.362 Mandatory Safety Standards. Underground coal mines. On-shift examination. Mine Safety and Health Administration, Department of Labor. Code of Federal Regulations. Washington, DC: U.S. Government Printing Office, Office of the Federal Register.

66 Fed. Reg. 27864 [2001]. Mine Safety and Health Administration: 30 CFR Part 72. Diesel particulate matter exposure of underground coal miners. Limit on concentration of diesel particulate matter; final rule. Code of Federal Regulations. Washington, DC: U.S. Government Printing Office, Office of the Federal Register.

71 Fed. Reg. 28924 [2006]. Mine Safety and Health Administration: 30 CFR 57.5060. Diesel particulate matter exposure of underground metal and nonmetal miners. Limit on concentration of diesel particulate matter; final rule. Code of Federal Regulations. Washington, DC: U.S. Government Printing Office, Office of the Federal Register.

Arnott WP, Arnold IJ, Mousset-Jones P, Kins K, Shaff S [2008]. Real-time measurement of diesel EC and TC in a Nevada Gold Mine with photoacoustic and Dusttrak instruments: comparison with NIOSH 5040 filter results. In: Wallace K, ed. Proceedings of the 12th U.S./North American Mine Ventilation Symposium. Reno, NV: University of Nevada, Reno, pp. 645–650.

Arnott WP, Moosmuller H, Rogers CF, Jin T, Brush R [1999]. Photoacoustic spectrometer for measuring light absorption by aerosol: instrument description. Atmos Environ *33*:2845–2852.

Austin CC, Roberge B, Goyer N [2006]. Cross-sensitivity of electrochemical detectors used to monitor worker exposure to airborne contaminants: false positive response in the absence of target analytes. J Environ Monit *8*:161–166.

Birch ME [2002]. Occupational monitoring of particulate diesel exhaust by NIOSH Method 5040. App Occup Environ Hyg *17*(6):400–405.

Birch ME, Cary R [1996]. Elemental carbon-based method for occupational monitoring of particulate diesel exhaust: methodology and exposure issues. Analyst *121*:1183–1190.

Birch ME, Noll JD [2004]. Submicrometer elemental carbon as a selective measure of diesel particulate matter in coal mines. J Environ Monit 6:799–806.

Brady, DM [2008]. The role of gas monitoring in the prevention and treatment of mine fires. In:Wallace K, ed. Proceedings of the 12th U.S./North American Mine Ventilation Symposium. Reno, NV: University of Nevada, Reno, pp. 509–513.

Cantrell BK, Rubow KL [1991]. Development of personal diesel aerosol sampler design and performance criteria. Min Eng *43*(2):231–236.

Cantrel BK, Rubow KL [1992]. Measurement of diesel aerosol in underground coal mines. In: Diesels in underground mines: measurement and control of particulate emissions. U.S. Department of the Interior, Bureau of Mines, Information Circular 9324, pp. 11–17.

Cantrell BK, Watts WF Jr [1996]. Diesel exhaust aerosol, review of measurement technology. In: The Canadian Ad Hoc Committee Proceedings of the November 6&7, 1996, Plenary Conference in Toronto, Ontario, Diesel Emissions Exposure Reduction in Mines. Toronto, Ontario, Canada: Canada Centre for Mineral and Energy Technology (CANMET), pp. 7.1–7.9.

Cantrell BK, Zeller HW, Williams KL, Cocalis J [1987]. Monitoring and measurement of in-mine aerosol: diesel emissions. In: Proceeding of Bureau of Mines Technology Transfer Seminar. U.S. Department of the Interior, Bureau of Mines, Information Circular 9141, pp. 18–40.

Cash DA, Ford RD, Haney RA, Kogut J, Lynch JG, Pomroy WH, Saseen GP, Stone RF [2003]. MSHA's report on data collected during a joint MSHA/Industry study of DPM levels in underground metal and nonmetal mines. United Stated Department of Labor Report. Washington, DC: U.S. Department of Labor.

Chakrabarti B, Fine PM, Delfino R, Sioutas C [2004]. Performance evaluation of the active-flow personal DataRam PM2.5 mass monitor (Thermo Anderson pDR-1200) designed for continuous personal exposure measurement. Atmos Environ *38*:3329–3340.

Chekan GJ, Colinet JF, Kissell FN, Rider JP, Vinson RP, Volkwein JC [2006]. Performance of a light-scattering dust monitor in underground mines. Trans Soc Min Metal Explor *320*:21–24.

Eatough DJ, Tang H, Cui W, Machir J [1995]. Determination of the size distribution and chemical composition of fine particulate semivolatile organic material in urban environments using diffusion denuder technology. Inhal Toxicol 7:691–710.

Elia A, Lugarà PM, Giancaspro C [2005]. Photoacoustic detection of nitric oxide by use of a quantum-cascade laser. Optics Letters *30*:988–990.

Gangal MK, Dainty ED [1993]. Ambient measurement of diesel particulate matter and respirable combustible dust in Canadian mines. In: Bhaskar R, ed. Proceedings of the 6th U.S./North American Mine Ventilation Symposium. Littleton, CO: Society for Mining, Metallurgy, and Exploration, pp. 83–89.

Gangal M, Ebersole J, Vallieres J [1990]. Laboratory study of current (1990/91) SOOT/RCD sampling methodology for the mine environment. Mining Research Laboratory, Canada Center for Mineral and Energy Technology (CANMET).

Gillies ADS, Wu HW [2006]. Evaluation of a new real time personal dust monitor for engineering studies. In: Mutmansky J, Ramani R, ed. Proceedings of the 11th U.S./North American Mine Ventilation Symposium. London: Taylor & Francis Group, pp. 167–174.

Gillies ADS, Wu HW [2008]. Evaluation of a first real time diesel particulate matter (DPM) monitor. Project final report. ACARP Project C15028.

Hamasha KM, Arnott WP [2009]. Photoacoustic measurements of black carbon light absorption coefficients in Irbid city, Jordan. Environ Monit Assess, DOI 10.1007/s10661-009-1017-3.

Hanrahan G, Patila DG, Wang J [2004]. Electrochemical sensors for environmental monitoring: design, development and applications. J Environ Monit 6(8):657–664.

Harren FJM, Cotti G, Oomens J, Hekkert STL [2000]. Photoacoustic spectroscopy in trace gas monitoring. In: Meyers, RA, ed. Encyclopedia of Analytical Chemistry. New York: Wiley.

Janisko S, Noll JD [2008]. Near real time monitoring of diesel particulate matter in underground mines. In: Wallace K, ed. Proceedings of the 12th U.S./North American Mine Ventilation Symposium. Reno, NV: University of Nevada, Reno, pp. 509–513.

Kirchstetter TW, Corrigan CE, Novakov T [2001]. Laboratory and field investigation of the adsorption of gaseous organic compounds onto quartz filters. Atmos Eviron 35:1663–1671.

Kittelson DB [1998]. Engines and nanoparticles: a review. J Aerosol Sci 29:575–588.

Lee K, Yanagisawa Y, Hishinuma M, Spengler JD, Billick IH [1992]. A passive sampler for measurement of carbon monoxide using a solid adsorbent. Env Sci Tech 26(4):697–702.

Mader BT, Flagan RC, Seinfeld JH [2001]. Sampling atmospheric carbonaceous aerosols using a particle trap impactor/denuder sampler. Env Sci Tech 35:4857–4867.

Mader BT, Schauer JJ, Seinfeld JH, Flagen RC, Yu JZ, Yang H, Lim H-J, Turpin BJ, Deminter JT, Heidemann G, Bae MS, Quinn P, Bates T, Eatough DJ, Huebert BJ, Bertram T, Howell S [2003]. Sampling method used for the collection of particle-phase organic and elemental carbon during ACE-Asia. Atmos Environ 37:1435–1449.

Marple VA, Kittelson DB, Rubow K [1986]. Methods for the selective sampling of diesel particulates in mine dust aerosols. U.S. Department of the Interior, Bureau of Mines, OFR 44-87, NITS PB 88-130810:94.

McCartney TC, Cantrell BK [1992]. A cost-effective personal diesel exhaust aerosol sampler. U.S. Department of the Interior, Bureau of Mines, Information Circular 9324, pp. 24–30.

McDow SR, Huntzicker JJ [1990]. Vapor adsorption artifact in the sampling of organic aerosol: face velocity effects. Atmos Environ 24A:2563–2571.

Miller AL, Habjan MC, Park K [2007]. Real-time estimation of elemental carbon emitted from diesel engine. Env Sci Tech 41:5783–5788.

MSHA [2002]. 30 CFR Part 57. Diesel particulate matter exposure of underground metal and nonmetal miners; proposed rule. Fed. Reg. 30:47297. Code of Federal Regulations. Washington, DC: U.S. Government Printing Office, Office of the Federal Register.

MSHA [2008]. Enforcement of diesel particulate matter final limit at metal and nonmetal underground mines. Washington, DC: U.S. Department of Labor, Mine Safety and Health Administration, Program policy letter No. P08-IV-01. [http://www.msha.gov/regs/complian/ppls/2008/PPL08-IV-1.pdf].

NIOSH [1990a]. Mineral dust and diesel aerosol measurements in underground metal and nonmetal mines. By Cantrell BK, Rubow KL. Pittsburgh, PA: U.S. Department of Health and Human Services, Centers for Disease Control, National Institute for Occupational Safety and Health, DHHS (NIOSH) Publication No. 90–108.

NIOSH [1990b]. Measurement of coal dust and diesel exhaust aerosols in underground mines. By Rubow KL, Cantrell BK, Marple VA. In: Proceedings of the VII International Pneumoconiosis Conference. Pittsburgh, PA: U.S. Department of Health and Human Services, Centers for Disease Control, National Institute for Occupational Safety and Health, DHHS (NIOSH) Publication No. 90-108, pp. 645–650.

NIOSH [2004]. O' Connor PF, ed. NIOSH Manual of Analytical Methods (NMAM), third supplement to NMAM, 4th ed. Cincinnati, OH: Department of Health and Human Services, Centers for Disease Control and Prevention, National Institute for Occupational Safety and Health, DHHS(NIOSH) Publication No. 2003-154.

NIOSH [2006]. Laboratory and field performance of a continuously measuring personal respirable dust monitor. By Volkwein JC, Vinson RP, Page SJ, McWilliams LJ, Joy GJ, Mischler SE, Tuchman DP. Pittsburgh, PA: U.S. Department of Health and Human Services, Centers for Disease Control and Prevention, National Institute for Occupational Safety and Health, DHHS (NIOSH) Publication No. 2006-145, Report of Investigations 9669.

NIOSH [2010]. Best practice for dust control in coal mining. By Colinet JF, Cecela AB, Chekan GJ, Organiscak JA, Wolfe AL. U.S. Department of Health and Human Services, Centers for Disease Control and Prevention, National Institute for Occupational Safety and Health, DHHS (NIOSH) Publication No. 2010-110, Information Circular 9517.

Noll JD, Birch ME [2004]. Evaluation of SKC DPM cassettes for monitoring diesel particulate matter in coal mines. J Environ Monit 6:973–978.

Noll JD, Birch ME [2008]. Effects of sampling artifacts on occupational samples of diesel particulate matter. Env Sci Tech 42(14):5223–5228.

Noll JD, Janisko S [2007]. Using laser absorption techniques to monitor diesel particulate matter exposure in underground stone mines. In: Cullum B, Porterfield D, eds. Proceedings for SPIE: Smart Biomedical and Physiological Sensor Technology V. Vol. 6759. Boston, MA: SPIE, pp. 1–11.

Noll JD, Bugarski AD, Patts LD, Mischler SE, McWilliams L [2007]. The relationship between elemental carbon, total carbon, and diesel particulate matter in several underground metal/nonmetal mines. Env Sci Tech 41(3):710–716.

Noll JD, Mischler SE, Schnakenberg GH Jr, Bugarski AD [2006]. Measuring diesel particulate matter in underground mines using sub micron elemental carbon as a surrogate. In:

Mutmansky J, Ramani R, ed. Proceedings of the 11th U.S./North American Mine Ventilation Symposium. London: Taylor & Francis Group, pp. 105–110.

Noll JD, Timko RJ, McWilliams LJ, Hall P, Haney R [2005]. Sampling results of the improved SKC® diesel particulate matter cassette. J Occup Environ Hyg 2(1):29–37.

Olson DA, Norris GA [2005]. Sampling artifacts in measurement of elemental and organic carbon: low-volume sampling in indoor and outdoor environments. Atmos Environ 39:5437–5445.

OSHA [2004]. Verification of calibration for direct-reading portable gas monitors. U.S. Department of Labor, Occupational Safety and Health Administration, Safety and Health Information Bulletins: SHIB 05-04-2004.

Palassis, J. [1999]. Portable infrared analyzers. App Occup Environ Hyg 14(8):510–514.

Pierson WR, Brachaczek WW [1983]. Particulate matter associated with vehicles on the road. Aerosol Sci Technol 2:1–40.

Quintana PJE, Samimi BS, Kleinman MT, Liu LJ, Soto K, Warner GY, Bufalino C, Valencia J, Francis D, Hovell MH, Delfino RJ [2000]. Evaluation of a real-time passive personal particle monitor in fixed site residential indoor and ambient measurements. J Exp Anal Environ Epi 10:437–445.

Roczko A [2010]. Photoacoustic infrared technology. MSA white paper. MSA. [http://www.media.msanet.com/NA/USA/PermanentInstruments/SafetyandHealthMonitors/ChemgardSeries/ChemgrdWhitePaper.pdf].

Rubow KL, Marple VA, Tao Y [1990]. Design and evaluation of a personal diesel aerosol sampler for underground coal mines. SME Preprint No. 90-132, 5 pp.

Stephenson DJ, Spear TM, Lutte MG [2006]. Comparison of sampling methods to measure exposure to diesel particulate matter in an underground metal mine. Min Eng 58(8):39–44.

Subramanian R, Khlystov AY, Cabada JC, Robinson AL [2004]. Positive and negative artifacts in particulate organic carbon measurements with denuded and undenuded sampling configurations. Aerosol Sci Technol 38:27–48.

Tucker SP, Pretty JR [2005]. Identification of oxidation products of solanesol produced during air sampling for tobacco smoke by electrospray mass spectrometry and HPLC. Analyst 130:1414–1424.

Turpin BJ, Huntzicker JJ, Hering SV [1994]. Investigation of organic aerosol sampling artifacts in the Los Angeles Basin. Atmos Environ 28:3061–3071.

Turpin BJ, Saxena P, Andrews E [2000]. Measuring and simulating particulate organics in the atmosphere: problems and prospects. Atmos Environ 34:2983–3013.

Verma DK, Shaw L, Julian J, Smolynec K, Wood C, Shaw D [1999]. A comparison of sampling and analytical methods for assessing occupational exposure to diesel exhaust in railroad work environment. Appl Occup Environ Hyg 14:701–714.

Volkwein JC, Thimons ED, Dunham D, Patashnick H, Rupprecht E [2004]. Development and evaluation of a new personal dust monitor for underground mining applications. In:

Proceedings of the 29th International Technical Conference on Coal Utilization and Fuel Systems. Gaithersburg, MD: Coal Technology Association, pp. 1–22.

Warburton PR, Pagano MP, Hoover R, Logman M, Crytzer K, Warburton YJ [1998]. Amperometric gas sensor response times. Anal Chem 70(5):998–1006.

Williams KL, Timko RJ [1984]. Performance evaluation of a real-time aerosol monitor. U.S. Department of the Interior, Bureau of Mines, Information Circular IC8968.

Wu HW, Gillies ADS, Volkwein JD, Noll J [2009]. Real-time DPM ambient monitoring in underground mines. In: Proceedings for the 9th International Mine Ventilation Congress. New Delhi, India: Oxford & IBH Publishing Co. Pvt. Ltd., pp. 821–830.

Yutaka Y, Akira N, Tatsuhiko G, Kenichi I, Junichi K [1999]. Development of measurement system for atmospheric gas concentration. Gas concentration measuring system by photoacoustic effect using CO_2 laser. J Min Mater Process Inst Jpn 115(2):77–82.

Zhu J, Aikawa B, Pigeon R [2005]. Measurement of fine particles in diesel emissions using a real-time aerosol monitor. J Air Waste Manage Assoc 55:978–983.

6.5 Section 5

30 CFR 57.5070. Miner training. Safety and health standards. Underground metal and nonmetal mines. Mining Safety and Health Administration. Department of Labor. Code of Federal Regulations. Washington, DC: U.S. Government Printing Office, Office of the Federal Register.

30 CFR 75.1915 Training and qualification of persons working on diesel-powered equipment. Mandatory safety standards. Underground coal mines. Code of Federal Regulations. Washington, DC: U.S. Government Printing Office, Office of the Federal Register.

30 CFR 75.338 Training, Mandatory Safety Standards. Underground coal mines. Code of Federal Regulations. Washington, DC: U.S. Government Printing Office, Office of the Federal Register.

66 Fed. Reg. 27864 [2001]. Mine Safety and Health Administration: 30 CFR Part 72. Diesel particulate matter exposure of underground coal miners. Limit on concentration of diesel particulate matter; final rule. Code of Federal Regulations. Washington, DC: U.S. Government Printing Office, Office of the Federal Register.

71 Fed. Reg. 28924 [2006]. Mine Safety and Health Administration: 30 CFR 57.5060. Diesel particulate matter exposure of underground metal and nonmetal miners. Limit on concentration of diesel particulate matter; final rule. Code of Federal Regulations. Washington, DC: U.S. Government Printing Office, Office of the Federal Register.

Caterpillar [2007]. Technology keeping workers safe in Australian underground mine. Caterpillar. Viewpoint: Perspectives on Modern Mining: 9

DeGaspari J [2003]. Armchair mining. Mech Eng, May: 1–9.

Emissions Advantage, LLC. [2005]. WRAP offroad diesel retrofit guidance document. Vol. 2. Emissions Advantage, 2.XIV-1–2.XIV-23 [http://www.wrapair.org/forums/msf/projects/offroad_diesel_retrofit/Offroad_Diesel_Retrofit _V2.pdf].

Haney RA, Schultz MJ, Rude RL, Tomko DM [2005]. Controls being used to reduce diesel particulate matter exposures in U.S. underground metal and nonmetal mines. In: Gillies ADS, ed. Proceedings of the 8th International Mine Ventilation Congress. Carlton, Victoria, Australia: Australian Institute of Mining and Metallurgy, pp. 249–254.

Hardcastle S, Kocsis C, Li G [2008]. Analyzing ventilation requirements and the utilization efficiency of the Kidd Creek mine ventilation system. In: Wallace K, ed. Proceedings of the 12th US/North American Mine Ventilation Symposium. Reno, NV: University of Nevada, Reno, pp. 27–36.

Larsson J, Appelgren J, Marshall J [2010]. Next generation system for unmanned LHD operation in underground mines. Reprints SME Annual Meeting. Phoenix, AZ: Society for Mining, Metallurgy, and Exploration, Reprint 10-001.

Meyer MA [2008]. Implementing a tracking and ventilation control system at Barrick Goldstrike's underground division. In: Wallace K, ed. Proceedings of the 12th US/North American Mine Ventilation Symposium. Reno, NV: University of Nevada, Reno, pp. 13–25.

NIOSH [1998]. Assessing occupational safety and health training. Cincinnati, OH: U.S. Department of Health and Human Services, Centers for Disease Control and Prevention, National Institute for Occupational Safety and Health, DHHS (NIOSH) Publication No. 1998-145.

Noort D, McCarthy P [2009]. Automated underground mining. Int Min, January: 50.

Wu HW, Gillies ADS [2008]. Developments in real time personal diesel particulate monitoring in mines. In: Wallace K, ed. Proceedings of the 12th US/North American Mine Ventilation Symposium. Reno, NV: University of Nevada, Reno, pp. 629–636.